Denbigh L
Memories of m

Julia Botterell

First published in Great Britain as a paperback original
By Julia Botterell   2009

ISBN 978-0-9563647-0-8

Printed and bound in Great Britain by
Think Ink
11-13 Philip Road, Ipswich,
Suffolk IP2 8BH

The best pleasure about dreams is

being able to

create them

The best quality about memories is

their

adaptability

Lacquer: n. hard glossy coating made by dissolving cellulose
derivatives or natural resins in a volatile solvent
n. hard varnish v.t. coat with it
n. hard glossy varnish v.t. coat with lacquer

Similar to : gild, daub, smear, cover, gloss, glaze, whitewash

Denbigh Lacquer: Memories of my Aunt Sally

Foreword

Where do you start when describing a life of contradictions layered with mysteries and wrapped in fanciful stories?

Someone once said that the truth is what we choose to believe. Indeed, during Sally's life there was one essential truth; that she lived it according to her rules and believed her own inventions whether or not they ran parallel to the facts or were diametrically opposed to them.

To unravel her life has been a joy and a frustration as she was a gifted story teller, having an almost photographic memory and able to squirrel detailed information away, to use when finding it to be a suitable embellishment. She did not, as they say, allow the truth to get in the way of a good story. As a child I was both fascinated by her huge personality and awed by her control, and now as an adult I am equally captivated by the eccentric life that she lived. It would be impossible ignore the impact that she had on so many people and too sad if her life went unrecorded.

These memories are by themselves only able to offer a glimpse into the person that I knew. We see, when looking in the mirror, the image that we expect, so my version of her life is the only one that I can tell. Perhaps this memoir, just like her stories, has been eschewed by my own inventions and mistaken memories. I have attempted to unravel her past but as I have looked at each photograph and letter they have thrown up more puzzles than answers; making me realise that what I thought I knew was in reality just one tiny part of her story.

Acknowledgements

This book, being almost a work in progress, as I have returned to it so many times to revise, threatens to be never finished if I don't let it go with all its faults and jumble of styles.

It would have never reached even this stage of completion had it not been for the encouragement of family and the sudden realisation that if I didn't hurry it along then it would be too late for our dear friend Ken to read a proof copy of the manuscript. For so many years I had told my stories of Sally and had not realised that anyone else could have been as seriously interested as I had been. Certainly I thought that some members of the family would be drawn to the subject, but as for a wider audience; I was doubtful.

Then, early in 2008 Ken found that he had terminal cancer and Sally's story was just a series of entries in the Family Tree file. I was still wading through paperwork, photographs and letters and there was no shape to the work. How was it to be organised? I needed to demonstrate the bewildering unravelling as it occurred; to take the reader through the confusion as if on a journey. But the pace was suddenly set. I had a few months at best to put all the parts together.

Finally I decided on a series of themed chapters which would describe some elements of Sally's character and then go backwards and forward in time to show how we can never be sure if reliable facts and clear memories will clarify or distort a truth.

I had imposed upon Sally's family in Nottingham to provide me with photographs and their memories of her life with them.

Tom and Nellie Payne allowed me to take notes as we talked of the past. We discussed Herbert and Chrissie and their life in Nottingham and his life in the army. Gladys Smith, the daughter of Harriet, Herbert's sister, allowed me some insights into the Payne family. This history was a complete revelation to me. I had not seriously considered how the interaction of this family had also formed Sally during her childhood.

Then there was Sally's first cousin Joan Sharp, daughter of Amos May, the railway clerk, down in Kent, who had granted me access to some letters that Sally had written to her in the 1970's. She was able to complete some detail of the May family and again provide some photographs that I had not previously seen.

Of course the internet site of Ancestry UK became an invaluable tool enabling me to trawl through the census documents of 1841 until 1901 and also provided verification of birth, death and marriage dates of various family members and pointed to where these events had taken place; sometimes confirming the information that I held and at other times being at odds with what I thought I knew. The latest 1911 census was an unexpected bonus. It provided me with locations for the Payne and May families and gave me more food for thought.

It has been gratifying to learn that various friends, having sneaked a preview of 'Denbigh Lacquer' have returned it with positive comments and varying degrees of enthusiasm which has encouraged me to feel that there is some merit in the enterprise.

However, my final acknowledgment and thanks go to my husband Al who has always provided unstinting support and encouragement throughout this project. His thoughtfulness, cups of tea and plates of nourishment when I was oblivious to time allowed me to concentrate on the task and for that I am in his debt!

Contents

Foreword   5

Chapter 1   Llanrhaeadr near Denbigh 2002   11

Chapter 2   Cranbrook 1915 Birth and early childhood   21

Chapter 3   Denbigh 1972   41

Chapter 4   Denbigh 1964   51

Chapter 5   The early 1950's   59

Chapter 6   Nottingham December 1928 from child to woman 75

Chapter 7   Tadek; her son, and Marion, the husband   93

Chapter 8   Fire, theft and burglary in Denbigh   120

Chapter 9   The May family myths   142

Chapter 10 Dear Sir, I wish to bring to your attention!   166

Chapter 11 Money, money, money   176

Chapter 12 Religion and politics   184

Chapter 13 Llanrhaeadr 27th May 2002   192

Chapter 14 Three Weddings and two funerals   202

Chapter 15 In this will I bequeath   212

Chapter 16 Denbigh Lacquer   220

Chapter 17 Confidences and discoveries   226

Chapter 18 Inheritance and history   248

Chapter 19 Pandora's Box   260

Chapter 20 Summer 2008   286

Index   298

Chapter 1   Llanrhaeadr near Denbigh 2002

The sky started to lighten and we watched as she lay there, half asleep, yet aware of our watchfulness and intrusion. She groaned low and soft. We wanted it to be her last sigh; for her to be able to leave this world in peace and yet were afraid that if it was, we would lose her forever.

Her thin worn sheet slipped, exposing a white bare shoulder. Hesitantly I went to cover her.

"Leave it!" she sighed with irritation and exasperation.

Guiltily I returned to the chair to sit and watch the dawn break; hearing faint bird song beginning, signalling the start of a new day and ending of one of the longest nights that we had known.

....

"As she doesn't want to go into the hospital I am not mindful to have her moved at this late hour". The locum doctor was kind and gentle.

"I have given her some pain relief but it is difficult to manage it here. In the morning we will see if we can arrange for her to be taken to Denbigh. Perhaps her GP can reassure her?" She turned to us with her query, her eyebrow slightly raised.

"It could be quite messy I'm afraid. The facts are that the faeces may well be present as she becomes sick and retches".

My stomach turned. I'm not going to be able to cope! Oh my God what are we to do? She will die and there will no one to help her through her pain. I silently panicked, unable to speak. Please don't let her die tonight! Oh my God! What are we going to do?

"She may be able to have small sips of water but basically we will have to wait until the morning and decide how best to proceed. She needs managed amounts of morphine."
"It's her cats. She is worried about them".
The doctor nodded and picked up her bag. I willed her to stay. Don't leave us! She walked to the door and we stared at each other as she left. The horror of the night was before us.
"We'll take turns to watch her, I'll get a chair". Al was as ever practical, but his voice seemed low and unsure.
"We need a bucket and some towels."
What else could we do? I tried to think.
"I need to ring work and say I won't be in tomorrow."

....

In the small cramped front sitting room I sat by the large gas fire. It whooped as it ignited and warmed the water for the central heating radiators. Despite the warmth from the fire it was unusually chilly. Shadows played around the room and I felt like an interloper as I looked at the familiarly strange artefacts. Dusty plates depicting a barely decipherable 'Wind in the Willows' story crowded the Welsh dresser and Edwardian Lady 'Months of the year' plates ringed the walls, whilst pictures vied for the remaining wall space. Some were nicely studied watercolours, others crudely painted oils. The room looked back at me sitting where Sally always sat. The window offered dark reflections of the room. The nearby table was littered with the usual paraphernalia of letters and bills, magazines and wrinkled fruit in a dusty old stringed fruit bowl. It had lain untouched for days. Black cat's hairs were not so noticeable in the dimly lit room but the air was tainted with their presence. I had never looked at the room so carefully before and felt an overwhelming sadness. Treasures and junk

12

were piled up giving the room a rounded appearance. An over packed bookcase was tightly crammed with business files and supported from the floor by VHS videos of recorded programmes slightly blocking the way to the wooden stairs.

Sally's flowery cursive script carefully detailed the contents of each video. Decades of programmes never watched selfishly guarded their own space on the floor.

"Okay?" we whispered to each other, our voices betraying our uncertainty.

"I'll go up now."

As Al took his turn by the fire I went reluctantly up the uncarpeted wooden stairs to sit by her bedside, my hands reaching out to the banisters to steady my ascent.

It was an intrusion to be here. Her thin back accused me as she turned, over facing the wall. Her manoeuvre excluded me, shunning my presence, shutting me out. We were going to betray her and she knew it. Her doctor would be asked to persuade her to go to the hospital and she would die there and not at home where she wanted to be. Dr Jones reminded us of her beloved son Tadek and probably did the same for her, so she allowed herself to be governed by him; a privilege not given lightly.

I found myself breathing in shallow bursts, straining to hear if she was still breathing and then being repelled as rasping groans and thickened sighs shook her body.

My eyes slowly adjusted to the darkness. I found a morbid curiosity had taken hold as I catalogued the piles of possessions heaped around the bed. Boxes distorted by age and the close proximity of other items reached shoulder level. Some of the contents had begun to leak from the more dilapidated boxes. Large ornaments, vases and books, probably purchased for someone in mind for Christmas, stayed resolutely contained in their mice- nibbled packages. Old cameras hung from the chair by the dusty cluttered

13

dressing table. Trailing loops of cobwebs heavy with black dust wafted from the ceiling.

Her bedcovers were worn and patched and the sheet which had become exposed by her turning showed large rents. I knew that the large trunks in the room contained new linen and bedding. A surge of frustration swept over me. Why, oh why! She could have been so comfortable. Her bed could have been softly covered with the new duvet and sheets that we had bought her only just last Christmas, which had been carefully selected according to her strict specifications of being made from pure one hundred percent cotton.

"As my skin reacts against anything man made; it just knows if something isn't natural."

Well it's a pity you didn't use the bedding we gave you then! I found myself taking in a sharp breath. No, no it was all too late now for silly petty recriminations.

A sudden screeching hoot jolted me back into the present; the owl reminding me of the surrounding countryside and her love of the visiting birds and wildlife. On the washing line stretching along the drive she had placed five large nut containers that were routinely visited and emptied each day. She had lovely red-headed green woodpeckers regularly tapping away on the trees surrounding the property. A flock of different birds would vie for the seeds and crumbs that she threw down; although some clever grey squirrels had found the large bag of nuts in the garage and had been stealing them from her for some time. Who would feed them all when she had gone?

She needed to be sick! Oh no, it's going to happen again! She grasped the bucket with surprising strength and black bile spurted, filling the bottom. My stomach quivered as I took the contents to the bathroom and tipped the mass into the toilet. As I flushed the pan the water swirled and stayed dark grey. This is going to happen again and again. I don't know what I shall do if she dies on me. Let her live until the doctor comes.

14

My cowardice shamed me all over again. Here was this strong fearless woman needing my help, in terrible pain, and I'm thinking of myself. Pull yourself together! I attempted to bully myself into regaining some control. Please let it be Al's turn soon.

However, even the thought of sitting once again alone downstairs also filled me with dread. Al appeared at the door and I willingly gave up my post.

I seemed to be surrounded by her ghosts, my head filling with dreamlike frights. Voices and accusations kept me anxious and unable to settle. Noises from outside made me imagine restless spirits, witches and other childish nightmares. I knew they were just the natural noises of the countryside but my skin tingled as I watched shapes, watching me, watching them. Tiny branches tapped and brushed against the window and I started at each sound. I prayed for the dawn to come quickly. The room seemed moody and cross. It didn't want me, the traitorous intruder, to be here. I drew my coat around my chest and attempted to bury my head into its folds. I dare not stir even to go into the crowded rubbish-filled kitchen to make a cup of tea. I was paralysed by my inadequacy and fearful of what the morning would bring.

I knew Sally was dying and that she would die with so many secrets left untold. I wished that I had had the courage to ask the questions that now would never be answered. Why had I been so reticent? Opportunities had been squandered. Secrets of my family would go with her. I would have to fuse together the half remembered conversations and perhaps would unwittingly create a whole set of new myths, not nearly as colourful and rich as those that she had spun. My father had always called her the Witch of Denbigh and he had been unwittingly right. She had cast a spell of deceit and clothed it so well; who was to know where truth ended and fabrication began.

I could begin with a long list of things that she had said that I knew to be wrong simply because they were devoid of her usual skill of weaving known fact with believable fiction. Within the last year she had stated that she was born at the foot of Snowdon to accentuate her Welsh heritage. That one was quite easy to unravel as her birth certificate was to prove. She also maintained that her maternal Nain and Taid May came from Ty Mawr, Conway; that they were both well connected and well-to-do, having owned a large slate quarry. She seemed to unconsciously imitate the imperious American actress Bette Davis who also maintained that she wished to trace her long lost Welsh cousins on one of her visits to Cardiff. Sally related stories of meeting Anna Pavlova, the famous ballerina, in London and Pope John the Polish Pope in Krakow, recalling that they had enjoyed quite a long chat. Apparently she had also enjoyed taking tea with Victoria Sackville-West, taken whilst her Taid was working at Sissinghurst Castle in Kent engaged in planting the nut grove for the authoress.

However, she was consistent in her adoration of her only son Tadek and love for her brother, my father.

....

Morning brought Dr Jones to the door. He was brisk, loud and jolly; filling the house with his presence. He listened to our concerns about her staying at home.

"I'll pop up and see her".

Whatever he said had had the desired effect as he returned back down to the kitchen.

"I told her that she needs some proper nursing for a few days and that you will be looking after the cats for her. I've also arranged for the ambulance to pick her up this morning and managed to make her a little more comfortable". He was reassuring although we all knew that the prospect of her ever returning to her beloved home was a charade.

Once again we watched as she refused to countenance the touch of fabric over her body and felt neglectful as she lay without clothing on her threadbare bed; her naked back reproaching our fearful gaze.

As the day got brighter she began to stir and moan. Her medication had not been strong enough keep the pain at bay. Dark patches stained the carpet around the bed as we had failingly endeavoured to contain the bouts of sickness in the bucket. The hours stretched longer and there was still no sign of the expected ambulance. Nine o'clock, ten o'clock, eleven o'clock, twelve o'clock passed. As each hour passed we found ourselves to be more and more desperate.

"Supposing they don't come! Should we ring the doctor again?" We were fearful that she could last much longer in such a condition. Finally the ambulance appeared at the side drive. They had got lost along the country lanes and not able to find her house. Relief overwhelmed us and we were close to tears with suppressed emotion. But then the next two hurdles presented themselves: how to manoeuvre her down the stairs in a stretcher, and how to persuade her to put a nightdress on. The unforgiving stairs had a tight dog-leg which meant that they were going to have to pass her almost over the banister and down into the crowded sitting room at an almost vertical angle. She didn't make a sound as they lifted and shoved and bumped their way over and round the stairs and banister, keeping up a steady reassuring banter between her and them, speaking for her as they attempted to squeeze past the bookcase.

"We'll have to shift that – it won't be a problem will it? We'll soon put it back again, no problems then, see!" Their cheerful voices filled the house.

Finally, as they loaded her into the ambulance she allowed the mask to slip and the pain froze her face as she tightly closed her eyes. We drove the bumpy unforgiving route to the Denbigh Infirmary; a journey of ten minutes that seemed to last forever.

....

Sally Rose Christiana Mary Payne was born in Cranbrook, Kent in the March of 1915 to her parents Christiana Edith May and Herbert Wilfred Payne, but in fact this Sally was never born; Sally was a fiction. Sally had chosen this name for herself as a young girl growing up in Nottingham. She had taken against the name of Rose and had decided that she would be called Sally instead. Rose was too soft, flowery and feminine for her.

Her death certificate incorrectly details her place of birth in Nottingham. I had unwittingly become complicit in her fantasies and had believed her when she had said that this was her name and the place where she had been born and bred so I duly repeated these details to the patient registrar, in wet bedraggled Denbigh, two days after her death.

I had been unable to find the office and had been sent to the bottom of the town by a well meaning passer-by and found myself queuing behind a large unkempt man who was loudly demanding his DHSS payment. By the time he was finally ushered away, the tired official just visible behind the tiny screen informed me that I needed to be at the other end of the town, and turning with evident irritation she disappeared into the office behind her. I arrived for my overdue appointment with the registrar ten minutes late, emotional, and consumed by frustration. After a cup of tea, sympathy for my loss and two abortive attempts to complete the form, I finally signed the flawed certificate compounding the myths of her life and death.

Bryn Llwyn a Godwys, Sally's cottage in the Glyn, Llanrhaeadr, just outside Denbigh town, in the Vale of Denbigh. The semi-detached property was extensively remodelled into one large house in the late 1970's.The interior room, being the front parlour, was situated to the left of the main porch.

Chapter 2 Cranbrook 1915 Birth and early childhood

Rose Christiana Mary Payne was born in Willesley Green, near Cranbrook in 1915, during the second year of the 1914 - 1918 World War. The country was in turmoil as more and more young men were being called up. England was changing rapidly. Women were clamouring for the right to vote. Suffragettes had been strident in their demands for emancipation. As the men disappeared into the mud and chaos of France, women assumed new positions of responsibility and freedom from home control. Despite their fathers' disapproval they were able to join the Land Army, following the "Back to the Land" call. The Women's Army Auxiliary Corps (WAAC) was enrolling young women to work at home and aboard as cooks, clerks, motor car drivers and transport mechanics. The Red Cross were calling for recruits to nurse, practise first aid or drive ambulances. The St John Ambulance and Red Cross were training women who wished to work as VAD's in the Voluntary Aid Detachment. Women who had been trained in the traditional roles of seamstresses, dressmakers, milliners or laboured in the lace and cotton mills in the north suddenly found that their services were no longer required. Demand for fashionable outfits and hats waned as the hardship of war impacted those at home. Women were required for the munitions factory and needed to learn the new trades of milling and making shells. A new world of engineering became everyday reality. Lady Parsons formed the Women's Engineering Society much to the disgust of the older men still employed in essential industries of mining or farming. Later they watched in disbelief as posters festooned the walls of the labour exchange. "British Women – the Royal

Air Force needs your help" depicting a young carefree woman sporting yet another uniform of the WRAF or WRNS.

Her father Herbert had spent some time serving in the British Army with the Kings Royal Rifles in India and was then working for the Midland Railway Company. His home was in Nottingham with his mother Mary Payne. How he met and courted her mother Christiana Edith May, who was living in Kent, is a mystery. It may be that, as by this time he was working for a railway company and having free travel, he could choose to visit different parts of the country. However, they were married in the April of 1914. Christiana was aged twenty three when she produced her daughter the following spring. They gave their child the name Rose Christiana Mary, taking her second name from her mother Christiana and the third name from her grandmother Mary Charlotte.

Herbert was twenty eight by this time and already his hair was beginning to recede. In later years his bald dome would sprout two very prominent ears. Christiana had the prettiness that youth afforded her but this began to quickly fade as she grew older and her large protruding front teeth began to spoil her looks.

Christiana, always referred to as Chrissie, was working as a domestic nurse before they met. Her family had lived in both Kent and Norfolk, as her father, Amos May, had been head gardener working predominantly on two large country estates, Eastwell Manor near Ashford in Kent, and later Lynford Hall in Norfolk. In the 1891 census they were living in the Gardener's House at Eastwell Manor and by 1901 the May family was accommodated at Bedgebury Lodge in Goudhurst in the district of Kilndown, Kent. It was whilst living here that Amos May worked in the Bedgebury Pinetum, which at that time had been sold by Philip and Evelyn Beresford-Hope to a Mr Isaac Lewis in 1899. The Beresford-Hopes were reduced to selling the prestigious estate and Pleasure Gardens due to the ruinous debts left by Philip's father. The Beresford–Hopes' family had owned the large Bedgebury House, the Pleasure

Gardens which contained the pinetum and a large walled garden, a vast area of the surrounding woodlands, farms occupied by tenant farmers and various lodges and smaller properties. Shooting parties were regularly invited for the weekends and the tenant farmers provided the family with their rents. But somehow the whole fortune had been lost. By 1901 Isaac Lewis employed Amos May to plant specimen pines and rare and exotic trees whilst liaising with gardeners in Kew, London.

Sometime later the May family had been photographed, in what appeared to be, the grounds of a large house, looking comfortably off and well dressed, although their fortunes would fade with the passing of time. It may have been Lynford Hall in Norfolk. In 1911 they had moved from this country estate and came to live here in Goudhurst, and by 1914 they were living in the High Street at Sissinghurst, Kent.

Her grandfather Amos, previously out of work in 1911 census, could have found employment at this time but as he was aged sixty by this time he was probably finding it difficult to find a job to suit his abilities as an experienced gardener. Large country estates were beginning to break up and the domestic staff scattered. The May family had always lived in 'tied' accommodation and the loss of a job would have rendered the family homeless. They were probably renting the property in Sissinghurst in somewhat reduced circumstances by the time that Herbert and Christiana met.

Amos appeared to have had a strong religious streak. Sally said that the family were Calvinists. His flowery letters often invoked God Almighty to look after the wellbeing of his family but the powers of the Almighty had not extended to protect his eldest daughter Charlotte Mary who found herself to be with child and unmarried. Sally had told me all about Charlotte, or Lottie as the family had called her. Lottie had been working at the St Thomas hospital in London, first as a Nightingale nurse and then as Matron prior to her unexpected return to the bosom of the family.

I spent some time writing to the hospital asking if they had kept records of their staff. It was not until I looked at the census for 1891 and found that she was indeed living away from the family home but not as a qualified matron in a large London hospital but as a Fancy Jewellery Assistant in Brighton. In 1909 she gave birth to a son, William, and by the following year of 1910 she was lying in her grave in Hartley, Kent. The only identity of her lover, wearing an army uniform, was to be found in a small photograph linked with her portrait in a velvet frame.

The family stories subsequently suggested that the father of her child had been a wealthy heir to the Coats Cotton dynasty and that he had been tragically killed in a car crash before he was able to ask for her hand in marriage. It was also said that indeed the man had not been in cotton at all but was heir to the Bryant & May fortune. Finally, the third story told of her heartbreak at the loss of her lover and her death being caused by a broken heart. She had been buried swathed in the folds of her unworn wedding dress.

This episode must have been very difficult for the family to bear but was the first of many tragedies to befall them.

Shortly after Christiana and Herbert were married he was called up to serve in the First World War. In the August of that year, Britain entered the war fray with its declaration against Germany and Christiana's parents were worried for their pregnant daughter. She had previously moved up to live in a distant northern Nottingham, away from all those whom she knew, and was soon to be parted from her new husband. They wrote to say that she should come home to live with them and that her Aunt Cissie would see her across London. And so it appears that she did move back to Kent as the location of Sally's birth confirms.

At some time later, Sally, Herbert and Christiana lived back in Nottingham but Sally always regarded Kent as her emotional home just as she came to regard Wales as her spiritual home. Christiana and her little family would often come back to visit

24

her parents and nephew Bill (Willie), as they were able to use the free travel tickets issued to employees of the railway company. Chrissie's brother, confusingly also called Amos after his father and grandfather, was an employee of the Southern Railway Company and was working as a booking clerk in Chatham so he too may have been able to provide free tickets for the family.

By 1919, when Sally was just four years old, her father had accompanied his wife and child on a visit to Cranbrook where Christiana's parents, Amos, Charlotte, their grandson Bill and daughter Dorothy Rose were living. The family were in serious trouble. Amos was reduced to having to seek out odd jobs for employment and they were finding it difficult to pay the rent.

Dorothy Rose, Christiana's sister, was an invalid. She had always been frail and often confined to a wheel chair. In 1901 the census had cruelly labelled her as "feeble minded'. She certainly had problems walking caused by some abnormality to her lower spine involving the vertebrae and sadly may have been academically quite slow. There had been earlier times when she was sent away to live away from the family. Whether she needed the air of a seaside coastal town or whether the family needed respite care for her is uncertain. However, that Herbert, her brother-in-law and she met can not be disputed. Some time during their June visit of 1919 Herbert seduced his vulnerable thirty year old sister-in-law.

Much to the consternation and horror of the family, Dorothy Rose was found to be pregnant. On the 20th February of the following year she gave birth to a boy.

Two days later her distraught mother, Mary Charlotte, wrote a frantic letter to Chrissie.

Station borough Cottages

My dear child'

You have been expecting a letter from me but I could not write. You know what you said at Christmas. You did not think that Herbert had been doing anything to Rose. I did not answer you for that had cross me [crossed my mind] but I put it from me as soon as it came for I thought what a wicked thing to think of him and you know Lottie did not see anything. Oh I cannot write but dear child do not let it make any difference in your home happiness, go to your heavenly father as I have done and ask him to help you as only he can, and I should like you to send three little nightgowns as I have the charity ones, the other things are flannel so I must make some before we go from here and bye two little vests. I have not known about this as only three weeks it is a little before its time. I can't tell you any more I am two dun up. I have not been out since I wrote a letter to anyone so none of your Aunties know anything about it or Amos,

Your loving mother

Swiftly Christiana assumed charge of the child and he was taken back to Nottingham to be brought up as Sally's younger brother.

What effect this must have had on Dorothy Rose having her child taken from her so suddenly is difficult to assess, but Amos, the grandfather was a broken man. He had lost his status in employment; his health was failing and he was trying to support his ailing wife, his young grandson Bill and was probably living with the severe disapproval of his neighbours who had known of his daughter's condition and may have also heard about Charlotte his eldest daughter. The family were accommodated at Rose Cottage in Wye, near Ashford. By the November they were being evicted from the house with nowhere to call home. The police had been summoned to ensure that they left. There was total panic. Dorothy Rose didn't understand what was happening; little Bill was only eleven and they had no means of removing their meagre possessions. Whether their married son Amos was in a position to support them is impossible to say. Help came at the eleventh hour from a Miss Poole who must have taken pity on the family. Another kindly soul, Mr Knight, quickly assessed their predicament and provided them with a wagon. Miss Poole facilitated their removal to Rectory Cottages in the nearby village of Cranbrook. An urgent pencil-written note sent from Mary Charlotte to her daughter Christiana in Nottingham detailed their desperate flight.

Dear Children,

thought that I would of had a letter before this to know how you were I ask you to get someone to write if you was not abel and I am sure you were not as I had no letter but Herbert could your father wrote to say we were moving on Monday but we could not have the rooms and could not get a cottage most of the things are in the cow lodge Mrs Knight has our piano Miss Knight and Miss Turner has the easy chairs and the six leather ones and we have some here your Dad says he dont see how I can come for we have not herd from Mr Allgrove and he says he could not be here with Miss Poole if I was not here people would talk so we did not get out of the house until yesterday and the police came but they see we were getting out it was poor litttle Willie dad and me had to do it Mr Knight was good for he brought a waggon down yesterday morning and told Dad to load it up and he would take it down to the farm for him he see him and Willie with the wheelbarrow taking things down on Tuesday Mr Knight was two busy to but he came and took that load and brought the waggon back for another load it was getting quite dark last night before we got the last 10 things in and oh I am tired do not know how to get about so I am afraid with a long journey I should not be much good and we cant lock up the bedroom so we dont like to leve our things to the mercy to other people I do wish your father could get work and a cottage it is a muddle here we brought our couch for Dad to sleep on your Dad went to see Miss Knight but Neasin would not let him see her and she charge 7/- a week .... for the weeks we have had the cottage and would not pay any more for our moving she said she engaged him and told him she would pay half she is the wickest person I was knew but that is enough so will leave off for Miss Poole and Rose is talking so fast at least Miss Poole is doing all the talking I will send the money back if we cant come if we had a cottage that I could lock up I might be able to come but I am to dun up now I do not know what to do hope you are better your loving mother

By the following October 1921 Amos was dead, leaving behind a sickly wife, a frail daughter and a grandson of twelve. Bill, always known as Willie by the family, needed to find paid employment to assist his aging grandmother.

Sally and her little brother Amos continued to visit their grandmother and their 'Aunty Rose', the frail Dorothy Rose, staying with them at Rectory Cottages during their summer visits. But once again death came to visit .When Sally was eight and little Amos was just three in 1923, their Aunty Rose died. Amos had just pieces of scrap pictures that his mother had used to write her name on and two very faded photographs of her; one of her seated on a wicker chair, and one standing awkwardly with her family outside Lynford Hall, leaning for support against the door jam. These provided the only means for him to use for recalling her memory in later years. He had been too young to form a lasting impression of her, but Sally had a powerful ability to recall vivid details of their stays in Kent and subsequently filled the voids with stories for her little brother.

Sally and Amos loved their visits to Kent. The surrounding landscape was in total contrast to their home in the dreary mining town of Jacksdale, Nottingham. The high street wound its way towards the windmill and featured the impressive building named the George Hotel. White painted clapperboard and orange rust coloured tiles fronted the houses and the surrounding countryside afforded views of meadows, hop fields, apple orchards, pastureland and the distinctive rounded oast houses. Just behind Rectory Cottages was a duck pond fringed with weeping willows and opposite stood Cranbrook Church. Sally and Amos slept in the little bedroom facing the church and would watch the procession of choir boys as they filed into the church for their practice. Who first had the idea to use a mirror to shine into the boy's eyes is not certain but they both took particular glee in dazzling the youngsters during the practice session and it appears that they were never caught despite frequently repeating the procedure.

However, the story changed to bell ringers when Sally, living in North Wales, in 1972 wrote to her cousin Joan in Kent.

I have vivid memories of many things which some day we can chat about (could fill a book). One thing I will tell you Bill and I once shone reflected sunlight in the eyes of the church bell ringers & disrupted Bell ringing practice.

Sally had tales of using wound sheets to shinny down from the bedroom and to prowl around the village after bedtime had been announced but it is not clear whether she did so and for what purpose. She once again changed the story to using fishing rods in the same letter, continuing........

29

Having been found out over that I then played a dangerous game of fitting all Grandad's fishing rods together (not very securely) and sliding down them from the attic window-might have killed myself if not caught in the 'Nick of time'.

They certainly made friends with the local children and visited the brewery yard and played games with them as Amos was to testify later. "We used to play with the Parker boys" she said but did not elaborate on the type of games that they enjoyed.

Whether Sally devised a particular torture for her little brother here or back at home in Nottingham is also difficult to ascertain but since she had a free rein during their trips to Kent it seems safe to assume that Amos's memories of being scared witless took place on the quiet countryside roads of Cranbrook.

Sally would suggest a countryside walk luring Amos away from the watchful eyes of Christiana and her grandmother. Once she had found a particular spot she would find little games to play until the opportunity arose. They would chase grasshoppers and try to catch butterflies until Amos was lulled into a false sense of security. Sally carefully ensured that the particular spot afforded her the maximum enjoyment. Suddenly she would alert Amos to the slow rumbling that terrifyingly started to increase in power and volume. Shrieking "it's the bogyman coming for us! "would then proceed to direct him into a clump of stinging nettles "so you won't be seen" and order him to lie down until the danger passed. The story of the bogy man having been told in graphic detail prior to this event involved the tortures that the bogy man inflicted on his victims. She would have already found a safer grassy place close by for herself and they would then both hold their breath and close their eyes as the dreadful goggled and leathered biker roared by. "I must have been a daft bugger" was the only censorious remark that Amos ever made about the incidents. And it was amazing that she was able to repeat the torture without Amos realising what was to happen, which proves that her powers of persuasion and the ability to enthral were quite well developed in a child of eight or nine years of age.

Sadly by 1925 their visits to their grandmother and their beloved Kent came to an end as Charlotte Mary died four years after her husband. Willie, aged sixteen, went to live with his Uncle Amos and his wife Edith. As time passed their memories of Rectory Cottages took on a more rosy hue having spent some of their best parts of a carefree childhood there.

Sally recalled that she was allowed to put the tobacco in the pipe for the local brewer Mr Willy Winche. She said that her grandfather Amos had worked for him and together they would puff away at their pipes, reminiscing about their time spent at Oxford university together, and that Billy Winche had seven pipes- one for each day of the week and that when she had visited the Cranbrook museum as an adult she had seen Billy Winche's pipe rack and had been able to tell them that they had placed the pipes incorrectly in the rack. There indeed was a William Winche, brewer, living at Baker's Cross, Cranbrook with his wife Catherine and their daughter Jane and son William in 1901. He was aged forty nine then and so would have been sixty eight by 1920 and Sally would have only been five. It was very possible that she knew him and that she remembered him as her grandfather's employer until her grandfather's death in 1925 when she would have been ten years old, but the idea that they had been to university together was quite whimsical.

Many times she would recount the time after Charlotte died and the family came down from Nottingham to find her Uncle Amos piling up all the possessions remaining from the May's onto a huge bonfire in the garden. Topping the pile was the

31

treasured heavy family bible that Sally was unable to rescue despite valiant attempts to do so.

"With that bible went all the details of our family history and our estates in Conway and North Wales", she would sigh.

"The family names had carefully been inscribed on the fly leaf for decades, but Uncle Amos was furious with Chrissie and Herbert for some reason. His eyebrows flew up exposing his fearful bulging eyes, but the bible was too badly scorched and Uncle Amos would not let me touch it".

She repeated these details, with some changes, in a letter dated 2nd June 1972, to her cousin Joan, her Uncle Amos's daughter, many years later, much to Joan's wry bemusement.

Oh how I wish we knew where that Bible was, it had all the family dates for hundreds of years in it, I remember being so fascinated with some of the vivid Welsh names and strange old writing, As I told you my mother always thought your father had it. So goodness only knows what happened.

She went on to compound the insults, seemingly oblivious of the effects of her story on Joan.

When grandma died in 1925 there was some unpleasantness between our parents which resulted in your father ordering my mother out of our grandmother's house. After a week or so (we stayed with friends in Cranbrook) he came to tell my mother she could go back to the house-he had claimed what he wanted (being the only son) you know how things were in that day. Well when mother, Moss (just a baby) and I returned to Rectory Cottage (Grandad & Grandma's) last place of residence, you can't imagine what it was like, so sorry this may not be pleasant for you but it is the truth and I was old enough to understand. Your mum had made a huge bonfire in the garden and burnt most of the things which were burnable, and some that were not. I remember retrieving some pieces of china which I had always liked from the ashes. Enough of that only now I think the bible must have gone on the bonfire perhaps amongst the books by mistake, though it was such a big one I really don't know how it could have been overlooked.

By 13th June she attempted to atone for the tone of her last letter saying,

re the quarrel between our parents as you say that is in the past nothing to do with you & I.

But she then added insult to injury by continuing,

The only clear knowledge I have of it was your father, my Uncle, standing like the God Thor, his eyes nearly bolting (he has prominent ones as you know) out of his head, and shouting "Get out of this house Chrissie". Mum then bundled Amos up and gave him to little Miss Povey & with me trotting along venting every curse (under my breath of course) against your dad we went to Miss Povey's cottage where we stayed until your father returned to Maidstone.

"With every retelling, the bonfire episode grew bigger, as did the family's past wealth in the slate mines of North Wales.

"Nain and Taid would have been devastated to have known what was going to happen to the family bible. I should have taken it back to safety to Nottingham when I had the chance!" She would exclaim. "Only I knew how important it was".

However, I was more impressed with the stories of Sissinghurst Castle and Victoria Sackville-West. As a child I had often visited the gardens of Sissinghurst and they held a special place in my affections, so I listened carefully to her stories containing meetings with the Sackville-West family.

"We had tea and buns and muffins in her drawing room when we met Vita at Sissinghurst Castle. Then we pushed Rose along in her chair as she loved looking at the herbaceous borders. Your Taid had planted the nut grove, which you can still see today, and Vita was so delighted with his work. She was quite an odd person though, quite a blue stocking, being part of the Bloomsbury group".

Vita and Harold bought Sissinghurst, which was, according to the guide books, in a poor state of repair, in 1930. The property had been owned by the Cornwallis family and then various farmers prior to the Sackville's purchase. Unfortunately Amos May died in 1921, nine years prior to their purchase, so unless Vita employed a medium she could not have provided Amos with instructions to plant the filbert grove. It was more than disappointing not to have a direct link to this fascinating family; I had loved our family outings to Vita and Harold's secret gardens, delighting in the profusion of plantings and the unexpected hidden areas that were discovered as we followed the pathways to find the fragrant white garden. The only part that caused problems for me was the overwhelming smell of curry from the small herb garden. I had romantically identified with Vita as she wrote her books in the castellated tower, and was somewhat mortified to have that family myth shattered so convincingly. I had been told that Amos had worked in Bedgebury Pinetum so the planting of the nut grove had made perfect sense.

....

34

Much later I began to research the story of Sissinghurst a little further, trawling through the internet and gardening books loaned by a friend in New Zealand. As I began to read, my conviction of Sally's fantasies was seriously challenged. The nuttery was thought to have been planted in 1900 according to Kirk Johnson in his book "Sissinghurst Castle" and one of the main reasons for Vita and Harold buying the property was the nuttery and orchard that captivated their attention. Suddenly I could hear Sally's voice and see her drawing herself up haughtily: 'you dared to doubt me?' Amos was living in Goudhurst in 1901 so he could have known the tenant farmer George Neve who was looking after the estate and farm until 1903.

In the book "Sissinghurst -'the making of a garden'" by Anne Scott-Jones, she wrote that a Sidney Neve, in 1937, aged 17 was taken on by Vita and Harold as a third gardener.

I found in the 1901 census that there was a Neve family still living in Sissinghurst but there was no mention of George Neve. The family consisted of a widow and her children, one of whom was named Sidney, aged 19. Then much later I went into the 1911 census and found the Neve family again but this time the head of the household was George Neve, aged 84, a retired farmer and Land Agent with Mary Eliza Neve, aged 69 and their sons, Henry, aged 51 who was also a Land Agent and Walter who had no occupation but was living on private means.

Anne Scott-Jones also described the history of the house and garden writing that the "Elizabethan priest's house and a tiny portion of the three sided Elizabethan mansion was known as the South Cottage and they were used from 1796 to 1855 as a workhouse, then degenerated into still worse repair and were used as farm buildings......then that the place had been on the market for several years since the death of the last owner, a farmer, who had not regarded the surroundings of the old castle as a garden, but merely a convenient dump for his rusty iron." This agrees with Tony Johnson's research, "in 1794 the Mann Estate rented the property to Cranbrook Poor Relief Trustees, and one hundred poor families farmed the estate while living in flimsy buildings that were tacked onto the ruins; this lasted until 1855, when the parish shut down the farm."

Anne Scott-Jones went on to write that Vita and Harold showed a huge enthusiasm for working on the garden and that they cleared the nuttery.

In "Gardening at Sissinghurst" by Tony Lord he sites that the planting of the nuttery and the orchard trees took place in around 1900, and that in 1930 the moat wall was unearthed and the nuttery cleared. Later in the book, "In April 1930 Harold's diary records: 'we came suddenly upon the nut walk and that settles it'. Thus the planting of the filberts inseparably associated with the rural life of Kent clinched that decision to make their home and garden there."

After the Second World War in 1946 the head gardener Jack Vass returned to Sissinghurst and made the restoration of the nuttery his first priority.

Tony Lord writes: "Believed to have been planted in about 1900, the nuts are all filberts (Corylus maxima); more vigorous than (Corylus avellana) and with the long calyx or husk extending beyond the end of the nut...........Though the nuts at the top of the azalea bank are a more vigorous cultivar, most of the planting here is of Kentish Cob (which is, paradoxically, a filbert). Its synonym, 'Lambert Filbert' is also a matter for debate: tradition insists that it was introduced by a Mr Lambert of nearby Goudhurst in about 1830. However, the great Victorian fruit expert, Dr Hogg, wrote in 1884 that it had only recently been introduced to Kent and that it was Aylmer Bouke Lambert of Wiltshire who first showed it at the Horticultural Society in 1812".

Whenever Sally came to stay with us in Kent she had a fixation about buying Kentish cob nuts and we would be presented with a large brown paper bag full of them. I loved the delicate frill that surrounded the almond-shaped nut case as it reminded me of the drawings of the flower fairies who wore clothes of the woods and meadows. Sally never left Kent without taking a quantity of these nuts back with her.

....

As a bright, vivacious young girl growing up in Nottingham the poverty of her family circumstances troubled her. Even with her friends in Friezeland in Underwood she felt ashamed of her poor home, so they played in the streets, which avoided the ignominy of letting them witness her shabbily furnished home, although there must have been many other neighbouring families sharing similar financial difficulties and having equally unkempt homes . One friend, Elvedor Kent, had a violent father who regularly beat his wife. Her mother's bruises were apparent for all to see once she ventured out to shop for the family groceries. Elvedor was cowered by her father's drunken outbursts but she and her mother had no means of escaping their life of deprivation and violence. Elvedor's only release was to be able to confide in Sally and tell how she hated her father.

In the street Sally befriended two boys who were viewed as an odd couple, being so different in looks and temperament. David Carling was short with a mass of fair curly hair whilst his friend Lawrence Levers was dark and lanky with his thin legs appearing at the bottom of his trousers. But it was her school friend Esme Daniel who was set apart from the crowd. She came from a relatively rich family who were able to afford chocolate éclairs. It seems that these were shared as a treat for Sally's family each Friday night, much to her delight.

For most of the time Sally devoted her spare time to the small menagerie in the small back yard crowded with hutches. The dogs and rabbits were fed on a meagre supply of scraps from the table. Sally diligently cared for them whilst dreaming of becoming a vet.

There was one incident which caused her much distress when it was reported that a family in nearby Bagthorpe kept some ducks. In order to keep them safe from the prying eyes of thieves they were put in a basket under a bridge each evening. Then, one dreadful night, after a particularly heavy downfall of rain, the river's waters rose, and the poor ducks were drowned, being unable to escape from their wicker confinement.

At school Sally was able to lose herself in her studies. Her love of books allowed her to live out her fantasies. She excelled in the work and found favour with her teachers who were pleased to have such a diligent and promising pupil. But at the age of fourteen she was forced to abandoned her studies for 'health reasons' and her dreams of further education were dashed.

The May family group: Rose, Chrissie, Mary Charlotte, her husband Amos and eldest daughter 'Lottie' at Lynford Hall in Norfolk, where Amos worked as the head gardener during the early 1900's. Sally paid for the slate headstone for the family burial in Cranbrook, Kent.

The George Hotel; Eastwell Manor in Kent; Amos and his family; *then below,* Rectory Cottages in Cranbrook.

Chapter 3   Denbigh 1972

By 1972 Sally was still living in the Nurses' Home in the grounds of the North Wales Hospital for Nervous and Mental Disorders. She had achieved the important position of Matron, with an impressive list of letters following her name on the hospital headed note paper; S.R.N., R.N.M.S., R.M.P.A, M.I.S.W... The hospital, commissioned in 1842 and opened in April1848 was a fine building much admired by the local people. For its day it was an enlightened institution. Most asylums in those days were formidable, being run as prisons with locked wards. The founding fathers passed a resolution that their hospital would be open, without walls and 'that all mechanical restraint and coercion would be replaced by kind management and moral discipline'. The original hospital stood on thirteen acres of land and took a large percentage of the town's people in employment with many people having members of their family working there. They were either nursing or occupying various positions in the kitchens, workshops, gardens and so on. It was a town within a town requiring skills and labour; taking from the town and beyond.

The name Matron inspired confidence and brought with it the image of starched uniforms and brisk no nonsense common sense. A Matron was expected to be all seeing and all knowing, with just the right amount of deference to the consultants of course. Patients, mentally or physically unfit were expected to toe the line and understand the rules.

Every Sunday all patients were required to attend the church service regardless of their religious preference.

"We always had a full house when Mrs Jay was around" confided an ex-colleague of Sally's. "Nobody dared stay away, and anyway it never did them any harm!"

Sally ruled with a rod of iron but was respected for her fairness, experience and dedication to the position. She ensured that her staff were equipped to do the job properly with staff education and training being one of her pet priorities; encouraging potential whenever she saw it. During her time at the hospital she started a Motor Club for the staff, annexed the old fire station to become the club's garage and demolished the old theatres.

As for her patients she believed that each one was a unique individual. She felt that nursing at her hospital should involve their whole care. They needed to be regularly assessed to ascertain their needs; and this included careful medication, meeting and treating physical needs and plenty of mental and practical stimulation to prepare them for the next step in coping with the world. She ensured that workshops were fully equipped for them to acquire skills that would prepare them for means to become self sufficient. The most aggressive patient wouldn't faze her. She met explosive anger and dangerous situations with equanimity.

When she had first been appointed to the post Sally's long hair was routinely tied up in a severe bun at the back of her head, but during the later years she had had it cut into a more gentle and modern style. She was the epitome of efficiency, order and discipline. Being about five foot six in height she always drew herself up and held back her shoulders so appeared to be much taller. Privately she was very proud of her trim figure and small waist.

"As a young girl my waist was just eighteen inches" she would announce. The implication being that a tendency to run to fat spoke of an inability to control; it was undisciplined and lazy. Her white starched cap and blue uniform meant business. She expected her orders to be obeyed without question, and as they invariably were she felt no reason to change her *modus operandi*. Her voice mimicked her statue. She spoke authoritatively with a slight Derbyshire twang which became huskier with age and the effects of her smoking habit which she attempted to conceal. Her skin was white and unblemished; her grey eyes looked through you, and beyond, and saw everything. The ability to raise just one eyebrow when questioning and appraising betrayed the family link with my father, but when he did it there was humour in his quizzical expression. When Sally did it there was reproach or looming interrogation to follow. I practised the technique of the lone raised eyebrow and was delighted to have perfected it during my childhood as it afforded me a physical link with them both.

She had an opinion on every aspect of life and would be happy to share them with those that she felt could enter into an educated discussion. Sally did not suffer fools gladly as they say. Little men irritated her, women who betrayed a more feminine side of their nature were considered inferior and children were generally avoided. She despised domesticity, regarding the business of cleaning, dusting, and mopping quite distasteful and trivial. The idea that any satisfaction could be derived from such occupation would be met with total incomprehension. That her hospital needed to be kept clean was obvious to her but then that was about keeping infection at bay and maintaining order in the wards, and nothing to do with aesthetics of a tidy and well presented home.

As a child I thought her to be fearless and brave. She certainly never betrayed a weakness. Her manner was forthright; you either liked it or lumped it. Her dreams were as grandiose as her pronouncements which she defied you to challenge.

....

'Care in the Community' was looming on the horizon and questions about the long term damage to patients being institutionalised were beginning to be asked. Sally was appalled at the uncritical enthusiasm for such radical changes and concerned about the untested impact on her vulnerable, clinically depressed, psychotic, unpredictable and troubled charges.

"How they will manage their medication without careful supervision I do not know" she argued.

"Who will directly monitor changes on a daily basis and be accountable? It's care on the cheap and there will be those who slip through the net left to fend for themselves sleeping rough in the streets, with nowhere to call home. It's a scandal and an abdication of responsibility. You mark my words. Care indeed! A disgrace; and we call ourselves a civilised society. It's politicians who want to make a name for themselves, with no ability to think things through and with no experience or qualifications in nursing who have these liberal views. It will be out of sight and out of mind."

Sally was an active fifty seven years of age but she knew that changes at her hospital were afoot and that her retirement was not too far on the horizon. The hospital had barely five hundred patients as a result of the government initiatives. She had already begun to look around for a home that she could call her own.

In the Nurses' Home she was provided with total care. All the domestic arrangements organised around her. Meals were served in her rooms; washing taken and returned crisp and starched, floors were polished, beds made, silver cleaned and furniture dusted but she aspired to own a house and some land. At first she looked at small holdings, then farms. Once she almost made a bid for a sheep farm before realising that perhaps even she would not have the time or skills to run the place single handed.

On the 19th November 1971 she received a letter from the estate agents Jackson-Stops & Staff based in Chester, confirming that her offer of £6,050 was to be accepted for a property.

Dear Madam,

Pen–y-Graig, Llanfair D.C.

We have at last received instructions that your offer of £6,050 for the above property subject to contract is to be accepted. Our client's solicitors are Messrs Barlett and Son of Marlom Chambers, 30 North Street, Liverpool and we have instructed them to submit a draft contract for the approval of your solicitors as soon as possible.

But at the bottom left hand side of the letter Sally wrote cryptically

only offered £4,500.

Perhaps she was unable to raise the funds and had to withdraw the offer.

"Oh how I would have loved that farm", she would often remark, "but it just slipped through my fingers, it was stolen from me".

Despite working throughout her adult life she had not the necessary capital to purchase a house that was big enough to fit her grand designs. Sally had always worked hard and spent well. Why buy one when two or three could be purchased? She needed to raise funds and realised that a bank loan would be necessary, but there were concerns over her pension as she needed to be sure that all her years of service, including those during the second world war, would be accredited to her.

She embarked upon a long campaign to have all the years reinstated at the correct value. Terse, complicated letters passed furiously from department to department culminating in accusations of incompetence and fraud. Sally would spend hours on her calculations, fretting over each response before firing off another written salvo. The unions were called in to add weight to her claims and so the process dragged out. She would frustratingly find another property that would suit only to find it snapped up before she could raise the money. Finally in 1974 she found two semi-detached cottages overlooking the Vale of Denbigh with a nice amount of land surrounding the property. She knew that the price and plans for improvement were beyond her means and that she would need to rent out one half of the property in order to pay for the work that she had envisaged. And as we were in the process of moving up to Wales an opportunity to share costs occurred to her.

……………………………………………..

Turning in past the high stone walls we walked up the long gravel drive to the hospital. The building was huge and impressive and I had faint butterflies tingling in my stomach; half excitement and a good deal of apprehension. It had been good of her to invite us to visit her. The offer of a position had come at the right time. Funds for us were extremely tight since moving up to Wales and only having one income. Everything was so strange; roads, signs and directions all in Welsh and totally incomprehensible to us in those days. Following the arrows we climbed the grand stone steps up to the main entrance.

"My God it's huge!" I needed to whisper." Look at all the windows and those bow shaped gables". It felt as if the windows were staring down at us, watching our approach. I suddenly wished to be somewhere else. The hospital had a reputation; everyone knew about being 'sent to Denbigh'.

She met us in her office. "We'll have a quick tour round, and you can meet some of the staff and patients".

We followed meekly, my heels sounded loud and clumsy on the flooring. She moved fast and we walked past groups of people, some sitting in chairs others around tables, one or two of the older people stared back, sloppy grins squinting at us, wanting to reach out and touch my hand. My skin crawled and I felt repugnance and guilt simultaneously. As we continued along the long corridors and into other rooms I realised that

46

Sally had not spoken or introduced us to some of the staff on the way.

"Oh," I said feebly "who was that?" indicating one of the staff as they smiled and walked purposefully past.

"That's John and he is making so much improvement".

With horror I realised that I couldn't tell patient from nurse or doctor. Everyone seemed so normal and yet it was not normal. I knew then that I was totally unsuited to work with any mental illness. My dreadful incomprehension and naivety, compounded by a distinct lack of compassion, made me ashamed. But my biggest concern was to have to tell Sally that I didn't want to work here. I couldn't do it! My whole being recoiled in terror.

It brought back my greatest nightmare that would come to haunt me through all the years of my childhood and even now had not lost its power to terrify me.

I was in the house belonging to my Grandmother. It was dark, sometime in the evening. I could hear voices downstairs and even though I knew that I shouldn't get out of bed and go down the stairs I needed to know what was being said. The murmurings grew louder but still I couldn't hear the words. They were all there in the gloomy kitchen. If I went down one more stair I would be able to bend over the banister and see into the badly lit room. I leaned over with the banister digging into my ribs. I didn't want to go down further and edged forward.

"She mustn't see this," someone said.

What mustn't I see? There was Gran, and Dad and Mum and Heather. I could tell it was them from their shapes even though their backs were towards me. But I didn't want them to turn round but then Gran began to turn. She started to put her hand up to her throat as if to tug at something. Was it her jumper that was tight around her neck? She grasped the skin at her neck and the folds seemed to be loose and thick.

Slowly she said "she will never know that it is not us", and continued to pull the face away from her face. I never knew what was underneath because I would awake at that point, in total panic, paralysed with fear and loathing.

The tour continued until finally we left, murmuring our thanks; the windows watched our departure.

Sally became Matron of Denbigh Hospital for Mental and Nervous Disorders in 1963. The hospital is now closed and falling into disrepair.

North Wales Hospital Denbigh

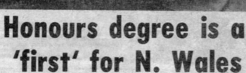

Honours degree is a 'first' for N. Wales

Steaming ahead in pursuit of further academic honours is Mrs Rose Sally Jay, senior nursing officer at the North Wales Hospital, Denbigh, who last week became the first Open University graduate in North Wales to gain an honours degree.

Mr Jay, whose home is at Bryn Llwyn, The Glyn, Llanrhaeadr, carried out a comparative study of the social and work patterns of Denbigh and gained her BA honours degree in arts and social science combined with technology and science.

Mrs Jay, who, at the age of 61, intends to study for further qualifications, has an unusual educational background. As a child she suffered from rheumatic fever with the result that she had only 3½ years formal education. She recalls that she did not have a Christmas out of her sick bed until she was 17.

Mrs Jay has strong connections with the administrative side of the Open University. She is a member of its general assembly and the Welsh representative in the senate. In addition, she is chairman of the Welsh Consultative Committee; and a member of the Cartrefle Study Centre, and of the Open University's geological and philosophical societies.

Outside her work at the North Wales Hospital, Mrs Jay has always been active in the British Red Cross Society and is at present nursing officer for Clwyd West. She is chairman of the local branch of the United Nations Association and, before re-organisation of local government, was a member of Denbigh Borough Council.

She is interested in photography, both still and cine, loves gardening and is a steam engine enthusiast.

ABOVE: Mrs Jay displays a pen and ink drawing by her brother of a traction engine, which he named "Sally," in honour of his sister, who is a steam engine enthusiast.

Chapter 4 Denbigh 1964

It was so exciting! Aunty Sally had suggested that we could stay for a week's holiday with her and we were going to stay in the hospital accommodation. Everything had been arranged. She was going to take us to the International Eisteddfod, whatever that was, and we were going over the Mersey on the ferry to Liverpool. Perhaps we would see the Beatles! When we got there she would be taking us out in her car. She had a caravan as well that was by the coast and we were going to see that and probably stay in it. The name of the place was in Welsh, of course, Abersoch, on the Lleyn Peninsula. There were going to be so many treats lined up. We were going to visit castles and see Snowdon and the little railway that went right to the top. And the hospital was just like a big hotel so we would have all our meals served up for us. So exciting! I could hug myself with happiness.

I couldn't wait for the journey to begin. We were to go through London, and then we had to change and travel across London to Euston, then on to Chester. I think we were going through a place called Mold, where we would have to change again, and finally onto Denbigh which apparently was a small town. Sally was either going to meet us at the station or she would send a car for us. We were going to be so important. We were the relatives of Mrs Sally Jay, Matron who was in charge of the whole of Denbigh Hospital.

It was only a pity that Heather couldn't come because she was working. We had two suitcases and Mum and I carried a smaller bag each. There were sandwiches for the journey wrapped in greaseproof paper and we had a flask with coffee in it. We would eat our food once we had got on the train at Euston as this would be the longest part of the journey.

I hoped that we had the right clothes with us because Wales had snow on their mountains because it was called Snowdon. So it could be very cold, and apparently Denbigh was close to the moors as well as the mountains. Dad said that town was high up and surrounded by sheep. And there was a castle which was either Welsh or King Edward's but I couldn't remember which it was. Anyway we would be visiting that as well because Dad loved castles.

We had visited Sissinghurst Castle which really wasn't a proper castle because it belonged to the National Trust and was important because of the lady who had lived there. She was a writer and had made lots of little beautiful gardens within brick walls with little archways and paths that led you all over the place. I had also been to Bodiam Castle that was so romantic with the water reflecting around the towers. Once, we had been to Dover castle and had climbed up so many round staircases they made you quite dizzy. And we had seen the dungeons. Perhaps Denbigh castle has a well and some dungeons too.

I wonder what my bedroom will be like and if there are toilets in the apartment or whether we have to go out into a corridor to the bathrooms.

It is just wonderful! Aunty Sally met us in her car at Denbigh railway station and we went up the steep hill until we reached the top of the town and then we drove past the Welsh castle which I couldn't see properly because the road was so narrow and a big wall hid most of the ruins from view. Then, just as we reached the top, we could see some fields and sheep and then down below us to the right were the huge grounds of the hospital laid out in front of us. We were to stay in her quarters. Once we had put our suitcases on the beds we went into her rooms to find a large tea laid out for us. There was a silver tray with a silver teapot, and silver milk and sugar bowl and then a plate of sandwiches and some yellow Madeira cake. It was just lovely. Tomorrow we will be having breakfast in this bright sunlit room and then we will be going to Liverpool. Aunty Sally has said that we will travel across the Mersey River on a ferry. It is a long journey again because we are in Wales and Liverpool is back in England.

Breakfast was lovely! We had tinned grapefruit segments in little white bowls, then corn flakes in another bowl followed by eggs and bacon with sausage and tomatoes which were on the tray keeping warm, covered with silver domes. When the domes were lifted off the smell of bacon just filled the room. We have never had tinned grapefruit. We just have the ordinary grapefruit which you have to cut up yourself and which always squirts into your eye just as you are trying to dig out the flesh with your spoon.

Aunty Sally said that the plates would be collected and all we had to do was just pile them back onto the little tray. The cutlery was quite heavy though and I found that they made a lot of noise as we were eating. I ate everything. Then we had toast wrapped up in a cloth to keep it warm and little pots of marmalade already spooned out into the little glass pots, with little curls of butter in another dish. It was so pretty. Aunty Sally eats like this every day I think.

Liverpool was very disappointing. It rained all day and the river was a dark grey brown. The wind whipped up the foam in the water and some seagulls tried to land on the sides of the ferry but kept on being blown away. There were a lot of very big grey buildings in the city and we walked by a building that had big stone birds on the top but we didn't see the Beatles.

Still, soon we are to have our dinner with Aunty Sally and as we are waiting to eat there is the sound of someone playing jazz on the piano. They are making the music come alive. So clever! Our piano doesn't sound like that. I am going to creep down into the corridor to see if I can see who is playing.

Tomorrow we are going to go into the town and then go to visit the castle as Aunty Sally can't be with us as she has to work. The next day I think we are going to see different people from countries all around the world singing, and being dressed up in their national costumes. I have a collection of dolls dressed in their national costumes. The first one that I had Heather gave me when she went to Greece. The lady carries a large wicker basket on her head and has gold jewellery at her throat and round her head. Not real gold of course. Then I bought a doll when we went to Calais for the day with our school. That was the time when one of the boys bought a penknife and the teacher took it from him. Aunty Sally gave me a doll from Poland and she was beautiful. Her skirt was patterned but it was her face that was the best part. Her face was so pretty and delicate, not like the Greek doll whose eyes looked too false. The doll from Aunty Sally looked very expensive and although I like the one I got from France, hers is the very best of the collection.

I can't remember if we ever did go to the International Llangollen Eisteddfod. Aunt Sally was always so busy having to keep changing the arrangements as different problems occurred. But the trip was a vivid chapter in my life. We were photographed standing by her caravan in Abersoch. One day we climbed over the broken stone walls of ruined Denbigh castle and peered through the rusty iron grid down the deep well into which the castle architect's son had fallen and died. We saw sunlight shafts gleaming on the cascading waters at Fairy Glen and searched for suitable woollen souvenirs in the crowded shops at Betws y Coed. Admiring the wooden love spoons and creamy thick folds of the sheep rugs we were astounded by the choice of such luxury goods. We had been treated like royalty and I believed her life to be a fairy tale of glamour and elegance. The hospital appeared to be more like a country estate than a working environment to care for the sick. I only saw it from the outside, set within well-kept grounds, green lawns, manicured shrubs, trees and crunchy gravel paths. I was a very impressionable teenager filled with romanticism. Sally did not approve of such nonsense. I was far too dreamy. My mother was not considered to be worthy of much attention but it was Moss, my father who she pampered, confided in, excluding Mum and I as she shared intimacies and confidences. They discussed and smoked together; her with her cigarettes and Dad with Erinmore mixture in his pipe. They resumed their close relationship of brother and sister which did not include us. Mum reacted with irritation but Dad seemed so happy that I became bewildered, not understanding her unhappiness. Sally flattered him; he had her undivided attention; they reminisced; she recalled childhood stories; they discussed trains, machines, religion, politics, space and the worlds beyond. I listened and watched as his chest expanded and he glowed. I suppose I was pleased that he was so happy and at that time didn't understand how selfish and exclusive love can be. Did Sally know that she excluded us? Probably she did. Did she care? Probably not. After all, what was a mere week of sibling time in the grand scheme of things? Hadn't she treated his family to a week of luxury, all expenses paid? What was there to complain about?

I don't remember the journey home.

Denbigh.
12th February, 1969.

Dear Matron,

Mayor's Charity Ball - Friday 28th March, 1969.

It is my intention to hold a Charity Ball in Denbigh on Friday the 28th March, 1969 in aid of "Save the Children Fund." I would be very pleased if you could attend this function and I enclose an invitation for yourself and lady.

The arrangements for the evening will be sent to you at a later date.

Yours sincerely,

Mayor.

The Matron,
North Wales Hospital for Mental
and Nervous Diseases,
Denbigh.

Sally received an invite to the Mayor's Charity Ball whilst she was Matron at the hospital. She also served as a Denbigh councillor during the 1970's. (Wearing a trouser suit on the front row)

Sally and her brother Amos and his wife Joyce on a caravan holiday at Abersoch.
 The caravan eventually returned to her home in Denbigh and slowly disintegrated during the passing years, still equipped with the camping paraphernalia that she had carefully acquired.

Evidence of her growing interest in the local steam railway societies.

LLANGOLLEN RAILWAY SOCIETY LIMITED

Cymdeithas Rheilfford Llangollen Cyfyngedig

Registered under the Industrial and Provident Societies Act 1965
Registered No. 21820 R

SHARE CERTIFICATE

This is to Certify that

.... Rose Sally Christiana Mary Jurayszyn Jag ....

is/are the Registered Holder(s) of .... £1 (one pound) fully paid shares in the Society, subject to the rules of the Society.

Registration Date ...... 8th March 1988   Chairman ....

Certificate No 112   Secretary ....

Registered Office: LLANGOLLEN STATION, LLANGOLLEN, CLWYD.

58

Chapter 5   The early 1950's

Christmas   Maidstone 1957

We have been waiting all day for the parcel to arrive and now it is here it is huge! Aunty Sally's writing on the front says, *"To Mr & Mrs A H W Payne"* and on the back she has written her own address. It is so big that Dad has had to push the arm chairs out of the way in the front room and has had to use his penknife to cut through all the tape. It is difficult to contain our excitement. Finally he opens it and it is indeed a box of dreams. There is soft yellow packing straw spilling out of the box. Nestling inside are tins and packages. Dad pulls out each one and we greedily devour his words.
"Tin of ham."
"Oh," we sigh.
"Dundee cake, tin of peaches, Christmas pudding with sherry, tin of cream, biscuits for cheese".
We savour the itinerary of treats. Once again we have received a feast of delights and it has exceeded our expectations. It is almost as if we can feel the wave of a Godmother's wand as the goods lay exposed on the floor. Our front room is filled with a glow. Our little Christmas tree which has been made from a collection of individual twigs with each twig wrapped with fringed green crepe paper receives the gifts as they are arranged around its paint tin base.
"Well, she's done us proud again," Dad announces and we all nod our approval. Our Aunty Sally only buys the best.

Summer   Maidstone 1957

Aunty Sally and her son Tadek are going to come down to Maidstone to stay with us. We have been waiting and waiting for her to be able to take time off work and come down to see us. Her shifts are so difficult to rearrange and she hardly gets any time to herself, and so it is lovely that she has at last been able to wangle it. It has been such a hot day and we expected her to arrive hours ago but despite watching and patrolling the road there has been no sign of her green Moggie Minor estate. Heather and I are to sleep together; with Mum's misgivings that we won't start arguing. Aunty Sally is to have my little front room and Tadek is going to have a bed made up in the front room downstairs.

Aunty Sally could sleep on a pin head as she is used to going without sleep. She has told Mum that on many occasions. Once she even slept in the attic in her house with huge spiders crawling around but she said that they didn't bother her. "Nothing to be frightened of" she said. I pray that I would never be expected to share a room with spiders and their clinging feathery webs. The thought was horrifying.

We run out again to watch the road. Still no sign. When will she be here? The morning has long gone. Sitting on the high stone park wall we have a good view of the road in both directions round the bend. Will the car appear from the Willington Street end or from the top of Oxford Road?

We haven't got a car yet nor a television or a refrigerator but Sally has heaps of lovely things in her big house.

It's thirsty work watching and waiting but if we go in we might just miss the moment so we have to stay put. I will practise a few steps along the narrow wall. If Mum sees us she will go mad. "You'll break your neck one day falling off that wall."

It's a good job that she doesn't know that yesterday we devised a new challenge and used our new skipping rope to

60

skip along the top. My heart had thumped and when we jumped down there was a strange jelly-like feeling in my legs.

"She's here, she's here!" The green car stopped, Sally glances in our direction and we feel exposed in her gaze.

We are to have tinned ham and salad as it is so hot and then tinned peaches and sterilised cream for afters.

Tadek is getting out of the car and they are taking out large suitcases. Sally is wearing green slacks and a cardigan and seems to be taller than I remembered. Her voice is loud too, but her scent smells the same, just so sophisticated.

"Come on then," we are summoned to assist.

Mum has been busy in the kitchen and looks flustered. Sally sits on Dad's captain's chair in the dining room and accepts a cup of tea. We are not sure where to sit and it feels as if the room is too small for us to just stand to watch, but I can't bear to miss a moment. Dad is beaming; his pipe is wedged between his teeth and swirls of smoke surround their heads. He is showing Sally a tiny wooden doll that he has been carving for me. All her limbs are jointed but she has not yet been painted.

"So you are keeping yourself busy then Wacker? How's the loco coming on?"

"Oh I've been busy over the park these last few weeks. We've had some problems with the track that needed replacing and Wallis wanted me to bed some bits and pieces down for him so I've hardly been in my shed this last month. We'll go out and have a butchers in a bit shall we, and see the old girl."

Mum comes in. "Shall we have some tea now, are you ready to eat something Sally?"

"Oh, you and food Joyce; always mythering, thinks of nothing else do you." I think that Sally is teasing Mum because she is smiling but Mum doesn't say anything. Sally and Dad are getting up to go out to his shed and Mum walks back to the kitchen. I think that something has gone wrong but I don't know what it can be.

Heather and I will lay the table for everyone; everything has to be pushed out of the way and the table leaf extended to make room for all of us.

Mum has sliced the ham but it has gone into bits as it is so hot and the jelly has not set. We were to have that with the tinned peaches but there is nowhere in the kitchen that is cold enough to put the jelly. We have crusty white bread which Mum has buttered and there is plenty of that but somehow there doesn't seem to be enough ham for six of us. We have got some tomatoes that have been quartered and cucumber and my favourite Heinz salad cream, and Mum is thinking about what to do.

"I'll open some sardines to go with it. I'm sure there's a tin in the pantry. Go and look Julie."

When Mum tries to open the tin the piece of thin metal snaps off with the key half turned across the top. Giving up with the twisted key she attacks the contents with a knife, gouging out the silver fish as they slither into a bowl.

"There doesn't seem much to speak of in that tin." Irritated, she takes the bowl into the dining room to join the rest of the fare.

"Tadek has such a good appetite." Sally returns with Dad and appraises the contents of the meal. She is still smiling but Mum doesn't reply and we are not sure about how everyone will fit around the table. Dad gets a stool from his workshop and Heather brings in the battered chair that is kept upstairs and we sit closely and uncomfortably together, conscious that we must keep our elbows in.

"Ham, Sally? Let me help you." Dad sits by Sally on his stool. Tadek helps himself to the ham and suddenly I know that there is not going to be enough to go round and I love ham!

"Julie, pass your plate." Mum puts a small piece on my plate, then Heather's and I watch as she takes a small piece of sardine for herself before passing the remaining small portion to Dad. Does any one else notice? I feel so embarrassed but Dad and Sally are laughing and talking together.

Tadek winks at us. "Both of you growing up so fast!"

The next day Tadek takes Heather's trike out onto the pavement and it caves in under his weight. He decides to take me on his shoulders and carry me around the front garden, following the little stone steps and paths that Dad has created. It is very high and I feel breathless; he is unsure of his footing and he is making me jiggle up and down which is very uncomfortable and I don't feel safe. He has been going round and round.

"She's coming round now." I look up to see Mum's face looking very grim and Sally is feeling my wrist. I have a loud banging in my head and each thump painfully repeats the beat in my ears.

"I don't think that there is any lasting damage," is Sally's prognosis. I survive the fall. Tadek doesn't meet my eye and my grazed lump is the only rebuke he receives.

We are going to Sissinghurst Castle in Sally's car and then having a dinner at the big hotel in Cranbrook. This is where Sally and Dad lived when they were little. We step into the little shops; Sally talks for ages to the wary shop owners; their replies are polite and I feel embarrassed as they smile and exchange glances with other shoppers. We troop past the church and the fire station, wandering up and down the raised iron fenced pavements, following Sally and Dad as they stride out together, arms linked. They are talking non stop and Dad's voice seems to catch her accent, blending in with her. They seem so close it is as if we don't exist. Dad points out the windmill at the top of the hill. We turn around retracing our steps. Sally says the Parker boys played with them in this yard.

"Do you remember Whacker?" We follow her finger and see an empty yard.

"Next time I'm down I'm bringing a gravestone with me Whacker. It's about time their remains were marked properly.

I'll have the best slate from the quarry and get it carved up there. Now time for lunch I think."

The George is very old and is dark inside. Our eyes take time to become accustomed to our new surroundings. We are given a large table and there is an enormous fire in the grate although it is a warm day. The meal is huge. We have a roast dinner with beef and puffy Yorkshire puddings and the gravy is passed around in a beautiful blue gravy boat. I begin to get very hot. Everything is so 'grand', which is a word that Sally uses. We have apple pie with thick fresh cream served in a pot with a silver spoon. I take out a huge dollop and it sits on the dessert then slowly melts, sliding around the pastry; creating a miniature moat around the pie.

When we step outside the sun dazzles us and it takes time again to see the road and pavement. Dad and Sally have been talking about everything and anything and names, dates; images have become a jumbled assortment of sounds and pictures in my head. I am so lucky to have an Aunty who knows so much and can talk for so long. We don't have anyone in our road, or in our family who is anything like her. Even across Mote Park when we go to see Dad with his trains there is no one who can talk about so many things and use such big words that I struggle to understand. Perhaps it's her accent that makes everything sound so strange and exciting. Mum says that Mr and Mrs Wallis are very well educated and they live in a very big house and he drives a very big car but he only seems to pass the time of day and say hello to us when Dad helps him with his train; and often it is Dad that is pointing out what needs to be done, then he just nods and agrees.

The visit has come to an end. Sally left yesterday and the house seems so quiet I can hear myself breathing. There is such emptiness around; Dad has gone back into his shed and Mum is busy in the kitchen. A saucepan lid has just gone clattering onto the floor and the cat has rushed out of the way into the dining room. I will get my paints out and do some colouring.

Summer   Nottingham 1958

The sun is so hot it has melted the tarmac on the roads. I can smell; newly painted creosote on the fences; smoke and coal. We are in Nottingham where miners work down in deep tunnels, their faces black with soot and coal dust. Dad remembers them as a child crouching down on the corner of a road to talk. He said that they crouch down to talk because they are used to doing that when they are down working at the coal face and so it has become a habit. We haven't seen any miners where Sally and Marion live.

Their house in 24 Charlecote Drive, Wollaton gleams robustly in the summer sun, guarded by a substantial wooden gate. It is so big and comfortable and bright. There is a large garden at the back. Sally has a greenhouse which she looks after and she has a small flower garden with a lawn at the back and then beyond that there is a big vegetable garden with huge onion seed heads and then further on is the fruit garden with masses of ripe raspberries. If you carry on going past the fruit bushes there is a stream that runs across the back and two large trees with branches that you can sit in. It is paradise.

Her house smalls just like her. Her perfume is everywhere. The carpets are thick and stretch from wall to wall. In the dining room the table has been laid for us. Everything is so clean and neat and new. Her large kitchen has a tall fridge in it and the cooker is set in with the other units so nothing stands awkwardly in its own space as things do in our kitchen. There is a big cooked ham joint cooling on the top of the fridge; the soft sweet smell wafts around the kitchen. My mouth is watering. Later on we are going to have this ham carved up and served with salad and new potatoes, but we can go outside and investigate first, "to see what we can see."

Sally is going to pick some of the fresh raspberries for our sweet and I might go and help.

I wander into the garden. Socks, her black cat with white paws, allows me to stroke him as he luxuriously stretches out his long limbs, his white whiskers shining in the sunlight, then he shakes himself and slowly, elegantly stalks towards Sally, his tail upright and proud.

"Are you coming to help me then?" she asks without turning. I feel so pleased and step forward quickly, only to realise that she hasn't seen me and is talking to the cat. I step back again, aiming for the path.

"Careful!" she freezes me in my tracks.

"I'm saving these seed heads. They need to be wrapped in some netting today. They are a new variety that I have been asked to trial this year."

"Go and fetch another box for the raspberries."

I dutifully return with the box and proffer it to her. She takes it impatiently and deposits a large handful of bubbled red soft berries inside. I wait uncertain, wanting to help but not sure whether this is allowed.

"Look! There are loads there," I try to be helpful and indicate where there are ripe berries hanging from the underside of the bush, perhaps hidden from her position. She glances in the direction but seems to miss the area that I have found.

"No over there," I step forward eagerly to point again and then on stepping back realise that my foot is not back on the path. I have brushed up against something.

"Oh for heaven's sake!" her eyebrows are raised and she has straightened up. I turn to look and find that I have trampled onto the onion head, its seeds are scattered over the earth. I turn and flee towards the house, a huge lump of pain caught in my throat.

My eyes are still puffy as we sit down at the table. Mum squeezes my hand and I feel silly and childish. Marion is out in the kitchen with Sally and I can hear his exasperation.

"It is not good to have this meat out in the open Sally. Not good at all. It could go very bad. It is too hot this weather and there are flies, they could contaminate. Do you want us ill?"

His delivery is mimicked.

"Not good, not good. It go very bad! Oh for goodness sake stop fussing. There is nothing wrong at all. I had it covered with the net. Anyway it was far too hot to put in the fridge. All you need to do is carve it, can you do that?"

"Yes of course, but you should be more careful Sally. We have fridge for this food. Why do we buy this if we are not using it? It is waste of money then, huh?"

"Oh you and money. Money, money, money. It's so important to you isn't it? And who has to go out and get the money for this household eh? I work all hours to put food on this table."

They seem oblivious to us sitting there trying to not listen; shamed by the row so public and raw.

Marion lowers his voice. "It's your choice Sally, you chose to have important work."

It sounds like an accusation.

"We could manage if you did not spend, spend. All the time; spending money. It is like confetti with you. Look! It blows away pouf, pouf!"

We glance at each other I feel a need to giggle and am torn between the emotions of being horrified at their anger and yet being guiltily amused at Marion's expressions. I can imagine him throwing the confetti around the kitchen; but this is a well rehearsed argument that promises to become more deadly as the exchanges cut deeper.

"I worked throughout Tadek's childhood. Missing out on all those years when he was so young and vulnerable. And what did he get from you! Nagging old man. Going on and on and on. It's a wonder how we both managed to put up with you over the years."

The wounding cuts slice our senses. I feel myself shuddering. How will he answer?

"You have very bad attitude Sally. Very destructive. I think that you do not know how to treat people. It is a wonder that I stay here and put up with such...."

"Put up with what! Me destructive! How do you think that Tadek has become so accomplished if I was such a bad person? Holding down two demanding jobs, skivvying for you, looking after this house, making the most of myself, scraping by on the pittance you bring home, ensuring that my son has good clothes on his back."

"He doesn't need all the things that you buy! Your son? Your son? Our son, I think. He tells me things that he does not say to you because you are so busy, busy with your nursing and important work. I am here for him. You are on this shift and that shift, always making arrangements, and we have to go hang. You even had your sick mother and all kinds looking after him. And now you are not caring about your own family, invited here and have to listen to you and all this."

Their voices lowered and the door cut out the remaining sound.

At the table with us all seated I glance around. The raging seemed to have been left in the kitchen and normality quickly resumed. Dad and Sally are laughing and Marion speaks kindly to Mum.

"So where do you want to go tomorrow Joyce?" He hands her a plate of pink thickly carved ham which she passes to me.

"I think Amos would like to go into Nottingham, Marion." She turns to Heather, passing the remaining plates across the table.

The white clothed table is laden with treats. A large salad, placed in the centre, has been arranged with generous portions of cucumber and tomatoes, there are little waxy new potatoes glistening with melted butter, sliced beetroot "from the garden" in a small dish, pickles, whole hard-boiled eggs, chunks of fresh bread, arranged butter in whirls, and salad cream, my favourite.

"May I have some salad cream please?"

Sally looked across as I self consciously spoon out a generous amount of thick creamy sauce. Everyone was served.

"Time to dig in then," Dad smiled.

I cover some lettuce with the salad cream and with horror find that it didn't taste right. It is mayonnaise and we had never had it at our house. What could I do with the remaining amount on my plate? It made me gag, being so rich in flavour. I carefully cover the remaining white blob, hiding it with a leaf of lettuce, and hope for the best.

We have time to ourselves in the morning until we go out this afternoon. It is still hot and we are going to sail Tadek's lovely little boats in the stream at the bottom of the garden. They are tied up with string to stop them floating away. Sally bought them for Tadek but he doesn't play with them very often; perhaps it's because he has so many other things. He has a shiny bike and a clockwork train set and upstairs there is a really big telescope, but I haven't actually seen it. You can see the smallest stars and planets at night. Sally knows their long strange sounding names. Sally bought it for his Christmas present this year I think and I know Dad wants to have a look through it.

Heather and I go down the path to the stream. The bees are buzzing around a blue-flowered bush. I think that Sally called it a 'boodullar' or something about it being a butterfly bush. Anyway they certainly love it and so do the butterflies. There are peacock butterflies and red admirals fluttering around. I know their names because I have an 'I Spy book about Moths and Butterflies' and we see them at home. Sally loves all animals, birds and insects and knows so much about them.

She has got so many big books with lovely pictures of them, especially on plants and flowers. I think it is strange that the bees don't seem to bother the butterflies even if they are practically on the same flower. Tadek was going to play with us but his friends have come round so he has gone out with them for a while.

It is really thirsty work sailing boats around but I'm not sure if we are allowed a drink before lunch. We call this meal dinner but dinner is in the evening when we would have tea, which is very confusing. Marion was cleaning the house first thing this morning. They have an electric vacuum cleaner because they have carpets. We have a carpet sweeper at home that you have to push over the carpet square but most of the time it picks some fluff up and then leaves it on the carpet again which is really annoying. Marion is from Poland and he was a pilot during the Second World War. He met Sally when she was in the WRAF and had to get special permission to marry her. He makes you feel very good and is very kind. He has a soft voice and a funny way of saying things. Sally always seems so irritated about things when he is around. When he was brushing up with the dustpan and brush in the kitchen she was tutting, I'm sure of it.

Tadek is back so we are going to play cowboys and Indians. There is a big branch that overhangs the stream and if I climb up onto it I can ambush him because he won't think to look up there. Heather has a big gun and I have a lovely silver one which is a bit smaller. Tadek said that we could borrow them for now.

"Bang! You're dead!" I shoot him from above and then my hand slips.

My gun is still in my hand but the barrel is in the water of the stream. How can that be? Sally is bending over me. She looks very worried; her cool hand is on my forehead. She is feeling all over me, gently stroking and squeezing my legs and arms, and now the back of my head. I feel a bit sick and my head is thumping. I want to sit up but she presses me down; feeling me all over again, her hand sliding down my back. It is nice, a bit like a cat being stroked I think. She looks into my eyes, holding the eyelid gently each time.

Sally carefully picks me up and carries me inside the house. I am laid down on the settee and she asks how I feel. I feel so safe with her there. She is so calm. You know that she will sort anything out.

"We'll keep an eye out for a while and just monitor her I think," she says to Mum who is standing behind Sally.

"There doesn't seem to be any sign of concussion and there's nothing broken."

Our game of cowboys and Indians is over for today. I lie there and wait for the afternoon to finish.

24 Charlecote Drive, Wollaton, Nottingham, Sally, Marion and
Tadek's home from the early 1950's. Heather and Julia playing by
the stream at the bottom of the garden.

73

Tadek (2nd left) with his friends and the children of Billl May in Nottingham.
The Payne family stayed with Sally and Marion at 24 Charlecote Drive. Sally and Tadek accompanied them around Nottingham during their visit in the early 1950's.

Chapter 6   Nottingham December 1928
from child to woman

Sally was just thirteen and aware of herself growing into an attractive young woman. She enjoyed her academic success at school, finding it easy to remember facts and figures and translate her thoughts onto the page. She was happiest at school rather than being at home listening to her father Herbert ranting at her mother Chrissie. She took solace in playing with her rabbits and the cats and dogs at home and would delight in rescuing injured animals and bring them back to nurse back to health. She and her little brother Amos would spend their time together chatting and playing. He had his paints and lead soldiers; she would organise games for them both.

She hated the family rows about drink and money. Her timid mother would cower before Herbert and Sally became more indignant at her father's unreasonable behaviour. Herbert decided to take in a lodger to help the family's finances stretch a little further, but this didn't extend to him handing the money over to Chrissie so she was expected to feed another mouth without extra funds. Herbert was mean but was able to find sufficient funds for his own pleasures which often extended beyond an odd drink or too. He would be in a foul mood after a drinking session, continually finding fault with Chrissie. It was hardly surprising that both Sally and Amos became teetotallers. Sally abhorred the very thought of alcohol and was vocal in her condemnation of drinkers throughout her life. She saw it as a terrible destructive and addictive habit. Amos had a more relaxed approach, although he never drank himself he was quite happy to see other people 'imbibe'. He would take a glass from Mum and sniff saying, "Mmm… smells like a good paint stripper."

Herbert's bad humour would extend to little Amos whose presence continually reproached him for his past unfaithfulness. He had not wanted to bring up Amos but for once the May family had exerted pressure and told him where his duties lie. Amos was a poor, thin specimen who probably wouldn't amount to much in his eyes and Sally seemed to be getting too big for her boots, beginning to argue with him, taking Chrissie's side and standing up for Amos when he shouted at the lad. Women were asserting themselves too much for his liking; the papers were full of their demands for this and that.

Arthur Fuller, their lodger, quickly saw how things were at Albert Avenue, Jacksdale. He had won Herbert's confidence becoming his drinking partner and found Chrissie's innate kindness easy to manipulate but Sally seemed to be made of sterner stuff despite her youth. She was clever, that was obvious, yet she was still naïve, being easy to tease, especially about her obsession with her animals. She was unsure about her budding femininity, almost being disdainful about her appearance as young girls often are; not wanting to acknowledge their sensuality, being half afraid of their new powers and yet secretly enthralled about themselves. Still a tomboy, Sally could be imaginative and amusing. He would listen to her stories as she entertained Amos; and yet with him she assumed aloofness; she held him at a distance. This presented a challenge to him and he set about gaining her confidence, drawing her closer.

He heard the rows between Herbert and Chrissie and saw how this affected Sally. He began to tease her and then to sympathise. Sally found that little by little she was able to confide in him. He seemed to understand her despair when things were going so badly between her parents. He bought her little gifts and asked after the animals. He would sit with her quite closely when she was cuddling the rabbits, flattering her, saying how pretty she was; that one day she would be a real beauty.

"Beauty and brains, what a rare combination Sal, you're something special and no doubt."

He would brush her arm and she felt a little shiver of pleasure. He was quite good looking in a funny way. Each evening she looked forward to him coming in from work and having a little chat. He made her feel so special and grown up.

One night he slipped into her bed. He thought that she needed an extra cuddle and that now, as a friend, he owed it to her to cheer her up. There was nothing wrong in it at all. Besides, she was looking so pretty and such prettiness deserved a nice reward. She would feel so good if he just touched her here and here. Didn't that feel nice? So nice; and just here too? He would just lie next to her and keep her warm. It was such a cold night. His fingers slipped between her legs and found her dampness.

When she began to struggle, sensing panic at his persistence, he used his weight to smother her protest. He entered her forcefully; his hand pressing hard on her mouth.

Sally did not say anything to Herbert or Chrissie the next morning. Feeling ashamed, she was unable to meet anyone's eye and felt a shuddering revulsion of her own participation. Had she encouraged him? Was it all her fault? Sally believed that by flirting with him she would be condemned by everyone that she knew. Wanting to blot out the episode she tried not to think about it but that evening Arthur winked at her as if nothing had happened. But what had happened? It was dirty and disgusting and best left alone. She would not let her thoughts control her. That night he came again into her room. His manner was frightening, aggressive; he seemed a different person.

Before she had a chance to draw herself up he hissed in her ear.

"If you say anything I'll kill those little bunnies of yours. Do you understand? This is our secret, so don't you say a word or their heads will come clean off."

By the following May it was painfully obvious to both Chrissie and Herbert that their daughter was pregnant. How Arthur managed to stay on as their lodger it is impossible to say. He may well have convinced them that Sally was not the innocent that she seemed and that in some way she had 'asked for it' despite her age. Certainly Herbert had always distrusted his clever, aloof daughter and the rent money was still needed; but there was the neighbour's condemnation to consider as a matter of some urgency. It was common knowledge in the neighbourhood that Amos was a bastard child and now there was to be another one in the family. Sally must have spent some time with some trusted friend of the family away from prying eyes.

On the 7th August of that year Sally gave birth to a healthy son, Thomas Arthur. Chrissie let it be known that she was the mother of the new baby boy and Arthur continued to visit the family for many years, bringing gifts for his little son. Herbert treated Tom kindly and they enjoyed a good relationship as 'father and son'.

How the family managed to conceal the truth is again difficult to imagine. Perhaps they said that Sally was unwell. She must have regained her figure fairly quickly. Then there was Amos; how did they hide the birth from him? Although he was only eight years old he was bright and quick for his age. Certainly no one, apart from the four involved, Sally, Arthur, Chrissie and Herbert, had any inkling of the truth. No subsequent whispered scandal reached Tom's ears during his childhood. He grew up as the youngest son of Chrissie's. Once again Chrissie found herself becoming a surrogate mother; another cross to bear.

Sally continued to live with her family, treating Tom as her little brother. Being so much younger than Amos and Sally he remained an outsider, never being invited to share their interests and conversations. Sally used her intellect to awe him into a feeling of inferiority. Tom grew up believing that Chrissie was his mother until, at the age of twenty one, he decided to get married to Nellie. A birth certificate for his wedding was required. The awful shock of finding that information about his real mother on this certificate must have been immense.

Throughout her adult life Sally never acknowledged Tom as her son, with just one exception.

Sally continued to blossom as a teenager, achieving such smouldering good looks that she decided to enter a beauty contest. There is a photograph of her in her bathing costume when she was about eighteen with the Daily Mail competition details on the back to annotate the unsuccessful application. She reinvented herself. After leaving school she went to work as a shop assistant, first at a milliners then at JV Hutton, a large departmental store and finally at Peacocks Bazaar in Nottingham and with her wages paid for a series of studio portraits wearing a variety of period costumes.
Once again the world for women was changing in England. The flapper era had arrived and for women over the age of thirty the right to vote had been won. Although the women, who had shed the constraints of living at home under the control of their fathers, had had to relinquish the jobs to the men who returned from the war, they were now rebelling in their mode of dress. The stays and tight waists had given way to straight tunic dresses, and for this fashion boyish figures were necessary. Chests had to be swathed, bound and flattened in elastic tubing, hair cut short in fashionable bobs

and some girls, even respectable ones, could be found smoking.

During the early and late 1920's the Great Depression had caused misery and brought hunger and hardship to many families, but worst was to come. Finally by the 1930's a world wide depression had set in. Factories lost orders, ship builders were signed off, miners lost their jobs and thousands of men found themselves out of work. There was no welfare state to support a family after just twenty six weeks when the handouts would cease. Soon a mood of desperation took hold as the men queued in long lines outside the Labour Exchanges only to find that there was no work to be had. Being 'laid off' became a hauntingly real fear. Those who had been neighbours or workmates now viewed each other suspiciously as the competition to obtain employment started to intensify. There were rumours of fights outside factory gates and of people marching down to London to protest to the Government. The Household Means Test was introduced in 1931 and for some men the indignity of submitting themselves to the test only to find that as their wives' and daughters' wages were all part of the test and that they were not eligible for any relief, was the last straw. For the first time in their lives they were not the 'bread winners' but were dependent on their own family for financial support. For some families they had to resort to queuing in the street for the arrival of the soup van.

At the age of sixteen, in May 1931, Sally registered as a pre-student at Retford Hospital for six months before enrolling as a student nurse at the Doncaster Royal Infirmary in November of that year. She worked hard at her studies, eventually achieving a successful pass in her Preliminary Examination.

1934 and the war years until 1944

It was on the 12th June in 1935, aged just twenty that she took on the awesome responsibility of nursing the criminally insane at the infamous Rampton Hospital. She must have been in contact with some truly frightening individuals in that bleak place. The nursing required nerves of steel and stamina, both of which Sally had in copious amounts. Her earlier years and trauma had provided her with the iron-like qualities that the job demanded. For the first time she found that she was in the company of other young women who were her intellectual equals.

In 1936 two events at home and abroad brought her life into sharp relief. The Jarrow March from Jarrow to London to petition Stanley Baldwin took over the front page of every newspaper and the war in Spain brought back all the reminders of the First World War to those who had been caught up in the fighting. For the first time she engaged in discussions about these events. Challenging alternative views were promoted. The Government's authority was questioned. Arguments about the threat of communism, the fight against fascism and the rights of the working man took place. She found herself drawn into the debates and then puzzlingly questioning her own conclusions.

She made a good impression on those around her; being able to cope with the most difficult patients whilst demonstrating an open ambition to further her knowledge of mental health. Her striking looks, perseverance and natural air of authority found favour. Each ensuing nursing exam was passed with ease. Promotion followed promotion until she finally resigned from the hospital as war was declared in 1939. She began as a Student Nurse, then Staff Nurse, and finally Nursing Sister, passing the Final Examination of the R.M.P.A.

Many women with her experience were looking to the armed forces as a natural progression, feeling that they needed to serve their country and also tempted by the propaganda to 'do their bit'.

Various opportunities opened up for aspiring young girls. Amy Johnson, the daring pilot, had shown them that being a woman was no bar to meeting challenges. She was a heroine in their eyes; to be emulated and worshipped. Once again posters displayed young attractive, carefree and laughing girls in their smart uniforms urging them to apply for the Auxiliary Territorial Service (ATS), the NAAFI, or the WRENS (with its provocative, 'up with the lark and to bed with a wren') providing the opportunity to work in meteorology, communications and on radar.

Life at Rampton Hospital had provided little opportunity to mix with an array of eligible daring young men, so the WRAF beckoned and Sally applied. It was a heady experience and she revelled in the demanding work and stimulating play, being able to blot out the everyday dreariness of meat rationing. Her leisure time was taken up in trips to the cinema and dancing with confident Americans and the polite, quiet Poles with whom she liaised on the base. They were equally charmed and fascinated by her alluring looks and powerful personality. Her diary recorded dates and meetings with them and letters from the young men which she kept safe over the years show how much fun they thought she was to be around. Her diary from January 1943,first at an RAF camp at Rigby and then in the April whilst stationed at RAF Hucknall, excitedly charted the number of evenings spent dancing, going to the cinema to see 'All that money can buy', the Walt Disney 'Jungle Book' and 'The Reluctant Dragon' or attending Polish concerts with her friend Ivy Humphreys. On 28th February she wrote

'went to the Sgt's mess with Sgt Bowen was bored to tears until a little Polish officer rescued me.'

82

By March she complained that she was being pursued by the Polish airman Marion and that he was far too keen. On Friday14 April she happily wrote

'Maria, Kay Dot and I all went to the Palais met Tadek and all waited at Nottingham for taxis which we got about 11.15 so home 11.45.'

After the weekend she decided to write Marion a nasty letter and then felt some remorse at her actions but said,

'still it had to be done '

On Saturday 8th of May she said, *'Duty tonight. Would have loved to have gone to the Palais to see if T. was there. I may be mad but I must see him again.'*

By the end of May she was worried that she had not heard from Tadek and that she had received no letters but then on the 8th June she wrote that she went to the Palais, found that he was there and had a lovely time.

On the 27th June she was feeling trapped by Marion once again.

'Marion came up to see me and talked his head off about the future nearly made me sick I felt like a caged bird its no use I can't go through with it. I shall either marry Tadek or remain a Nurse. Actually I am sure that I should prefer to remain a nurse anyhow!'

Throughout July and August she pined for Tadek, who did not contact her, and became irritated with Marion who continued to see her. Then on the 2nd September she had a phone call from both men. By this time she had started to take lessons in Polish.

Although she let down her hair at times she was always in control until she met Tadeusz. He was a dashing Polish flying officer possessing fine, taunt, good looks, a wide smile and the extra appeal, having an aura of mystery. She was captivated. As he was flying on dangerous missions it was uncertain that he would return to her after each flight. Each time that he returned was like the first time that they had met. A passion grew inside her. Despite the murmurings of disquiet in her head telling her, 'remember, be careful', she continued to seek him out. On the outside she continued to appear carefree and assured but her stomach managed to knot itself each time he held her hand and whispered his longing for her. Taking on extra nursing duties made her feel responsible and fulfilled; it sanctioned her liberty, allowing her to take her pleasure without guilt. A career in nursing was her ambition; she despised domesticity and wanting to 'settle down'; besides, war made any such commitment absurd. Who knew what tomorrow would bring. 'Live life to the full' was the mantra of her friends and she happily complied with that dictate. Besides there were the injured and sick who brought the horrors of war and the vulnerability of life so vividly before her on a daily basis. Efficiently and skilfully she nursed each patient, giving them her warmth and kindness that she kept hidden from her healthy compatriots. It was the tenderness that she had previously kept especially reserved for her injured animals in her earlier years. By the October of 1943 she had risen to the rank of Flight Sergeant.

Sally had been badly scarred by Arthur's seduction and now was fearful of losing her hard-won reputation. Other nurses looked up to her; she was popular. Despising the conditions of her working class family home and her bullying father she never wanted to place herself in a subservient position of being financially and emotionally dependent on a man. And yet there was a fierce sexual longing inside her that fought for control. How to reconcile the two parts of her personality was her dilemma. The 'here today gone tomorrow' made it more necessary to seize the moment before any chance of happiness was taken away. So many pilots and aircrew were being lost in action. She dreaded losing Tadek.

On the 16th September her annotated diary suddenly stopped. Across the page she wrote diagonally *Blank; Brain & Body*. On the 17th *Blank,* on the 18th *Blank* and again and again *Blank* on each day until the 23rd. On the 24th she wrote *'I wish I knew for sure & really what to do.'*
She left October and November totally blank until finally in across the pages for the first week in December she wrote mournfully
'The blanks will never be filled in all need is, that song titters'

1. *Jealousy*
2. *You are my sunshine*
3. *My Blue eyes(I am thinking so much of T)*

It was whilst Sally was on duty in 1943 that a plane came back to the air base trailing a stream of smoke and flame. As the pilot desperately fought to steady the machine it crashed onto the airstrip, exploding into a ball of fire. There was no chance for either the pilot or the aircrew to evade the impact or the ensuing flames despite the best efforts of the ground staff. No survivors escaped the wreckage. After the flames were finally doused the bodies were removed. The pilot was later identified as Tadeusz.
She may have seen the crash. She could have been informed of it whilst she was working. Everyone may have rushed out to witness the tragedy. For her it was an unspeakable loss. A month later she found out that she was pregnant.

Sally never spoke of Tadeusz. Even her brother, far away on a Royal Navy destroyer in the Middle East, whom she kept so close, had no inkling of this special relationship.

Amongst the debris a scrap of his uniform and a badge was retrieved, the only tangible physical link to his life.

What was to be done? She was unmarried and pregnant. She was granted some compassionate leave but time itself was now her enemy. Tadeusz had been part of a larger group of Poles with whom she had mixed and her thoughts reluctantly turned back to Marion Joseph Jurczyszyn. He continued to adore her despite her coolness but never had a chance to make any impression on her whilst the flamboyant Tadeusz was there.

Sally returned to work desperate to resolve her dilemma. Marion was just twenty two years old. Sally was now twenty eight. She saw her chance. Marion was still besotted and she needed to move fast. Marion applied for special permission to marry. Their wedding took place on the 4th November 1943, and there were just two witnesses; her friend Ivy Humphreys and a Polish friend of Marion's named Rudolph Scatkowski. No member of Sally's family was present; even her adored brother was not informed of her marriage. No photographs were taken. Complete secrecy cloaked the event.

Six months later on the 6th May 1944 Sally presented Marion with a son. They named the child Tadeusz John Jurczyszyn.

Wars have always created so many human tragedies. For those who survive they have to live with the consequences. Sally and Marion were totally incompatible. She realised it within weeks of their marriage. She found him dull and oppressive. He was utterly bewildered by her coldness, at first assuming that the care of a baby was taking its toll on her vitality. He forgave her sharp words and fault finding, hoping that it was just a phase of early motherhood. Sally took his compassion as a sign of weakness and despised him for his gentleness. Marion's bewilderment made him seek assurances from her and receiving none he started to cajole and badger her, which in turn exasperated the situation.

She was desperate to escape the confines of motherhood and being a dutiful wife. Her whole being was revolted by her position. Suddenly realising that if she didn't act quickly her prized independence would be lost for ever she made a decision. Tadek, her son, could be looked after by her mother Chrissie and she could return to work. They needed money to buy a house. There was also the real fear that all Poles were to be denied access to permanent residency in the UK so she needed to have her own income. Her arguments were so strong poor Marion didn't know how to refute her reasoning and was left having to accept her decision.

From working in a temporary capacity, whilst expecting Tadek,,at Mapperley Hospital from November 1943 to August 1944 she applied for a full time position as a Staff Nurse from the August onwards. This hospital for the mentally insane was built in the 1880's, set in one hundred and twenty five acres of land. It had comprised of a bakery, butchers, church and recreation hall. Formerly the hospital was known as the Nottingham Lunatic Asylum and had locked closed doors to confine the inmates. Sally went to work under the directorship of Dr Duncan Macmillan who advocated an open-style hospital with unlocked doors. This was part of a new and exciting venture in the care and treatment of the mentally insane and Sally embraced it wholeheartedly.

Together as a staff they organised ambitious theatre productions with the patients; encouraging them to sew costumes, audition for roles in light operettas, learn stage management skills, build the scenery, rig up the lighting and take responsibly for rehearsals. The summer brought a variety of competitive sporting occasions, fetes and carnivals and tableaux. Classes were arranged to create an interest in woodwork, joinery, needlework, painting and gardening. Careful mental stimulation combined with supervised medication and counselling brought out qualities and confidence that some patients had not experienced before.

Marion had to accept a five year contract with the RAF in order to be granted British citizenship. He was often away, stationed both in Malta and Gibraltar during the late 1940's up until 1951 and then became stationed in Cornwall and then at RAF Swanton Morley in Norfolk.

His absence didn't bother Sally. He would send her loving letters whilst she carefully noted the contents and catalogued them in date order, methodically writing across the envelope the date received, provided it with a number and annotated that a reply had been sent.

The May family were not informed of her marriage and confinement and she made excuses why she could not attend her brother's wedding to Joyce in the April 1944. Marion was Amos's best man, and her cousin Joan was the bridesmaid but Sally was conspicuous by her absence. The family had no idea that by that time she was eight months pregnant. Marion and Sally did not attend her cousin Joan May's wedding to Charles in May of that year since Sally had just given birth seven days prior to that date. Her brother Amos acted as best man for Charles.

Strangely, both sides of the family did not think to enquire into the reasons for her absence nor question why they had not been invited to her wedding to Marion. It was as if she was able to deflect searching questions by making the enquirer self conscious and somehow bad mannered in pursuing such information. Even Joan, who was always forthright and quizzical, was left in the dark. Somehow the information of her wedding and Tadek's birth came out piecemeal and the facts were left deliberately hazy.

Many years later she maintained that Tadek had been one of twins, his brother dying at birth, and that the survivor had been covered in thick black hair. Why she invented this strange story I had no idea until by chance during a conversation with her cousin Joan I found out that Joan had lost twins when she was five months pregnant. A brief record

88

of his birth which she scribbled on a small slip of paper stated that she was violently sick; that the birth was difficult and that Tadek came out '7/8th dead and just 1/8th alive', and then went on to detail very elaborately the flowers that she received from family and friends, with little mention about Tadek's wellbeing.

		REGISTRATION DISTRICT				CRANBROOK				

	1915		BIRTH in the Sub-District of		Cranbrook		in the County of	Kent		

No.	When and Where Born.	Name, if any.	Sex.	Name and Surname of Father.	Name and Maiden Surname of Mother.	Rank or Profession of Father.	Signature, Description and Residence of Informant.	When Registered.	Signature of Registrar
468	Fifteenth March 1915 Willesley Green Cranbrook R. D.	Rose Christiana Mary	Girl	Herbert Wilfred Payne	Christiana Edith Payne formerly May	Rifleman 7363 2nd Battalion Kings Royal Rifles Railway Watchman	Christiana Edith Payne Mother Willesley Green Cranbrook	Twenty seventh March 1915	A. Gilbert Registrar

Chrissie & Herbert with
Sally; her birth certificate,
working at Peacocks; and a
photo that she submitted for a beauty competition.

№ 234971   *(Printed by Author...)*

CERTIFIED COPY of an ENTRY OF MARRIAGE.
Pursuant to the Marriage Acts, 1811 to 1939.

The Statutory Fee for this Certificate is
7s. 6d. If required subsequently is registration, a Search Fee is payable in addition.

Registration District   *Bingham.*

1943   Marriage Solemnized at *The Register Office.*
District of *Bingham* in the County of *Nottingham* in

No.	When Married	Name and Surname	Age	Condition	Rank or Profession	Residence at the time of Marriage	Father's Name and Surname	Rank or Profession of
118	Fourth November 1943	Marian Joseph Jurozgyzyn	22 years	Bachelor	Leading Airman under training Pilot 780 no 1 Polish Air Force	Shelford Home Address Poryland Lopscwski Kopshire Poland	Hilary Jurozgyzyn	Locomotive Engineer
		Rose Christiana Mary Payne	28 years	Spinster	Hospital Nurse.	29 Albert Avenue Jacksdale	Herbert Wilfred Payne	Railway Lengthman

Married in the *Register Office* according to the Rites and Ceremonies of the   by *Licence* by

John w. Linley Registrar

This Marriage was solemnized between us: *Marian Joseph Jurozgyzyn / Rose Christiana Payne* in the Presence of us: *Joy Humphreys / Rudolf Szatkowski*

W.B. Birch Superintendent Registrar

I, *John Marrison Linley*, Registrar of Marriages for the District of *Bingham* in the County of *Nottingham* do hereby certify that this is a true copy of the Entry No. *118* in the Register Book of Marriages for the said District, and that such Register B...
now legally in my custody. WITNESS MY HAND this *22* day of *November 1943.*

CAUTION.—Any person who (1) falsifies any of the particulars on this Certificate, or (2) uses it as true, knowing it to be falsified, is liable to Prosecution.

Chapter 7 Tadek, her son, and Marion, the husband

Throughout her life Sally never acknowledged that she had had two sons. Everyone who knew Sally believed that the spoilt and idolised Tadek was her only son. Each time she signed a new version of her will she stated her intention that her only son Tadek would inherit her entire estate. Emotionally she held him close and yet was happy to leave the everyday care of him to others. As a small boy he was led to believe that the world revolved around him. Shamelessly, she spoilt him with gifts on a regular basis and yet deprived him of her company for much of the time. She was uncomfortable in the company of young children. Her way of connecting with him was to seek out expensive presents regardless of birthdays and Christmas treats. He was so used to receiving a gift each time that she returned home he expected similar treatment from other members of the family. My mother can recall him asking, when she returned from a shopping trip whilst he was visiting them in Maidstone, "And what have you bought for me?"

Chrissie was left to look after him whilst she was at Mapperley Hospital and later his cousin Janet May and her siblings became his young playmates.

Photographs of Sally and Tadek picture him with his latest acquisition: a new bike, a new sailing boat, an expensive train set, and a telescope; her arm draped protectively around him shielding him from the world. He was provided with piano lessons, becoming an accomplished jazz musician.

At Tom and Nellie's wedding in 1950 he is pictured like a portly little Lord Fauntleroy in a dubious sailor suit made in white silk parachute material by Nellie. And yet despite his cosseted existence he had an ability to relate well to other children and was a good playmate.

Whilst Marion was stationed away from home in 1954 Sally asked Edna, a colleague whom she had known since 1952, to lodge with them at their new home at 24 Charlecote Drive. Moving away from her parent's house meant that she needed help with Tadek and the despised housework. Sally and Marion corresponded regularly but most of the time they argued about money, that Herbert Payne was not taking care of Chrissie and about the care of Tadek. They put him into a private school and the expensive fees were taking up money that was required for the house. Tadek would need cricket whites or new shoes and even the 30/- that Edna was giving them each week was not enough to see Sally constantly descending into debt.

Sally would write to Marion saying that they need to buy hose pipe to water the garden, that they needed a fridge, a garden shed, Marley tiles for the kitchen floors and that she was worn out with the effort of looking after Tadek, working night shifts and doing Chrissie's washing. Often her letters were punctuated with the frustration of Marion telling her what to do and of shouting at her. She blamed him for being like all men and shouting to get their own way when all she could do was to acquiesce to his demands and settle for a quiet life. He would blaze back and write that she had never known what it was like to be an obedient wife and do as she was told and that she always got her own way despite all her promises to compromise. Their letters would be peppered with 'sweethearts' and 'darlings' and 'pets' and yet they both seemed to be bedevilled by a form of schizophrenia as they developed a pattern of cajoling, bursts of bad temper and name calling and ending with an 'all my love' as if all the threats and blatant anger could be lightly dismissed. She would complain that they had no money, that she couldn't get a decent rest and that the family were wearing her out equally Marion would rage and say that she never considered him

94

suffering such bad health and that his legs were getting worse.

He wrote;

you know as well as I do that you do not take the slightest notice of what I say............I am not allowed to say my piece, if I say anything in normal human manner no notice is taken then I have no alternative but shout, hoping it will ring a little bell. As I told you many times before my sweet you do note me as if I was mentally unbalanced or imbecile, and I think to tell you once more that your theory is wrong I am perfectly sane.........if you drop that attitude you will find me quite pleasant. I mean business Pet, and now it is up to you. Now sweetheart I do not intend to enter into Russia kind of diplomacy over this little incident because it will drag on for ever. I promise to comply with your request on the understanding that you comply with mine.

Sally responded, angry at his suggestion that she had been unreasonable.

Goodness knows why you men have to fly up in the air to prove your point- it is so unnecessary- I spent weeks of training Tadek and Edna not to shout and rave and to conduct themselves in a quiet manner then just when I get them to a nice quiet phase home you come finding fault with everything shouting and raving like a madman and the whole house is in an uproar again in no time. The times I have come home during your stay here feeling tired yes but not completely finished and as soon as I put one foot over the doorstep, instead of peace I find bad tempers-rows, grumbles, about this one not pulling her or his weight and me not running the place efficiently etc-

95

what little energy I did have just floats way in a few seconds I feel like a piece of wet rag- why Marion? It is so unnecessary I have done my best with money, cooking, cleaning,keeping Tadek and Edna up to scratch etc, but when you start to pull everything to pieces and moan I feel too fed up and tired ....I keep my mouth shut to keep the peace........I have the horrible feeling that I am a failure and no good as a wife and mother- do you realise that?

She turned the argument around to infer that Marion and her own father were so alike and to express her loathing for her father,

.....the fact that I could not stand father and ran away from my responsibilities at No 61 is my business and I have been a good daughter — when mother went into hospital I would have packed up work and looked after No 61 but I was too big a coward because I cannot stand people who shout. Please darling think this over and don't develop into a bawling husband as you are now — because though I love you very, very much — I shall eventually run out on you. I can stand anything but shouting —help me, do not make life harder,- you shout, then Tadek and Edna shout then I find myself shouting and then I feel like a caged animal and want to run away from it all.

By the middle of 1955 Chrissie was becoming more and more frail during her stay in hospital. When she was discharged she went to live with Sally, Tadek and Edna the lodger. Sally worked on night shifts and was home during the day whilst Tadek was at school and then she could go out to work in the evening. Sally and Edna were at loggerheads, constantly

96

arguing about how heavy handed she was around the house whilst doing the housework. And then a complete turnabout! Sally had complained to Marion about Edna damaging a mantelpiece tile and on his return home he set to and ordered Edna out of the house. Sally then turned the tables on Marion and sided with Edna. For the first time Marion wrote to Sally without his usual 'sweethearts' and 'darlings' and Sally, to spite him, showed his letter to Edna with the caustic remarks written across the envelope,

Dear E,

just read this. Ye Gods I am thankful he is not here I feel like thunder but I guess you will have to go if he does it he will go to the papers and you know what folks will say we are like a couple of (Like Auntie Alice and Great Kate) [lesbians] it could even be the means of losing our good names he will kick me out indeed does he flatter himself I want to stay the moment I can fix T J [Tadek] up I shall follow you but not at his order God he thinks I want to stay and grind away in this hole one thing I do know I shall smash all I can't carry away with me when I do clear out see you Sat, love Sally

Marion had written;

Dear Sally,
No doubt you will be surprised to receive letter from me so soon but I assure you that I am not writing to express my love to you. During my stay at home you did not want to listen to me so I hope you will read and read carefully because I mean every word I am putting down, those

days I was talking and not acting are over and you will soon find out it is true.

Now as you know I told Edna to find digs by Monday of course she as usual ignored me and rolled in Monday evening when I asked her what she was doing here she never answered I did not imagine she was ignorant to such a degree if somebody had told me to remove my body from his home my pride would not allow me to stay however she proved herself to have no pride or personal dignity she is terribly clumsy and untidy and her tongue is awful. She does not respect somebody's property therefore as an individual she represents no value and in my eye she is just a miserable parasite. All this will have ill effect on her life and she will make some poor chap unhappy- however all this is none of my business she will probably discover all or some of her faults but it might be too late, anyhow in order to protect my property from her careless hands she is definitely going. I know that you think that sun shines out of her bottom may be she has good points but they do not compensate for her bad ones. ....after she goes Sally I expect to see the house clean ,tidy and with out the whole regiment of shoes in the kitchen, at the moment my kitchen looks more like the cobbler's shop when I come home next and I find no improvement you will follow your precious Edna

Their relationship continued on a dizzy downward spiral. Chrissie was brought home to stay at 24 with a bed put in the lounge. She could not go back to her home at Wagstaff Lane in Jacksdale, as Herbert was unable to care for himself, let alone a very sick wife who required a suppurating sore in her side to be cleaned and dressed. By the August of 1954 Edna was told to remove all her belongings from 24 but then there was the problem of the housework and care for Chrissie. The district nurse came to support Chrissie but Sally did not believe that she should be doing any housework as she was working at the hospital. Perversely Marion agreed with her after berating her about the state of the house in a previous letter saying,

damn it you are not just ordinary house wife and now that Edna has gone I do not expect you to do housework
surly with us both working we can afford domestic help.

They decided that they could afford to employ a cleaner for seven hours each week and not eight hours as this would render them having to pay a national insurance contribution. After ordering Sally from his house Marion's next letter headed 'my darling' said that they needed to send for a bottle of holy water from Lourdes to help alleviate Chrissie's condition. In September Marion decided that Sally needed to have some extra money to help with Chrissie's care and sent her a further £1 each week. Sally had a fit of conscience and wrote back to say that she had needed to spend the money on a new pair of Wellington boots.

Finally they both agreed that they could not have Chrissie living at the house and decided to prevail on their sister-in-law Nellie, Tom's wife, to look after Chrissie once she was moved back to her home. Herbert had reduced the house to a filthy condition. His clothes were dirty and Nellie was expected to clean and prepare the meals, often having to pay for the food herself. Chrissie was alarmed that they had decided to move her back. Her time at No.24 had allowed her to see how well they lived. She saw the new fridge, the rustic shed; the new vacuum cleaner and the huge amount spent on the garden as Sally took possession of exotic flower bulbs and expensive lawn treatments. The idea of moving back to the squalor of No.61 must have appalled her. She confessed that her time at 24 had made her feel 'jealous and bitter'. Despite this Marion and Sally would not be persuaded and ensured that they had made friends with Nellie to ensure her co-operation and then arranged for a district nurse to come in twice a day to attend to Chrissie's needs. By the middle of October Sally decided that although her mother was no longer living with her she still required the cleaning help and the £1 a week extra funds for Marion had written to tell her that she couldn't be a 'professional woman and a house wife at the same time'. Marion sent an extra 10/- to Chrissie but Herbert Payne had to be threatened before he would part with any money towards the housekeeping. Nellie had to provide her own cleaning materials as well as the raw ingredients for each meal.

Around this time Sally needed to have an operation and Marion wanted to spend more time in his very comfortable home. He demanded that Sally spoke to the Soldiers, Sailors and Airmen's Family Association (SSAFA) to see if they could exert some pressure to have him posted closer to home. Sally dreaded having him home full time, despite her entreaties for him to be with her, as she could manage her life as she pleased whilst he was away. When he did finally come out of the Air Force the death knell was sounded for their marriage. He applied for a job with the Coal Board.

Sally despised him for taking such a mundane job that held no glamour or romance. Although he was an intelligent man, having also obtained a private pilot's licence, she increasingly ridiculed him for being emotional and inadequate in every way.

In 1956 Chrissie died. To their horror they found that Herbert had installed a local couple to look after him and had gifted his house to them. Having been gifted the house, the couple unscrupulously then did as little as they could for Herbert. Herbert realised with growing fear and far too late what an error he had made. He was abandoned in his own home and not one member of the family wanted anything to do with him.

Emotionally they had no attachment to him and financially there was nothing to be gained in supporting him.

As Tadek grew up Sally ensured the best opportunities arose for him. He had a large circle of friends, formed a jazz band with some of them and, on one occasion, he and his friends decided to play for twenty-four hours non stop as part of a charity event. The feat made the local papers. He also learnt to hide his love of alcohol from her. Whether or not she knew that he drank or she chose to ignore it I am not sure, but he developed a good appetite for the good things in life and alcohol formed an integral part of his lifestyle.

By the time that he was a youth she became quite open in her ridicule about Marion in front of Tadek, challenging him to have any respect for his father. She sneered about his abilities to drive a car or navigate a route, even though he was still piloting bi-planes over Britain. She called him an 'old woman' for wanting the house to be neat and clean, she raged against his nagging to her to rein in her spending and Tadek would be caught in the crossfire of her vicious attacks. He was encouraged to side with her against this 'ineffectual, weak and useless' father. Tadek had to tread a fine line in appeasing her and yet still maintaining a relationship with 'the old fella' as he called him.

It was as if she hated Marion for being there and yet she didn't want to let go. It was a cat and mouse situation; somehow she was compelled to torment him and yet still needed to receive his adoration and love in return.

At school Tadek was doing well but had not decided on a career. Sally made some decisions for him, first pushing him into banking, then nursing, until he finally decided that Social Services work was his forte. His friendships with other youths posed no problems for her and she delighted in being in their company, but when he started to form a serious relationship with a young girl she felt seriously threatened. He wrote to her saying that he was going to bring Yvonne home to meet her. The relationship seemed quite strong and they were well

101

suited. Yvonne was pretty and intelligent with a good sense of fun. He took her down to Kent to meet his Uncle Amos and his family. It was a successful trip. Yvonne was unpretentious and fun to be with. And yet soon after meeting Sally in 1968 she and Tadek parted company.

Sally and Tadek enjoyed photography and so the best camera had to be purchased in order to pursue this hobby. They filled copious albums with dubious quality pictures but then in those days the whole film had to be developed and Sally never allowed an image to be discarded. They loved steam trains so Tadek was provided with a miniature train and track to run around the garden.

Only on their family holidays to Poland did Marion come into his own. It took some time before the family could be granted permission to travel to Poland. Soviet Russia had a strong hold over Poland and the secret police still spied on the citizens. Sally loved the life that was led by Marion's family. His father had been a locomotive engineer and other members of the family were working for the Forestry Commission and lecturing at college. Tadek, Marion and Sally revelled in seeing this part of the world, still quite mysterious and foreign at that time. It gave them both some cache amongst their peers and colleagues back in Nottingham.

With the name Jurczyszyn Sally used to refer to Tadek as TJ (TJay) as people found the pronunciation of Jurczyszyn so difficult and we used TJ in place of Tadek. When Sally finally fled to Wales to leave Marion once and for all, Tadek and his father became a little closer and their relationship flourished.

It was also at this time that Tadek began to resent any claims on his mother's purse strings that he had singularly enjoyed for such a long period. Now that she was so far away it was difficult for him to let her see how he required certain things. It was awkward and rather obvious to write about money and so it meant tedious journeys to Denbigh when he could acquaint her with the necessities that he desired. He told her how tricky things were at home with so little money to call his own but sometimes a more positive approach needed to be taken.

He was therefore horrified when he found out that his Uncle Amos had written to Sally asking for a loan of £25 pounds to put towards the purchase of a new car and quickly put pen to paper.

..Now regarding the letter to you from Amos, much as I like Whacker, I really do think that he is a bloody fool to even entertain the idea of running a car, After all mum, let's face it you know how expensive it can be EVEN WHEN YOU HAVE ALREADY PURCHASED A CAR I put that in capital letters to emphasize my point. What the blazes he wants to get rid of the Bond for I do not know. Now if he was going to buy a new Reliant I could understand his reasoning. Really mum I am both very surprised at him and also very disappointed in his reasoning. I am also glad that you are not handing out £25 to him; remember you really must do your best now to get out of your Bank Managers bad books. I know things here have been difficult and I really do thank you for all the sacrifices that you have made in order that I may be well situated in my future life. But now you must look after NO. 1 & do your level best to square things up your end of the world.

Going back to Uncle Amos I really think that if I was to lend him the money so that he could buy a car I do not think that I would be doing him any favours. I think that I would be only helping him on the way to a downward path money wise regarding in running a car, what with the extra Road tax and insurance etc. I hope mum that you see the point that I am illustrating to you.

Now regarding Easter if everything goes as according to plan we shall leave Ilkeston just after breakfast and depending on traffic I hope to be in Denbigh early Friday afternoon, possibly just after lunch. Oh by the way my old love, do try to be in your uniform, so that my young lady will be able to see you, in all your glory; te he he. Anyhow I must admit myself that you do look an impressive figure in your "DRAGON'S outfit",

Now mum I really must close and you will have to excuse my scribble.

GOD BLESS & lots of love T. Jay xxx

PS// BE GOOD!!!!!

PPS/ In any case, I wonder what Auntie Joyce would say about his silly idea. If he wants the money that bad let him discuss the matter with her first.

The hypocrisy of the letter and his blatant attempt to flatter her was breathtaking in its transparency but it obviously worked since Amos never received the money.

Marion had been working for some time with the Coal Board and had joined a Polish club. They were still living at Wollaton at number 24. Some time during the middle 1960's Marion went back to Poland on his own and met Barbara and began a romantic liaison. Barbara's husband was in prison and she was finding life difficult in the small community where everyone's business was transparent. Sally did not find out for some time what was happening. Marion finally realised that Sally was never going to come back to Nottingham and allowed himself to develop the relationship with Barbara despite his strong Catholic upbringing and twingeing conscience.

It may have been that Tadek allowed it to slip out but somehow Sally found out and was furious; absolutely incandescent with rage. That she didn't actually want Marion seemed to have no bearing on the matter. Suddenly she was a wronged woman. He had betrayed her love and devotion. She wrote to his family passionately pouring out her grief at the utter betrayal. The Polish family were appalled. Sally had always been such a good and treasured daughter-in-law they were aghast at being implicated by association with such a

104

scandal. The incensed family immediately wrote to Marion telling him that they were shocked by his treatment of Sally. How could he have been so cruel to this distraught woman who loved him with every fibre in her body? Marion was unsure. Was this the same person who had mocked him throughout their marriage? Did she indeed love him and want to be with him? There was only one course of action, he had to give up quiet and caring Barbara and return to his one and only true love.

Marion's brother Zygmunt wrote affectionately to Sally in the September 1967 hoping to heal the wounds created by their family,

My dear Sally!

.....first I must answer your questions; 'when did the love affair between Marion and Barbara start? Yes sally I have observe the love is starting in August 1966. I spoke at once to Marion about, and therefore we (Marion and I) have quarrelled. I wrote not to you about, (while we have quarrelled). It may be right what Marion tells you' there was nothing between him and Barbara before August 1966, but he was really in correspondence with her in autumn 1965. This time (in November 1965) was by me (visit me) mother of Barbara and she tells me about their correspondence.

You are right Sally, Marion has a very nasty temper, the same was our father, my mother tells me. It is very hard to live with him, but I hope now past all this affair will be all right. You both shall be happy.

Yes Sally, Marion has a big fault in all this affair. They (he and she) are not children, they both have fault, but what has happened has happened. So is better for you and Marion to forget all this things.

Our mother is happy to see you and Marion together; she was often to pray for harmony in your marriage. I wrote to her; as I receive letter

105

from you both, she start crying so most was she glad. Sally be positive, I do not tell our mother as Marion about you have asked then you want know I can answer your questions all time. I want ever and will help you in all things. Mother will be helping you too.

Sally I am very very glad to see you next year. It is the highest time to meet you. I also love you sally. I have and I will. You was and are ever my darling. I am looking forward to meet you too so we can meet and talk.   Plenty of kisses for you,

Yours Zygmunt xxxx
Love from Ludlia and Marek
Love to Marion and Tadek.

Zygmunt endeavoured to finalise his travel arrangements by the beginning of 1968 and wrote again to Sally outlining his plans for the journey and then telling her of the profound effect Marion's affair had had on their mother.

My dear Sally,

I thank you for your letters from 6/2/68, and 6/3/68 with a photograph. The photograph is wonderful and like me [liked by me] very much. Last week I have received the documents for my journey to England and I have sent my petition of visa to the British Embassy. Now I must wait, but I don't know how long. I have sent petition of passport too. I do hope that all shall be happy. I wish to meet you quickly but I am afraid my English isn't enough well to speak and to understand. I hope we will have a good time.

Sally I am very sorry about Marion's bad habits in all. I have know Marion since 1939 when he was a good boy at that time. His education has finished far from home between his friends by Air force and now I know him not as adult man. Since 1966 he even wrote and spoke there is all right in his marriage. The affair between Marion and Barbara was for me and for mother terrible. I never thought Marion is so silly and frivolous. Now I think he regrets the Barbara affair. I forbade him write to me nothing about and he ought not to write to her but I am not sure he is writing to her or not. He really has now the hard time, he did understand what he has done, and he knows what to do but in one time he has many of ideas.

I think the worst time is over, now he will be better, and past my visit shall be all right, although I will have with him the heavy conversations. I do hope we may put him in the right way; he shall not hurt you any more and must be a good husband.

This time three weeks ago I was by [with] Mother I did not say of this all to her, but it seems to me that she knows all about. Mother is very sorry that her own son was for you so wrong, when you get here we shall have with her a long talk and I will be the interpreter for her and you therefore it will be very good if I come to you first and I shall pray to keep my English better. I suppose the first time will be heavy for us you will do not understand my conversation but past a short time it shall be well. I promise to be your obedient and polite schoolboy.

I enjoy that you have made arrangements for going to the International Eisteddfod (Marion wrote me that you have bought the tickets).

I am very happy to spend the first week in Denbigh by you.

My congratulations to Yvonne for her first step on the road to becoming a trained Nurse.

107

Give my live to Yvonne, Marion, and Tadek,

Good night and many kisses to you,

Your ever loving brother,

Zygmunt xxx

P.S Love to you from Ludlia and Marek xx

As soon as Marion promised to give Barbara up; sought forgiveness from his Polish family and wrote to Sally of his decision, she informed him that she had been so badly hurt that she and decided to remain in Wales and would not be returning to Nottingham. Oh cat, look how your claws have torn the mouse! Why keep him just within your grasp? Poor Marion believed that he had profoundly wounded her and spent years writing of his undying devotion to her, endeavouring to regain her love; quite pointlessly as it turned out.

By the October of 1968 she once again wrote to change her will.

I give and bequeath;

£500 to my husband Mr Marion Joseph Jurczyszyn-Jay 24 Charlotte Drive, Wollaton, Nottingham

this being the sum he gave me as a share of money jointly saved and invested in the building society during our twenty years of marriage, and before he decided to enjoy the company of another woman. When it seems we were to come together again he insisted I had the said sum. I however have never regarded it as mine, it was to me an insult to expect to 'pay me off for all my years of devotion to him and our son plus spending all my earnings in the household of 24 Charlotte drive with this money-therefore herewith returned.

Angrily she wrote of 'ten points to remember'; an *aide memoire* for her fury.

1. *You brought her to Wales and asked me for married quarters (if she was a friend why?)*

2. *You told me I had no family at Glan Llyn (the Cottage) (If you had not completely intended to cast me out why?)*

3. *You stood in the Church at Tissington admiring a gravestone which was inscribed in such a way that is read as though the two persons buried there were man and mistress and told me that you admired him for an honest man (If when you asked her to have you, it was not as a wife or a mistress why?)*

4. *You told everyone I had left you to make your actions seem justifiable. (If you did not want to get rid of me why?)*

5. *You did your best to turn Tadek against me again to justify your action with the hope he would accept her.*

6. *You told me you loved her to my face (If this was not true why?)*

7. *You deliberately went into the bedroom in your pyjamas to kiss her goodnight, yet knocked on the bathroom door, to me your wife. (if this was not to show me she was your new wife- why?)*

8. *You did not want to give her up; and said you would always remain friends and send money to her and the children (If you were not determined to live with her why?)*

109

If that is not enough to show that it WAS NOT friendship you wanted then I must be completely insane. PTO

The next sheet continued;

9. *You had no hesitation in telling me to P & F off, but would not say such things to your mistress. Why, why, why?*

10. *You had regard to her feelings and believed every word she spoke-yet never ever thought of my feelings and regarded me as the biggest liar ever born. (If your love for her was not greater than for me-why!)*

It is easy for you to forget these things because I really believe you are now ashamed of them but remember they are burned into my very soul and when you upset me, all come flooding back like a tidal wave which may one day push me over the brink completely. I am no longer stable I can no longer hold myself apart and ignore the facts. I loved you and trusted you too well. You try to justify your actions, by saying others do this or that, maybe they do but I think if you really stop to think few persons have so little regard for another person's feelings as to act so utterly ruthlessly and then completely forget the things they have done and said.

Sally spent hours writing numerous suicide letters addressed to Marion and Tadek. They were never sent; remaining unopened amongst her paperwork. Some of the letters to Marion stretched to fifteen to eighteen neatly written pages speaking of her emotional turmoil and grief at losing him. Some adopted a brave self sacrificing tone. She would depart this earth leaving the path clear for Marion to be with his one love Barbara. Her love for him was so strong, and knowing had she had his happiness in her hand she knew she had to give way. Her greatest pain was in having to contravene the edicts of her Christian faith and of her deeply held belief in the sanctity of life, and yet she felt compelled to disregard her own torment. Some letters spoke of her frank realisation that they had never been sexually compatible. That he had seen her as a 'mother figure' and had found it difficult to make love to her with out arousing himself with lewd and 'dirty' stories, which had disgusted her. During the 'act' of love making he said that it was impossible to bring her to a climax and that she needed to let go and 'enjoy' herself. Little did she realise that he had been comparing her with his precious Barbara. Her love for him transcended the sordid level that he sought to bring her to and she had had to fight to maintain and cherish her love for him despite his shortcomings.

Tadek finally sided with his mother and made Marion's life very difficult. He openly condemned his 'abhorrent' behaviour and betrayal of his blameless mother. Besides, he enjoyed the freedom of living in on his own and found domestic scenes between his parents tiresome, especially as his own love interest with Yvonne was starting to blossom. Marion had been able to conduct his affair with Barbara without Tadek's intervention but somehow his letters from Barbara had been intercepted, copied and translated for Sally. Amongst her numerous suicide letters were Barbara's letters to Marion. At first the letters spoke of her relief to be loved and to love in return. Her life had been so terrible after the imprisonment of her husband for theft, but now she had a reason to hope that they could finally be happy together and that the blackness of the past would be finally over. Once their affair had been exposed and Marion had agreed to return to Sally, Barbara's letters were filled with recriminations. Marion had rescued her only to throw her back to the wolves. Her life was miserable. She had no money and no means of escaping the scandal and persecution visited upon her by his family and her neighbours. They branded her as a fallen woman; a dirty, despicable adulteress, a harlot. It would have been better if she had never met him than to have loved him so dearly and then lost him.

Sally must have read the translated letters with some satisfaction. It was, after all, what they both deserved. They were both damaged goods whereas she was untainted by their exposed deception. Her reputation was beyond reproach; a wronged and noble woman who could be magnanimous in her final hours upon this earth. However, just as her letters never reached their intended destination, so she too decided to remain solidly earthbound and not take the dictated route of her correspondence. She knew that he would now live an unfulfilled life without Barbara in his tiny bachelor flat, hopefully ignored by Tadek and abandoned by his precious family.

Marion had previously agreed to move out of 24 into a flat after Sally had ensured that only Tadek's name was on the deeds for the house.

The solicitors from Woodland Chambers, Nottingham wrote on the 1st September 1965 to Sally to confirm the gift.

Dear Madam,

24 Charlecote Drive

Wollaton,Nottingham

We thank you for your instructions, received through Mr Jurczyszyn-Jay to act for you both in connection with the gift of the above property to your son.
The necessary document has been prepared and we understand that any documents requiring to be witnessed can be sent to you via Messrs Kerfoot Owen of 1 Crown Place Denbigh.

We have today sent the deed of Gift to them for your signature and they will no doubt be getting in touch with you very shortly.

 Unfortunately Tadek also had other plans for his future and when finally in 1981 he announced his intention to marry, Sally was astounded; she had not seen it coming at all. His intended, Charlotte, was a quiet 'mousy little thing'. Sally consoled herself that it would all be over and that he would see sense. She attempted to find little faults that he might not have discovered for himself but it was to no avail. Tadek's mind was made up and being so far away she couldn't find a way to influence him.

After a few years of marriage and producing a son Tadek soon found that family life was not compatible with his free and easy bachelor style of living, spending and enjoyment.

They decided on a separation and to Sally's fury this meant that his wife was legally entitled to half the proceeds of the house. She saw 'her house' having to be mortgaged in order to pay the ex wife off. It maddened her that a lifetime of investment had gone so easily and determined that she would ensure that he never got married again.

She continued to spend huge sums of money on him saying that his ex-wife was 'bleeding him dry' and that he had but £20 to live on each week. Surprisingly this meagre amount enabled him to continue his relaxed life style, eating out, drinking, buying new miniature trains, travelling around the countryside and generally having a good time.

At work in the Nottingham Social Services Department he played the perfect part. Dealing with disenfranchised aggressive youths or mentally unbalanced drug fuelled individuals gave him no qualms. He, like his mother Sally, faced potentially explosive situations in their professional life with equanimity; her with her powerful personality; him with his sizable presence and good humour. They were both able to weigh up a situation and defuse it; they could both think on their feet.

Sally continued to work to make more and more money to secure their futures. She imagined him inheriting her home in Wales and encouraged him to visit as often as he could. He did not enjoy being torn from his train enthusiast and drinking friends and told her how difficult it was being 'on call' at work so often. When he did visit she would serve up the proverbial fattened calf. He would be given a whole chicken to eat at one meal. The table would groan with specialities purchased from the delicatessen food shops.

They would travel around the locality taking photographs and purchasing hand-made goods. Sometimes she would buy him a whole wardrobe of clothes at a time as he was always finding it difficult to 'make ends meet'; as he would cheerfully explain in case you thought that he was bemoaning his fate. As she purchased his clothes, his glasses, his shoes, and his petrol for his journey over to her and met any unexpected bills it was difficult to imagine what he actually did pay for in the end.

As he entered into his forties, sporting a full set of beard and whiskers he bore a striking likeness to Amos May his great grandfather. This pleased Sally as she continued to cherish the fantasies around this family. That Tadek so closely resembled this ancestor enabled the family link to be maintained and her ancestors to be kept physically alive for Sally. When the two met together they could chat for hours, thoroughly enjoying each other's company. Tadek was sometimes awed by his mother's depth of knowledge and her unerring ability to recall facts. It was almost impossible to enter into a discussion or raise a topic that she had not either researched or held a principled view upon. They enjoyed visiting National Trust properties and she would be able to regurgitate the names of the families who owned the property when other lesser mortals would have to resort to reading in the guide book. Many times she would be able to insert other facts not contained in that particular guide; linking families together from one property to another.

Just as Sally could squirrel away possessions, papers, artefacts, so she could squirrel away bits of information, but the trick was being able to recall them at will, and she managed to do this over and over again.

In 1987 Marion died aged just sixty six years old. What effect this news had on Sally is difficult to say. She never mentioned his death or spoke of her regret about their fractured relationship. He seemed to have just slipped out of her life.

Meanwhile Sally was invigorated by Tadek's infrequent visits and was so convinced of his love of her property in Wales which made all her hard work, to build and expand the house, worth while. She was building up his inheritance and he would be lord and master of all he surveyed. But we knew in our heart of hearts that this was a pipe dream. Tadek had no intention of establishing his Welsh identity. When she died we knew that he would sell it without a moment's hesitation. His life was in Nottingham, not in the backwaters of Llanrhaeadr in Wales no matter how beautiful the spot.

When the news of his early death reached Sally in May 1996 she was devastated. Suddenly all her dreams and aspirations were scattered, blown away by the tragedy. It was the very worst thing that could have happened to her. Even losing her beloved home would have been a trifle compared with the awful loss of this cherished son. Within weeks she seemed to wither, her magnificent spirit was crushed. Where she had always drawn herself up, holding herself erect and confident, appearing to tower over others; now she seemed to stoop and sag. She became smaller overnight. Determined to see Tadek, she told us that she would never believe that it was him until she had seen him with her own eyes. It was as if she felt that there had been a terrible mistake and that when she looked into the casket it would not be her son but a stranger mistakenly identified as Tadek looking back at her. When she came from the undertaker's, leaning on Allan's arm, her face wore a mask of unimaginable grief. She now had to live with that lasting vision. He had been purple and bloated despite the best efforts of the undertaker to make him more presentable. Tadek had suffered a massive heart attack; his life style had secured his fate.

Sally gave up her grandiose schemes for the property. She allowed the mice to rifle through the drawers making their nests wherever they chose. A library of books was left for them to nibble and chew. In the kitchen pots of preserves and pickles blackened; contents in jars became anonymous; the table that used to be set for feasts stayed covered with unread papers, wizened fruit and tea cup stains. A Miss Haversham gloom descended as spiders were left undisturbed to spin their tracery webs across the ceilings.

We attempted to take her out on visits and momentarily the old sparkle would return but increasingly she would refuse an outing, only venturing out when cajoled and pressurised.

She would still drive her car to shop and to make essential trips but now resorted to mail order catalogues, buying jewellery, shoes, and clothes that would never be worn and expensive ornaments, coins, china and plants that would be stacked upstairs in a bedroom half forgotten. She had a wooden casket made in which to keep a picture of him.

Then in April of the following year another tragedy came; the death of her dear brother Moss. Now there was no one in whom she could confide and keep close to her. She felt the gnawing signs of cancer and chose to ignore it. The cancer could only kill her body; her soul had already died.

Polish Officer Commanding
R.A.F.Station,Newton,Notts.

Certificate.

This is certified that according to our records 783714,
LAC Jurczyszyn M. is of Roman Catholic religion and not married
and that he has been granted permission to marry Rose Christiana
Mary Payne.

Group Captain,
Polish Officer Commanding
R.A.F.Station,Newton,Notts.

From the top:
Certificate of permission for Marion to marry Sally. A family portrait when Tadek was about three. Sally and Tadek at 24 Charlecote Drive and on holiday during the late 1940's.

24 hours of jazz; Sally & Marion on holiday in Poland. Zygmunt with the family. Tadek in the back yard in Denbigh.

118

Chapter 8   Fire, theft and burglary in Denbigh

Prior to her purchase and the renovation of the property in Llanrhaeadr her paperwork indicates that Sally took over the tenancy of Tŷ Gwyn, Clawdd Newdd, Denbigh, in the May of 1969. A Rev. Trevor Jones from Caerwys owned the property and the outgoing tenant made some arrangements regarding the furniture and fittings that were to be sold on for a fair price of £50. There was some dispute regarding the dining room chairs which were not part of the sale. Sally wanted all the good furniture along with the other bits and pieces and appealed to the Rev. Trevor Jones for some support. He agreed that it seemed unfair for the outgoing tenant to agree a price and then not include the 'good' dining room chairs but wisely remarked that the issue was strictly between her and the other tenant. The outgoing tenant had already provoked his displeasure by losing a set of keys, not leaving the property vacant when her tenancy had expired by two months and allowing the garden to become unkempt.
Sally soon found that she had met her match when she received a final letter regarding the chairs from Ms Cooper with a nice sting in its tail.

Dear Mrs Jay,
Thank you for your letter received this morning. I fail to understand why you are bringing up the matter of the Dining chairs. In my first letter to you I mentioned them & in the second letter also & yet in your reply (14th) you agree. They are not to be sold but to be brought here for our own use; you knew that from the start, because I said I would replace them. You would be walking into a fully

furnished house& in your letter you state it is a 'fair price' I don't think a woman in your position would go back on her word & I can only guess reading all your letters again its the money problem that is a worry for you, if this is so I am quite willing to wait, as I hoped you would understand, money is a problem to us all.

The rent was to be thirty-six shillings a week exclusive of rates and the notice to quit was set at three months.

There is a strange set of circumstances here, as to my knowledge Sally did not move out of her accommodation in the hospital until she bought a property. Perhaps she decided not to go ahead with the move but just gave the stipulated three months' notice.

By 1974 Sally had bought her two cottages, renaming them, Bryn Llwyn â Godwys, and installed a local couple to rent the left-hand-side cottage whilst she resided in the right-hand-side cottage. As we had just moved up from Goudhurst in Kent we were also looking for accommodation but after the visit to Denbigh Hospital we decided to stay with college friends and buy a house in Mynydd Isa, near Mold. The couple paid her rent which helped her to save for the building project. After leaving the hospital she took on a variety of part-time jobs. In the winter of 1974 she applied for her pension. She informed the DHSS that she was still married but living apart as no court order had been applied. The bank reluctantly agreed to provide a substantial loan but this had to be paid back within ten years. Her pension and lump sum was not going to be sufficient to meet both the loan and interest that accrued during that time and so she decided to take up a local milk round, delivering to her neighbours in and around Denbigh.

Angrily finding that her finances were inadequate for the plans that she had put in place she rounded on the hospital authorities in 1975, writing a flurry of letters detailing her length and years of service and demanding more money. This dispute regarding years of reckonable service to qualify for the Health Service Superannuation Scheme had been rumbling on since 1966. At first she was unsuccessful in making them agree to a more generous settlement. Things finally turned nasty when, in 1977, they scrutinised the hourly rate of pay that she had received in the course of her permanent night duties as the Senior Nursing Officer. She was scandalised to find that they had accused her of fraudulently accepting an amount that was in excess of what she was due. They wrote asking for the alleged overpayment to be repaid.

Dear Mrs Jay,

Arising from a recent check of salaries paid to staff on protected scales, it has been brought to my notice that you have been overpaid a considerable amount in salary from a date early in 1976. This apparently occurred when you took over the duties of Senior Nursing Officer on permanent night duty, for which you were authorised under the Whitley Council, Nurses and Midwives Conditions of Service to be paid an additional allowance of £4992 and the Psychiatric lead of £165 per annum, giving you the total salary of £5847, which is clearly shown as the annual rate on each and every payslip.

It has now been discovered that you have, in addition, received payments in respect of all the night duty hours you have worked. These details were extracted from the North Wales Hospital monthly staff returns and involve a total of 1664½ hours x ¼ time = 416⅛ hours at £2.80335 per hour = £1166.50 overpaid.

Again I would point out that these unauthorised payments were shown separately and quite clearly on your payslip as enhanced payments and in view of your vast experience in the nursing profession, I feel you could not have been unaware of the excess pay you were receiving.

This is a grave and serious matter, since although the employer makes every effort to ensure the correctness of salary payments, there is also an obligation on the part of the employee to thoroughly check the payslip and to report to the employer any apparent discrepancies. In this particular case, the unauthorised payments were clearly visible and should have been reported immediately.

In view of the circumstances I must ask you for your immediate observations and to indicate how you propose to repay this overpayment.

In 1966 the Ministry of Health had also informed her categorically that her years working at Rampton and later Mapperley Hospital, from 1935 up until August 1944 did not qualify for the Superannuation scheme.

Previously in the February 1977 she had requested details of her salary and they had written to confirm the annual salary of £5157 together with the annual night Duty Allowance of £690 and the Annual Earnings supplement of £312 which amounted to a final salary of £6159 which did not equate to the threatening letter that she received in the July of that year. She tried to explain that the post of Deputy Principle Nursing Officer, created for her in 1969 did not appear to have an official pay scale and that she had been informed by the hospital administrators that she had an entitlement to the enhanced pay due to her agreement to accept night duties of 40 hours each week.

Her rage exploded through her correspondence.

The tone of your letter is very unpleasant, if not insulting.........................in the past I have queried each step when I thought it to be in error. However now that I no longer hire personnel my interest in pay scales etc has declined.

The years of frustration led her to end the letter to the District Finance Officer with the words;

I am sending details to the executive body of my union and you will doubtlessly hear from them in due course.

In 1980 she received the support from the Royal College of Nursing. They sympathised with her plight and felt that she had indeed been treated unfairly by the Superannuation Division. They believed that she was entitled to the full 40 years of reckonable service from 1935 until 1975 which would have equated to 45 years in 1980. Kept with the letters were her frantic jottings trying to make sense of the figures. She worked out her lump sum and pension entitlement based on 40 years and knew that she could raise sufficient funds to secure her cottages but not to carry out her proposed improvements.

The work commenced at Bryn Llwyn â Godwys once the tenants installed on one side of the property had moved out. Sally had by this time taken on night nursing duties, first at a nursing home in Runcorn and then one in Rhyl to supplement her income.

The stairs were removed from the left-hand side of the property leaving a large beamed room pleasantly lit from two windows and a back door. Set in the door was a beautiful stained glass window with a sailing ship sentimentally inscribed 'East or West Home is Best'. This room became the lounge with a large log-burning fireplace to provide the focal point. She brought in two pianolas; complete with a large box of music rolls, an upright piano and a modern grandfather clock, a large oak sideboard with the lion face details, a large glass cabinet, settee and two armchairs, an occasional games table, her Last Supper tapestry and a profusion of knick knacks. Always on the lookout for old things to add to her house she managed to acquire some wood block flooring that had been taken out of a school and they were laid and polished for the floor; their warm chestnut glow took on the rainbow colours from the stained window during the late morning sun.

Before this was completed she had to live in the restricted space of the right-hand cottage with her whole collection of books, paintings, pottery, kitchen ware, and her assorted menagerie whilst the rest of her possessions brought from the Nursing Home were piled in trunks and suitcases in the outhouses. She never bothered to lock her doors, feeling that she was far away from the 'criminal classes,' and her cats had the run of the outside yard, fields and the two rooms downstairs. She wanted to install a Rayburn for cooking and heating the hot water but had to also accommodate an old electric cooker by the back kitchen door until the renovation would allow more space to use. She placed her cooking oil in large plastic containers on the floor by the cooker and in another small ante-room she had squeezed in a washing machine.

....

It was very dark when she stirred; awoken by a sound that she didn't recognise. Sleep threatened to overwhelm her but again a noise brought her back. She turned over, dragging the covers over herself, trying to settle back. Suddenly she sat up. Something was wrong. The urgent crying of her cat stabbed at her chest. It was in distress, yowling and meowing, whimpering and calling for her. As she switched on the light she slowly realised that there was a strange greyness around her although the light was on. Smoke was filling her room, swirling lazily, then rising as she stood there unsure and perplexed. Panic gripped her. She could hear the cat and realised that the other rasping sound was the sound of its claws tearing at the door. It was trying to get out. It must be

125

trapped. Black thick smoke billowed up the stairs and she tried to cover her face whilst her other hand felt for the banister. There was a roaring crackling sound coming from the kitchen. She stumbled down the wooden steps. Her throat started to contract as the gagging acrid smoke filled her mouth, stinging and choking her. She wanted to gulp in air but each breath rasped with smoke. Reaching the bottom of the stairs she pushed against the door and felt a rush of heat and saw the flickering flames. The room was enveloped in black smoke. She had to reach the sink for water; towels to throw over the flames. It had to be stopped.

After the flames had been doused the electricity failed. Plunged into darkness again she felt around the cupboards until she found her large torch and surveyed the scene. The fire engine arrived some time later and the crew reassured her that the place was safe. Everything was either charred and blackened or dripping with water.

It had been the plastic container filled with cooking oil that had caused the fire to spread so quickly. The blackened soot-streaked walls resembled the aftermath of Dante's inferno. So much was ruined. An investigation of the cause would have to be carried out before an insurance claim could be made. Sally looked at the kitchen door leading into her parlour. Huge scratches marked the bottom panel. "If it hadn't been for Socks I would be dead" she declared.

The fire brought the new work to a standstill and caused her much unhappiness. Many of her purchases had been destroyed; the rewiring had to take priority and she couldn't now accommodate Tadek for his proposed visit with the place in such an awful mess.

Not long afterwards we went over to see her. The place still reeked of soot and stale smoke. We stood looking at the damage; we couldn't sit down as everything was still covered in oily grime. It was a grim scene. Sally seemed vulnerable for the first time. I realised that she was not invincible. We offered help to clean up and temporary accommodation with us in Mynydd Isa but of course this was rejected out of hand. She would manage; she always had done. It was just a matter of waiting for the insurance and then she would be able to sort things out.

The work eventually recommenced. A centre porch entrance graced the front of the house and the chimneys had been repaired. In the dark kitchen she had arranged for thick hand-made burr walnut cupboards to be fixed to the walls and the Rayburn was installed in the corner. The garage, complete with an 'inspection pit', was built onto the side and a new door led from the garage into the private back yard. She arranged for a lean-to greenhouse to be put against the lounge wall and already had managed to plant some fertile peach trees inside. A border of soil on top of the wall retaining the orchard beyond the yard had been planted with narcissi and daffodil bulbs. Someone had cut the long grass underneath the trees and the mossy damp path leading to the outhouses were worn and used. Thick stable doors with large black wrought-iron latches had been hung at each entrance. Inside the vast garage new purchases, strimmers, patio chairs, a parasol, shears, garden forks, rakes, rope, twine, bird baths, outside temperature gauges, a pond pump and fountain, a rotovator, trench digger, boxes of seed, nuts, garden pots, paints, varnish, assembled along each wall, still in their boxes and packaging and tins. At one end she had installed a large chest freezer and an upright fridge freezer which was packed with home grown and shop purchased produce.

Paintings from grateful patients and friends hung on her walls in the parlour and a fat Denbigh eight-day long-case grandfather clock marked Rich'd Griffiths, the dial delicately decorated with two birds took up residence in the corner behind the priest bench. Radiators had been fitted in each room and upstairs a shower room fitted on the landing area between her room and the other three bedrooms. Tadek's room boasted a large black-grated fireplace, a double bed, an imposing large black ebony wardrobe, a newly upholstered *chaise lounge* and a window that afforded magnificent north-westerly views of Denbigh and the surrounding countryside.

Gradually more brown swirled jugs, potato keepers, bowls, and goblets purchased from the befriended potter David Frith and the local Anvil Denbigh pottery appeared. A railway station clock took up its timely position by the kitchen door and heavy multi-coloured Tiffany styled lampshades hung from the ceiling. Traditional Welsh woollen throws in vivid lilac and purple adorned chairs and beds and as the cottage took on a bohemian air of eclectic style so Sally worked harder and longer hours to sustain her growing need for cash. Her racing-green MG sports car would wind its way along the narrow lanes its headlights picking out transfixed rabbits frozen in its headlights. During the day she started to work on the garden, planting walnut trees, greengages and quinces to the left of the property and a prickly Araucaria in memory of the monkey puzzle trees planted by her grandfather in Bedgebury National Pinetum in Kent. She spent longer hours away from home as her night duties grew into twelve-hour shifts and then the inevitable happened.

One early morning she reached home to find the back door wide open. Stepping into the house she sensed all was not well. The place had been ransacked. Upstairs the drawers and cupboards had been carelessly turned out and emptied onto the floor; all her jewellery, watches, sentimental treasures had gone. Expensive cameras had been found, the television, along with other gadgets still in their boxes in the garage had been taken.

Sally had been too trusting. She had allowed workmen, gardeners, postmen, visitors, and new acquaintances to witness her cavalier attitude to security. Everyone in the locality knew that her doors were never locked. Someone spoke to someone and so the story reached the ears of a thief who gladly took advantage of an opportunity to thoroughly search a property so full of saleable treasures.

It was a wonder that the insurance company paid out, but they did and so she took the opportunity to restock the house and buy Clogau Welsh gold jewellery, and pieces set with emeralds, a new television set and some watches. Unfortunately she forgot to invest in security and a few months later she came home to find that she had been burgled again and this time the thief, whilst finding new treasures to fence, had been more haphazard in his approach, which led the police to believe that the burglar probably had a serious drug habit to support. Sally maintained that the thief could not have been a local but had used the A55 coming from over the border in Liverpool in order to plunder properties in North Wales. Once more she replaced the stolen items with the insurance money but she had learnt her lesson and good locks were put on the doors and windows were no longer left open.

Increasingly she found constraints on her free time but we were always amazed at how much she achieved despite the long hours working at the different nursing homes. The homes were quick to snap her up. Her vast experience and qualifications in both general and psychiatric nursing was invaluable. Back in 1948 she received her Certificate from the General Nursing Council stating that she was "qualified by virtue of having obtained the certificate of the Royal Medico-Psychological Association to take and use the title of 'Registered Nurse for Mental Defectives'." She was qualified to administer medication, could relate to her confused patients suffering dementia or Alzheimer's disease and her quick and decisive manner gave the staff and patients the reassurance that all would be well. Aggressive clients caused her no alarm; she calmed down explosive situations with equanimity, she nursed these frail and often very frightened vulnerable old people with skill and kindness.

Once back home in her beloved Bryn Llwyn â Godwys she set about the herculean task of moving large items of furniture unaided. She painted and decorated, having a dubious preference for lime green paint that splattered wilfully on the backs of the furniture. She catalogued her videos, bought, read and stacked a library of reference books on steam trains, photography, stately homes, history, astronomy, woodwork, gardening, art, antiques, birds, zoology, religion, stories of The Mabinogion, Tales of the Arabian Nights, bibliographies, autobiographies, and flora and fauna until the bookcases groaned under their load.

Her full address book was testament to the daily correspondence that she undertook; her local postman never came empty handed, bringing with him a succession of thick envelopes, parcels and the unwanted bills.

Each Christmas she would proudly count the number of cards that she had received, triumphant that the figure never once fell below one hundred.

One Christmas as she was rushing around after returning from a gruelling night shift she fell headlong across the parlour as she carried in a heavy bucket of coal. Her arm snapped under the pressure of the fall. We found out from her neighbour later that day that she was in the hospital and hurried to see her. We found her cross and indignant at the inconvenience of being there.

"I have so much to do!" she blazed. "And what are you here for? I shall be home soon. The cats need me." She viewed our presence as 'fussing about nothing'. Annoyed at us seeing her in such a vulnerable state she fought to take control of the situation.

Her arm was swathed in a thick plaster with just her long fingers peeping out at the bottom and her face, although defiant, seemed to be steeling itself against the waves of pain.

130

The doctor confirmed the bad break and that it would be at best six weeks before she would be out of plaster.

Despite her protests Al took a stern line. I realised with surprise that she was going to agree to his proposals.

"I will come over after work Sally and bring in the coal. I can feed the cats and do what is necessary but you will have to stay with us for a couple of days until we know that you can cope. And don't say no because that is settled. Once you have had a bit of time to recuperate then I will bring you back home and we will…."

She tried to wave away his words, shaking her head, but he fixed her in his gaze and continued,

"When I bring you back home I can still do the ashes and coal and feed the cats but we will need to get some ready-meals for you."

She pressed her lips together in a grimace and attempted to draw herself up.

"I am a vegetarian and cannot eat meat," she announced imperiously.

"We will get vegetarian ready-meals Sally, there is no problem," I intervened.

"I can only eat natural products, not that chemical mess." Her right eyebrow arched.

I shouldn't have said anything; Al was doing quite nicely without my interference and now the struggle would be uphill.

"Sally, we will get proper quality meals and Julia can cook some suppers which I can pop in your freezer. There is no problem at all. The sooner we can sort this out the quicker you will be back home looking after your cats."

She sniffed and considered the last remark. Being back home with her beloved cats 'sooner rather than later' had an appeal.

"Mmmm", her nostrils flared slightly, "Mmmm."

This sounded like a qualified agreement. Al took the opportunity to press the point.

"Give me your house keys today and we will get another set cut just in case you are not too good again. Now we can go back to yours and feed the cats...."

"The cats don't know you.......you will scare them off."

"No Sally, of course they don't know us that well, but I will fill up the bowls and they can help themselves after I have gone. Now where's the problem.... Huh? I will ring you here at the hospital tonight; give you an update, and then we will come tomorrow and get this sorted. Right?"

She pressed her lips together again and allowed a quiet grunt to act as an acknowledgement of her agreement.

Each evening that Al visited so a special relationship developed. He became captivated by her enquiring mind and her interest in the world about her. She looked forward to his trips over to feed the parlour fire and sweep out the ashes. Sally began to admire his no-nonsense approach. She approved of his strength; his ability to deal with the many odd jobs that she had not been able to fix. She respected his technical prowess and practical knowledge, even allowing him to offer practical solutions to things that she had put to one side. He considered the cobweb loops of electrical cable in the garage.

"Who left it like that, Sally?"

"Oh, yes I need to have it rewired in there," she reluctantly agreed, declining to answer the query. The prospect of cost hanging between them like the trailing loops of cable.

"That's no big deal just to get this area sorted. I can come at the weekend to do it. You will need a new fuse and termination box, a 13amp ring for the garage and I can get hold of a roll of cable. It will take no more than two days tops. And then it will be safe. You can't go on like that; you will end up being electrocuted!"

Her eyes widened, seeing an end to a nagging problem. He was as good as his word. A fuse box was fastened to the wall and the trailing cables replaced with neat wires running straight and close to the walls. New light switches and power points replaced the blackened ones. Sally was delighted. She saw progress and improvement as she sat there massaging her fingers, willing for the plaster to be removed. Her depression of being confined, and worry about her lack of earnings lifted as she found that her daily routine was getting easier to manage.

Once the plaster was removed she continued her Witch Hazel massage treatment and the arm regained its original strength without sign of any injury. Sally delighted in resuming her regime and being able to drive once again.

"Have the poor devils been advised that she is back on the road?" was Dad's response to the news. And we grinned at his humour. Sally had twice crashed her MG although she had tried to keep the incidents quiet.

In the first incident she had been returning home and had taken a corner too fast. Her car had ploughed through a hedge, ending up in the field. The cost of the repair and the look of her crumpled bonnet upset her more than the crash. On the second incident the side of the car was damaged but the details of the accident were not forthcoming. Once again she was probably driving along the narrow country roads at the time. She didn't seem to have involved another driver so perhaps as Dad remarked "the hedge jumped out at her".

Although she used to mock Marion and his ability to drive or navigate she did seem to take the long route whenever she came to visit us. We would wait impatiently as her MG finally roared into view.

One Christmas she decided that she would be able to take some time off and come over to us in Mynydd Isa for the day. Most of the morning had disappeared by the time she arrived and it took some time to divest the car from its parcels, bags and boxes. She accepted the freshly brewed coffee but declined the proffered mince pies. Actually we were relieved as we realised later that they were special ones laced with fruit and sherry.

We had not begun the opening of presents as we had wanted to wait for her. Scissors were handed out and places taken. Al and I ended up on the floor and Mum flustered around looking for bin sacks for the ensuing rubbish.

One at a time the boxes and packages were opened and ribbon, sellotape and wrapping paper covered the floor. Portia, our Labrador, opened one eye at each unwrapping until sighing, losing interest and settling down to sleep with her head resting on her outstretched paws. Al opened a large box to us both from Sally. I watched excitedly as he pulled out thin sticks. They looked like masts. He drew out a large shell sailing ship fixed to an urchin shell. Inside the orange shell resided an electrical lamp and coiled cable. We were speechless. Globules of thick glue ensured that the pearly shells adhered to the stick-like masts and trailed from shell to shell. We found a plug to switch it on. The orange urchin shell glowed pink.

"How unusual," I managed to murmur and dare not meet Dad's eye.

"What is it?" Mum queried, not having seen it being switched on. I couldn't answer her. She looked around at each of us until the silence was deafening. Portia raised her head sniffing the air.

Al came to the rescue. "Sally's excelled herself this time. Well, I've never seen a lamp like this before." He managed to sound as if it had given him great pleasure.

I found that I needed to turn the oven on and made my escape into the kitchen. Once I had regained some composure I managed to rejoin the family.

The sailing ship passed into family folklore. Whenever we couldn't think what to give someone Al would say "we could always give them a ship!" and we would double up, remembering that Christmas and wondering if Sally really ever knew how horrible we thought the object was. After we threw it away, as we couldn't get rid of it in any other way, we were sad that we had never taken a picture as a reminder of the awful thing. We had previously attempted to sell it for 50p at a school fair and it sat there on the table until the end of the afternoon.

It was a couple of years later that Dad and Mum were with us for Christmas when they opened a large box from Sally. Inside nestled another shell ship. We rolled about the floor with Mum reproaching us with,"it's the thought that counts" and us shouting "but what was she *thinking of* at the time, Mum!"

I don't know what happened to this ship but we never fail to giggle when we recall the 'second coming' of the ghost ship.

………………………..

During one of our many visits to see her we could see that she was looking particularly thin. She finally admitted to feeling unwell and that it was her gall bladder playing up. Although she was a vegetarian she enjoyed dairy products and relished eating fresh organic produce before organic had been a word in general usage, and certainly long before supermarkets had specially designated shelving for that food. She mournfully announced that she could no longer eat butter, cream or cheese because she then suffered so much pain and felt so queasy. Eventually she was admitted into the Princess Alexandra Hospital in Rhyl and had her gall bladder removed. It was after this operation that she seemed to mellow in her approach to us. We had shown a willingness to look after her cats while she was there and she was unable to return to work whilst recovering from her hospital stay and so quite enjoyed having us as visitors to relieve the boredom of her enforced incarceration.

It was around that time that she realised that Al and I had been quite badly hit financially, having to pay for his divorce, selling and giving all the proceeds to his ex-wife and paying a large monthly contribution to his two children. I had made my own clothes for a number of years and so she decided that she would step in and give me a warm winter coat. I was presented with a zigzag patterned Welsh wool coat that would have stopped the traffic and caused a minor accident; you could have seen me coming a mile off. It was warm and it did fit, but I hated the coat with a vengeance, despite mum saying how well it had been made.

She also presented us with her home-made jellies and jams; her specialities being the jam from her greengage tree and her Denbigh Plum tree. Her young walnut tree refused to produce nuts but the little fig tree managed to show a modest crop of green figs and her peach tree, cordoned in her lean-to greenhouse, managed to give her massive fruits. Every so often they would develop so quickly that they would fall to the ground before she was able to pick them, quickly drawing in the wasps.

When Al was still ill one morning after a sleepless night following our attendance at a Ball at RAF Sealand, I rang her to ask her about the symptoms that he had shown. "I don't think it is appendicitis," I said, "because he hasn't been sick.'

"Sick! He doesn't need to be sick!" She railed

"Get him to the doctor; he needs to be in hospital!" she snapped.

Al owes his large appendix scar to me and his life to Sally. His appendix had burst.

During Tadek's lifetime she had always ensured that he and his son David would enjoy the various visits to theatre Clwyd to see the magical Christmas productions. After he died and David was no longer invited to spend time with her we took her to the theatre to see the popular musical rock and roll pantomimes.

She sometimes bought tickets for the Gilbert and Sullivan productions which were to be performed in Ruthin and asked if we would accompany her. But it was our trips to Bodnant Gardens that delighted her. On one occasion we had spent so long in the grounds examining all the plants and trees that we didn't notice the time and realised with horror that closing time had been and gone. I envisaged having to haul her over the high wall that enclosed the grounds as Al grimly helped her along the narrow difficult pathways away from the river valley. Thankfully the turnstile still operated to allow visitors to leave the gardens. I had been overcome with panic but Sally was completely unperturbed by the experience, once again demonstrating our different natures.

As a child I had always been fascinated by the distinctive perfumes that people wore. For my father the smell of pipe tobacco and cigar smoke brought him tantalisingly close to me long after his death. Sally had worn a mysterious delicate fragrance and her perfume often lingered in the air after her departure. It was not one that I have ever managed to find despite sniffing various samples at Boots counters and at airport duty-free shops. Then one day I was buying a perfume for a friend at the Browns store in Chester and stopped at the expensive Sisley counter. The fragrance was the nearest that I have ever experienced as being able to replicate that individualistic smell that used to delight me as a child and yet it wasn't produced until 1976. Perhaps she wore the older perfume of 4711 which also reminds me of her, and this was certainly available and affordable in the 1950's, having been created way back in the 1880's. The perfume was distributed to German submariners during the Second World War to address the problem of the lack of bathing in the submarines. The submariners in turn gave the bottles of perfume as gifts to their wives and girlfriends. By the 1980's she no longer wore perfume and I found nothing in the house that pointed me in the right direction but I rather like the idea that even her perfume has remained a mystery and that I still can't decide between one of the oldest and one of the youngest products.

Towards the end of her life she took a keen interest in the expensive orchids which had finally begun to be imported and could be found in some specialist nurseries. Of course now they are available in every supermarket, but at that time they had had an aura of being exotic and very foreign. Sally took great delight in nurturing these plants which still manage to wither in the hands of the average householder once they have shed their waxy flowers.

When we cleared the house we found a particularly different looking yellow-green Phalaenopsis in the kitchen and an equally fabulous cream green Cymbidium. Once the Phalaenopsis was positioned on our kitchen window sill it continued to flower for three continuous years, much to our amazement and the Cymbidium flourished in the conservatory. Having been enthralled by their beauty we continued to purchase other orchids and due to Al's green fingers they flower for long healthy periods, ensuring that somewhere in the house there is an orchid to remind us of Sally's orchid legacy.

Interior views of Sally's house in the 1980's and 1990's. The first burglary took many family pieces including jewellery, cameras and electrical items so she purchased replacements from the local jewellers in Denbigh and sent for the Clogau Gold catalogue to buy the amethyst Tree of Life ring and pendant. By the year 2000 the unkempt lounge began to fill with unopened boxes. Her glorious Cymbidium continues to flower to this day.

Chapter 9   The May family myths

The May family's history was wedded to Wales. Our illustrious mythical ancestors on our maternal grandfather's side had the family name of Wynne and had owned large properties in North Wales, including the country estate and Plas Mawr in Conway built for Robert Wynne, a Welsh merchant, in 1576 plus a slate quarry at Whistling Sands which had afforded them great wealth and status. Sally had completed the circle by returning to Wales, and by doing so had preserved our Welsh heritage. The large Welsh family bible passed from father to son had carefully recorded each name on the fly leaf in beautiful copperplate. This was the same bible that had been so wantonly destroyed by her Uncle Amos, an employee of the railway, in 1925; consumed by the flames of a garden bonfire in Cranbrook. Sally had been unable to rescue it and had only the scanty recall of conversations with her grandfather, Amos May, her dear Taid, to enable her to piece together the broken family history. This grandfather had been able to benefit from a good education at Oxford University, reading science and botany, which had helped him to achieve an astounding knowledge of horticulture. This sound understanding opened the doors of large country estates up and down the length and breadth of England, from Wildgate, Jedburgh, Old Layton Norfolk, Wisley, Kent, Hartley and Cranbrook. These owners were keen to extend their gardens and grounds and to grow more exotic species in their greenhouses to be the envy of their peers.

Amos May had been the head gardener, at Eastwell Manor in Kent, and at the equally prestigious Lynford Hall in Norfolk. He frequented the gardens at Kew, conversing with the gardeners there whilst researching species of plants and trees that would be compatible with the soil on the estates. He advised the owners of Bedgebury Pinetum, establishing a wonderful arboretum for them. And then of course there was the celebrated association with Vita Sackville-West and Harold Nicholson when he planted their Nuttery.

Before him, his uncle, John May, had been a ship's surgeon or a sea captain and had sailed to Malta. John brought back exotic presents for the family and at some time had given a fine Macaw parrot to his sister. Earlier, during his seafaring days serving in the Navy, he had chased ships away during the Abolition of Slavery. In Sally's cousin Joan's house there was a fine oil painting of John and his brother demonstrating how wealthy and important the two men were. As Sally said, "it was only those of consequence with wealth and position who could afford to have such a painting commissioned." (Her cousin Joan was the daughter of Amos May the railway booking clerk.)

Sally spoke of how she and Tadek had visited the family's Plas Mawr estate and that Tadek had been so surprised to find the statuary in the grounds just as she had described. The bronze stag being one of the most celebrated pieces, standing at the far end of an avenue of fine oaks.

When she had visited the slate quarry at Whistling Sands to find a suitable piece to mark the May burial ground in Kent she was astounded and delighted to be shown the old accounts written in her ancestor Wynne May's own hand. They had wanted her to take the headstone as a gift but she felt that she couldn't accept such a generous offer, despite their many protestations. Instead she took it back to Denbigh to have it inscribed before taking it down to Kent.

Sadly it was while the young Amos May (her grandfather) had been recuperating from a chest infection at the seaside in Brighton in 1874 that he had met the barely literate Mary Charlotte Gilbert. They corresponded for ten years before they were finally married. He had had to complete his university studies. Amos was able to write beautiful letters in his educated hand but poor Mary could only produce sad little notes, badly constructed and often illegible. It was a poor match for Amos but he was such a generous and kind hearted man that he took pity on the girl and married her. Of course she held him back so he was never able to take his place in the best society.

Sally's letter to Joan in 1972 flowed with Celtic romanticism as she replied to Joan's query about receiving a Welsh love spoon,

now why did I give you the spoon and card, because you, like me have a strong (very strong) streak of Welsh blood, the romanticism, we feel, judging things with our heart rather than our head is purely Celtic and I for one thank God for it. I pity those who can only see things in the light of £.S.D and utilitarian function, they miss so much. You and I feel and experience, they only judge and balance. Therefore I know you would appreciate a small example of local industry. Around here one can still obtain hand made goods pottery, leather etc. I wish as I said before I had a house so that I could say 'come and stay' and I will show you the spots. The remainder of your question yes your Paternal & my Maternal grandfathers; Mother was a Wynne of the famous lineage. It was Constance JOHN (not Joan) apparently a boy was wanted so when she was born the John remained and the Constance was put in front for convenience. I did not mention Sarah Ann May, because I never met her, I am not sure where she lived apparently she did not but was Grandad' (our) little sister. She was NOT Aunt Cissie- I did not meet Aunt Cissie, she lived in Maida Vale London, Aunt Kate of Scotney was Grandmother's sister (a Gilbert before marriage) she I knew very well. Yes, Grandfather

144

was born on Conway, but as I said whether Plas Mawr or Plas Newydd (Not the Anglesey Newyddon) I am not sure. The fun of probing back will be ours.....................

Sir John Wynne of Gwydir is a long way back BUT his offspring's are still the Lord Lieutenant of the area. The reason I was given for granddad being in sent to the Gilberts family was to recuperate after Rheumatic fever. Anyhow whatever the reason it was how he came to meet Mary Charlotte Gilbert. They were writing for ten years (by letter).

Her earlier letter written just eleven days prior to this attempted to demonstrate more accurately the Welsh heritage by providing dates.

I have worked out the following:- Amos May born 10-12-1853 Caernarvonshire (Conway)

Mary Charlotte May (nee Gilbert) born July or August 1854. The date that they were married was 29/5/1884 (this may be up to 4 years out because I remember Grandad saying they had met when he was 16 and Grandma 15 and married 10 years later, on the other hand I always understood that the brooch I have with the day May 29th 1884 was a wedding gift).

Finally on the back page she drew a family tree, gathering together the entire mythical lineage and compounding the story with the more recent events, incorrectly attributing parentage to illegitimate children.

She headed up the tree putting the first Amos May, her great grandfather, as a May Wynne having two marriages and a brother John Doan May. Down the line followed her

145

grandfather Amos May, born in 1853, and his wife Mary Charlotte with their four children; Charlotte Mary, Amos, Christiana and Rose. She then provided Christiana and Herbert with three children: Sally 1915, Amos, her brother, 1920 and their younger brother Tom 1929 and finally Christiana's brother Amos with a daughter Joan. Charlotte Mary had Bill (William)

It was during the middle 1960's when my sister Heather expressed a casual interest in the family history and wanted to know more about our father's ancestors. Unbeknown to Sally Dad started to unravel some of the stories; feeling that enough time had passed for those long dead. He then explained that there were other truths whose exposure would cause a good deal of anguish, heartache and some anger so we should keep those things private and to ourselves. We couldn't understand why Dad's accent was so different to his sister Sally's. Dad then explained that he did spend a good deal of time visiting his family in Kent, often staying with his Uncle Amos, his cousin Joan's father, and that Joan was the school friend of our Mum.

Then he dropped the first bombshell. He was not Sally's brother but was her half-brother. His father Herbert, after marrying Chrissie, had made Dorothy Rose, his sister-in-law, pregnant. We were speechless. Although the 1960's were said to be liberated and swinging this was something quite shocking to our family who had never experienced divorce let alone illegitimacy. Sitting around the glowing fire in the front room Dad proceeded to tell the May story. As a child he had been taken to Nottingham to be brought up by Herbert and Chrissie. Herbert had been an aggressive father to him; frightening him with his drinking and threats rather than actual physical violence but the family lived in his shadow of tyranny and meanness.

146

"If there was an egg to be had then he would have it," Dad spoke so bitterly about him and so we in turn judged and condemned him for hurting our Dad.

The next bombshell fell.

Sally had given birth to a child when she was just fourteen years old. Our Uncle Tom was in fact our cousin. Chrissie had not had three children, just one. Dad's mother Dorothy Rose had been an invalid and quite incapable of looking after a child. Dad opened a smooth wooden box and went through his childhood treasures. There were tiny scraps of paper covered with black ink spidery writing,

"Dorothy Rose May, Dorothy Rose May" written as a child would, practising their letters. It seemed so sad to us that this grown woman was struggling to master writing her name, and then there were more scraps, she had used a little rubber stamp to print out little flowers on the page. The innocence of such an activity caught at our throat. Here were Victorian style paper scraps stuck on the next piece, stuck in random, haphazardly, as a very young child would do it. Carefully he held up a tiny photograph. There was his young mother as a girl, her pretty thin face staring wistfully out at us. Her hair swept up and caught at the back; her tucked pinafore dress covered with a little apron and her dainty little ankle boots crossed, just showing beneath her skirt.

Next he brought out a few chess pawns. "All I have left from the set," he explained. "The old man would play and when he realised that he was about to lose he would grab the board and snap it shut," he remarked with a sad smile. "When I came home to collect my things after the war they had all been thrown out."

The whole idea of constructing a family tree was quite out of the question. We were profoundly saddened by Dad's revelation and his subsequent stories of his childhood in Nottingham; of the long illnesses that he suffered, being in hospital for nearly two years being bedridden after contracting scarlet fever and rheumatic fever and the fact that he was perpetually frightened by his own shadow and threats of the 'Tall Agrippa'. We also couldn't bring ourselves to believe that Sally had suffered such a trauma. She seemed so fearless and bold. To think of her as a little thirteen year-old being seduced by a grown man was quite horrifying. She would then have discovered her pregnancy and given birth; it made my blood run cold. She must have been in despair and so frightened. It was impossible to hold an image of this young girl next to our Aunt Sally and to know that at one time they had been one and the same.

It was not until Sally moved to the hospital in Denbigh, North Wales that the stories of our Welsh heritage started to emerge.

"Bloody nonsense," our Dad would be indignant. And when the Welsh terminology of Nain and Taid appeared he was beside himself. "Where the hell does she get such rubbish from, I don't know," he would explode. But despite such censure he could not bring himself to challenge her in front of others. When she finally bought the two cottages in Llanrhaeadr near Denbigh and told him of her plans to restore the cottages back into the one large house as they had been in the past he did allow his frustration to spill out.

"Look Sal", he would try to soften his words. "The beams in the attics show how these two were constructed. Look at the stairs on both sides and windows; look at the symmetry love". But she would not be persuaded. Her quest was the restoration of the property to its former glory. Minor facts of original construction were irrelevant in the grand scheme of things.

"Thank God she didn't get the farm," he would murmur with a wry smile. "Just think of that!" And he would roll his eyes whilst we would try not to giggle.

We stood outside looking at the two stone cottages from the road side. The property was a fair size already. On one side to the right were two stone outhouses requiring some urgent repair. The two box hedges lined the paths running up to the cottages' separate front doors. On the left leading to the back of the property were old sheds cobbled together with metal sheeting for the roof. A tangled collection of thin sinewy apple, pear, plum and greengage trees was all that remained of the little orchard at the back. Rotten fruit, seeping wet syrup, oozed on the ground, the fruits still held on the branches had been ravaged by drowsy wasps. There was stillness but an enchantment about the place. It had been sleeping for years. As we walked around to the back following a beaten-down soft grass track we found a little wall separating the two back windows and the two back yards. The doors were placed at the end as an exit from each kitchen. There were two rooms at the top and two at the bottom. A shoulder-high brick wall covered with moss and delicate trailing ivy leaved toad flax held back the higher ground containing the orchard, a rusty tin bath, and pink rosebay willow herb, tall grasses and stinging nettles. At the front, to the right, there was a cesspit. Fresh water came from a pipe further up at the back from a well or stream or from a farm. From the front bedroom windows on the far left we could see the ragged ruined remains of Denbigh Castle and the hills of the Clwydian range on the right. In front of us, on the other side of the quiet country road, a hedge kept in the sheep that dotted the surrounding fields.

 Excitedly Sally showed Dad the architect's plans; they were grandiose and costly. She would need a bank loan to cover even some of the minor alterations.

"I want a main porch at the front. The staircase will be on the left side and then we'll dispense with the other staircase. I'll knock the two rooms in this left cottage into one which will be the lounge and I'll have a coal fire in there. This side will be left in two with the kitchen at the back, with an Aga, and then this will be the dining room where we are now." She announced her plans with great satisfaction. A local builder, Mr Rizzle, was to carry out the alterations.

Dad looked more closely at the carefully detailed drawings.

"What's this for Sal, on the left here?"

Sally looked over his shoulder, "oh that's the garage and the inspection pit."

All the way home he kept up a staccato of terse remarks. "What does she want a pit for? An inspection pit! What the hell for! One house, my arse! Two cottages they always were. Bloody foolish woman! More money than bloody sense! And a bloody fool of an architect to encourage her too! Know what he's after; probably charging her a fortune for those plans. It will all come to grief. You mark my words! She'll work herself into an early grave!"

We knew that his anger masked his concern for her. She had an unerring capacity, despite her intelligence, to be flattered by unscrupulous sycophantic people. Having such a vivid imagination it was strange that she did not spot this ability for exaggeration in others.

As she became established at the hospital and the surrounding area her outside interests expanded. Meeting various local dignitaries during the course of her work was routine and she gradually developed a keen interest in the affairs of the town and county. Becoming a councillor seemed a natural step to take and she relished the responsibility of representing the town and discussing the issues with fellow councillors. It was during this time when she began to speak more and more about the family's Welsh roots. Fiction and fact began to blur as she associated more closely with those having titles and property. Meeting Lady X or Lord Y, when they met her at the hospital or at local charity functions, enabled her to visualise places of local importance. She began to learn and understand the history behind these families. Being a member of the Denbigh Red Cross, supporting local animal charities, participating in archaeological digs all contributed to her ability to fraternise with people of some influence. Her depth of knowledge and experience percolated through her conversation. She was a

150

persuasive and impressive conversationalist. She joined various organisations and became a shareholder in the Llangollen Railway and later the Norfolk Railway. She had always been a competent and regular correspondent, keeping in touch with those she had met during the course of her work and this expanded to her writing to all kinds of societies and groups.

It was after she moved into her beloved Bryn Llwyn that she decided that she had always been a vegetarian and to take up the opportunity to further her studies by enrolling in the Open University. The lack of a university degree had always troubled her. She wanted to have her intellect finally acknowledged. She had passed all her medical qualifications and achieved status in promotions but she hankered for a degree with honours, nothing less. At the age of sixty one, in 1976, her picture appeared in the local paper with the headline "Honours degree is first for N. Wales". Holding aloft a pen and ink picture drawn by her brother Amos the article went on to describe her success quoting the 'facts' of her education and childhood in Nottingham.

Steaming ahead in pursuit of further academic honours is Mrs Rose Sally Jay a Senior Nursing officer at the North Wales Hospital Denbigh, who last week became the first Open University graduate in North Wales to gain an honours degree.

Mrs Jay whose home is Bryn Llwyn, The Glyn, Llanrhaeadr, carried out a comparative study of the social and work patterns of Denbigh and gained her BA honours degree in arts and social science combined with technology and science.

Mrs Jay, who, at the age of 61, intends to study for further qualifications, has an unusual educational background. As a child she suffered from rheumatic fever with the result that she had only 3 ½ years of formal education. She recalls that she did not have a Christmas out of her sick bed until she was seventeen.

Mrs Jay has strong connections with the administrative side of the Open University. She is a member of its general assembly and the Welsh representative in the senate. In addition she is chairman of the Welsh Conservative Committee and a member of the Cartrefle Study Centre and of the Open University's geological and philosophical societies.

Outside her work at the North Wales Hospital Mrs Jay has always been active in the British Red Cross Society and is at present nursing officer for Clwyd West. She is chairman of the local branch of the United Nations association and before reorganisation of local government was a member of the Denbigh Borough Council.

She is interested in photography, both still and cine, loves gardening and is a steam engine enthusiast.

Our bursting pride in her achievement was tempered by the mirth that the newspaper article induced. That she had decided to 'adopt' my father's childhood illness of rheumatic fever provided some amusement and we wondered why she had not gone on to compound the myth and given herself the two years of being bedridden in hospital as Dad, having contracted both rheumatic fever and scarlet fever, had been. He used to regale us with stories of his confinement and the boyish tricks he devised to stave off the numbing boredom of his illnesses whilst lying on the hospital bed. Sally and my father had suffered from the normal childhood complaints but according to Dad she was a fit, robust child whereas he was always a 'weakly specimen'. She loved the outdoor life and attending to the many household pets and strays that found their way to their door. There were the two dogs, Peter and Nimo, who managed to worm their way into the photographs taken at the back of the house with Chrissie and their Uncle

152

Willie (Bill). Various cages housed the rabbits, and stray cats were often prowling around thoughtfully watching the progress of various rescued birds.

Sally developed a huge compassion for animals that finally led to the remarkable announcement that she had always been a vegetarian. Once she established herself in Llanrhaeadr she soon assembled a menagerie of stray and wounded animals. A white rat enjoyed her hospitality until he finally succumbed to a malignant tumour; a seagull named Sydney with a damaged wing took up residence in one of the garden wired cages, a tame Phileas the pheasant, with a gleaming aqua green neck, vivid red wattling and long mahogany and chestnut brown tail feathers strutted around the orchard, hoarsely declaring his presence each morning, and a selection of feral cats found their way to her door. Each was named often according to its physical appearance just as Socks had received his name when she was living in Nottingham. The local vet was constantly patronised as she brought each new case to be treated, wormed, splinted, examined and x-rayed. It was whilst she was studying with the Open University that she had found that she had to use a frog in order to look at nerve response and electrical stimuli. She was horrified that an animal was to be used for her research.

"I said to them there is nothing that can't be done by using a human," was her indignant response, "so I used by own thumb instead." We didn't question the validity of this statement as was so often the case when she 'got on her high horse'.

Still, vegetarianism grew to become her passion, but as she wasn't a domestic goddess her meals became fairly limited. She allowed herself eggs, butter, milk, cheese, and cream but these dairy products had to be curtailed when she suffered from a gall bladder complaint, leaving her with nuts, fruit and vegetables as her main staple diet. Having remembered her wonderful meat feasts that she and Marion had provided when we stayed at Nottingham we decided once again to connive with her stories and allowed her to convince us of her lifetime aversion to meat eating.

While sitting in her parlour surrounded by books and files she would recount her experiences.

"I remember meeting Anna Pavlova in London in the late twenties," she sighed, closing her eyes to capture the pictured memory. "She was dancing in Swan Lake at the time; her dying swan was a masterpiece. I went to the stage door and although I was only a thin little scrap she still found time to talk to me and gave me her autograph. I do believe that she lived in Hampstead Heath in London at the time as she couldn't go back to her native Russia. She lived her life as an *émigré*. It was this sadness of being away from her beloved homeland that gave her performance a special pathos. I could identify with that even as a child."

We murmured our wonder of her having had such a cherished memory whilst privately trying to work out how old she would have been and who would have taken her down to London and managed to pay the price for a ballet performance. We decided that perhaps she had just been reading about Pavlova as we couldn't find fault with any of the facts. It just seemed so far fetched that Sally had been taken there at all, never mind the stage door conversation and autograph. The family were certainly not flush with money and why would Sally, who never seemed to show any interest in the theatre or arts, have wanted to have gone to see a ballet? In 1925 she would have been just ten years old; would she have known about a famous ballerina coming from a fairly impoverished working class background? From what Dad had said the family didn't seem to have 'gone in' for that kind of thing. Their father Herbert was musical as were many people of those times. The area boosted quality brass bands linked to the collieries which resulted in my father having a passion for their sound, buying Decca records during the 1960's, but for Herbert it was the violin and the pretty mandolin decorated with inlaid mother of pearl which he played at home, causing

154

their dog Nemo to howl throughout his performance. Herbert may have developed his musical ability whilst serving out in India but Sally had no such musical gift. She did not sing or play an instrument; neither could she paint although she did produce a tapestry of 'The Last Supper' which hung in her lounge until the late 1980's, when the moths managed to eat their way in and laid bare the table. It was her accomplished 'brother' Tom who was able to read music, playing both the organ in church and the piano at home. Amos also played, but not having music lessons, played 'by ear' and enjoyed 'tinkling the ivories'. As a young lad he had an appreciation of fine art, and enjoyed painting, sending off to Reeves for brushes and water colours.

During her time in the WAAF's she attended dances, went to the theatre and saw the films of the day but then again all her contemporaries were doing this so she probably went along with them as the 'thing to do'.

As she studied for her degree it brought her into contact with books, paintings and plays that she had not previously examined. Sally had fixed ideas about Literature and what she regarded as Art. Having selected novels from the eclectic reading list she was quite dismissive of the French authors, especially Zola. She found his earthy realism repulsive,

"quite pornographic; what a sordid little man," she scathingly declared. Flaubert and Balzac fared little better; she waved away my protests as I endeavoured to come to their defence. I declared that their ability to paint grim pictures of the basic struggles of the working class men and women in the mines and fields of France was quite outstanding; that Flaubert could describe the hunger of love and lust. But the complicated and twisting relationships plunged her into a place that she did not want to go. I wondered how the tutorials went at the summer school that she attended and would have loved to have been a fly on the wall to have witnessed her verbal tirade on lecturers, more used to youthful compliant students, and her tsunami assaults on the modern classics.

155

Her blatant subjectivity would have done 'Educating Rita' proud. Having such a photographic memory enabled her to quote at length so she would have been able to have given 'chapter and verse' references to support her dubious reasoning. No doubt the sympathetic lecturers, having first foolishly allowed her some modicum of respect, believing that her age warranted it, would then have found themselves on a back foot during the unexpected attack and then found it difficult to regain ground.

But back to the Welsh myths. Why did she decide to abandon the facts of her upbringing and dismiss her paternal Payne heritage? Why did she reject it all? Was it because by accurately remembering her childhood it brought back all the history that she wanted to conceal? She had left her husband, child and Nottingham home behind and had forged out a successful, respectable career, reaching the pinnacle of her profession. She had established a sense of real worth, and saw that reflected back in the eyes of others. How had she done this if she had not had, like the Dickensian Oliver, some heritage of gentility and aristocracy? This power and influence must have had its roots in some strong ancestor. She could not change the facts of her Nottingham family but her Grandfather Amos had worked with gentry. He too had a propensity to embellish as his flowery letters demonstrated. Since by this time all his children: Chrissie, Charlotte, Dorothy Rose and Amos had died there was no one to refute her assertions of his privileged upbringing. There was only her cousin Joan, living in Kent, whom she needed to convince; her brother Amos had been too young to have known his grandfather and therefore would not have been able to recall conversations.
But where to place this family? What better place than Wales where she was able to garner information and investigate the large estates and families living there.

The Payne family had little to commend itself to her. A brutal grandfather, Charles Payne, had produced ten children in the mining town of Daybrook, Arnold, Nottingham. One day, whilst he was working on his shift at the coal face, his Scottish wife Mary summoned up the courage to bundle all their belongings onto a hand cart and race away from the family home, taking her children with her. When Charles returned to find them gone he spent the next few days searching for them and on finally banging on the door of their refuge he was met by the two oldest lads who proceeded to fly at him with raised fists, beating him off so thoroughly that they successfully ensured that he stayed away for good. Charles found himself another woman to provide him with his home comforts and they heard no more from him. There was just the one visit from his common-law wife who turned up at their home after he had died to see if there had been a life insurance paid on him. Sally had heard an account of this incident and this, coupled with her own father's oppressive presence, provided her with enough repugnance to reject them all. How could she, a clever and intelligent woman, be part of that sordid past? It had to be her maternal side of the family that had provided her with her talents and superiority. As she sat in her new home planning its new shape she grew with it and phoenix like adopted her new Welsh persona.

And yet it was the Payne side of the family that had natural talents and intellect which she chose to ignore. Of the ten children born by Mary Smith, her paternal grandmother, many went on to produce children who were musical and clever; some going on to study and enter professions in teaching and forge successful careers in engineering and commerce.

Had she known what power the internet had with its ability to disentangle and trace family trees she would have been as devastated as my father would have been elated.

The 1901 census showed the Mays, Amos and Mary Charlotte, living in Goudhurst in Kent with their two youngest children, Dorothy Rose aged eleven and Chrissie aged eight.

It confirmed Amos May's occupation as a gardener but more tellingly it provided his place of birth as Turnham Green in Middlesex. Sadly the 1911 census showed that the little family, of Amos aged fifty seven, his wife Mary, Dorothy Rose aged twenty one and little William, nearly two years old, were living in Goudhurst, in the district of Cranbrook, Kent, at White Stock Cottages, and although Amos proclaimed his status as a head gardener he also completed the next section which stated the ignominy that he was 'Out of Work'. His daughter Chrissie, Sally's mother, aged nineteen was living at 16 Beachboro Villas in Folkstone, working as a domestic nurse to three very young children, in the household of Mr Frederick Sidney Upton and his wife Mabel. He was in trade as a fancy dealer selling furniture, toys, stationery china, glass and hardware. Herbert Wilfred Payne was stationed nearby. He was listed as being in the military in the same district of Elham, Folkstone, Kent as a Rifleman 'Y3 RKR's (Royal Kings Rifles), although his father Charles Payne had incorrectly included him on their census sheet in Nottingham.

However, going back to the May family, the census of 1871 demonstrated that Amos as a youth was living with his father, also confusingly named Amos, a nursery propagator, and their children in Paddington, London. Having found that connection, a much earlier census of 1841 then detailed his father Amos as a child, living with his father John, and mother Mary, both born in Kent, together with their family in Hollingbourne, just outside the Medway county town of Maidstone.

So much for the Welsh heritage.

And as the great, great, grandfather John was an agricultural labourer, the grand idea of inherited wealth and influence fell by the wayside. All the Mays had their roots firmly planted in southern English soil with not a Welsh landowner or stately home in sight. It was one thing to trace the family's roots but quite another thing to accept them. I was actually acutely disappointed to have disproved the myths but unable to

158

continue the research on the internet due to 1841 being the earliest census to access. I endeavoured to search at the Maidstone Town Hall, looking through the faint, almost illegible microfiche records for births, deaths and marriages but had to concede after hours of going dizzy that I had found nothing to add. Each census had produced a prolific amount of Mays living in and around Maidstone; in fact the whole area seemed quite overrun with them.

So it appeared that her grandfather Amos May had, like his father, been accepted for an apprenticeship as a gardener and had received some training which allowed him to work on some large estates. He had had a successful career until the demise of the estates and had finally lived in much reduced circumstances just prior to his death in the October of 1921. Sally must have been a very precocious child to have been able to recall long conversations with him when she was merely five or six years of age. She would have spent more time with her grandmother, Mary Charlotte, who died when she was ten years old. Perhaps it was she, mourning the loss of a husband and grander living accommodation, who allowed Sally to fantasise and imagine a more illustrious past, hiding some of the more painful memories of illegitimate children with stories of manufacturing dynasties courting their eldest daughter. Perhaps it was her father Herbert who allowed the family to believe in these stories to deflect his own part in the family's ignominy. There were certainly shared family stories that gave them more status than their circumstances allowed, that had been passed around with the retelling compounding and cementing the details until it ingrained in the family lore much as coal dust cleaves to the miner.

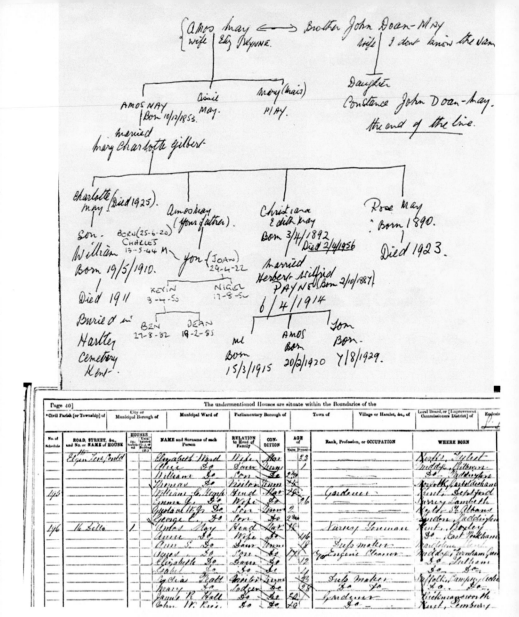

The mythical 'May Wynne' family tree composed by Sally for her cousin Joan. She listed Amos May (DOB 1853) as having a Welsh mother, Elizabeth Wynne, but the 1871 census shows Amos aged 17, born in Turnham Green, as living with his parents Amos and Anne at Elgin Terrace in Paddington.

Standard Pedigree Tree

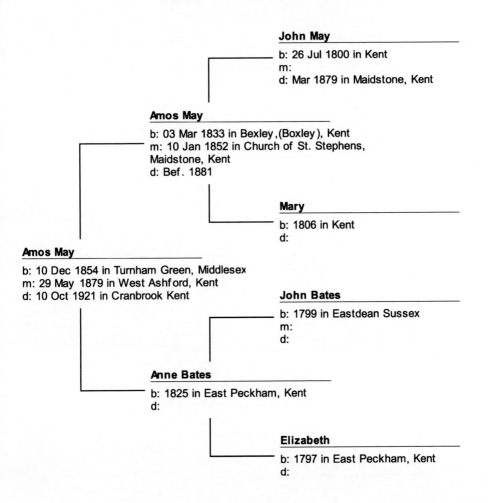

John May

b: 26 Jul 1800 in Kent
m:
d: Mar 1879 in Maidstone, Kent

Amos May

b: 03 Mar 1833 in Bexley,(Boxley), Kent
m: 10 Jan 1852 in Church of St. Stephens,
Maidstone, Kent
d: Bef. 1881

Mary

b: 1806 in Kent
d:

Amos May

b: 10 Dec 1854 in Turnham Green, Middlesex
m: 29 May 1879 in West Ashford, Kent
d: 10 Oct 1921 in Cranbrook Kent

John Bates

b: 1799 in Eastdean Sussex
m:
d:

Anne Bates

b: 1825 in East Peckham, Kent
d:

Elizabeth

b: 1797 in East Peckham, Kent
d:

Notes:

Standard Pedigree Tree

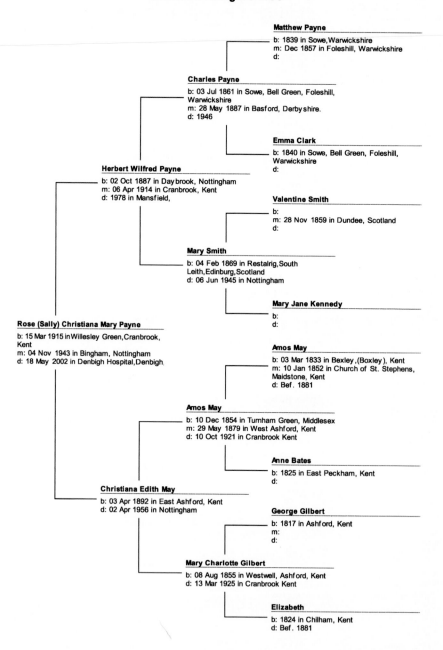

Matthew Payne

b: 1839 in Sowe, Warwickshire
m: Dec 1857 in Foleshill, Warwickshire
d:

Charles Payne

b: 03 Jul 1861 in Sowe, Bell Green, Foleshill,
Warwickshire
m: 28 May 1887 in Basford, Derbyshire.
d: 1946

Emma Clark

b: 1840 in Sowe, Bell Green, Foleshill,
Warwickshire
d:

Herbert Wilfred Payne

b: 02 Oct 1887 in Daybrook, Nottingham
m: 06 Apr 1914 in Cranbrook, Kent
d: 1978 in Mansfield,

Valentine Smith

b:
m: 28 Nov 1859 in Dundee, Scotland
d:

Mary Smith

b: 04 Feb 1869 in Restalrig, South
Leith, Edinburg, Scotland
d: 06 Jun 1945 in Nottingham

Mary Jane Kennedy

b:
d:

Rose (Sally) Christiana Mary Payne

b: 15 Mar 1915 in Willesley Green, Cranbrook,
Kent
m: 04 Nov 1943 in Bingham, Nottingham
d: 18 May 2002 in Denbigh Hospital, Denbigh,

Amos May

b: 03 Mar 1833 in Bexley, (Boxley), Kent
m: 10 Jan 1852 in Church of St. Stephens,
Maidstone, Kent
d: Bef. 1881

Amos May

b: 10 Dec 1854 in Turnham Green, Middlesex
m: 29 May 1879 in West Ashford, Kent
d: 10 Oct 1921 in Cranbrook Kent

Anne Bates

b: 1825 in East Peckham, Kent
d:

Christiana Edith May

b: 03 Apr 1892 in East Ashford, Kent
d: 02 Apr 1956 in Nottingham

George Gilbert

b: 1817 in Ashford, Kent
m:
d:

Mary Charlotte Gilbert

b: 08 Aug 1855 in Westwell, Ashford, Kent
d: 13 Mar 1925 in Cranbrook Kent

Elizabeth

b: 1824 in Chilham, Kent
d: Bef. 1881

Notes:

Descendants of Christiana Edith May

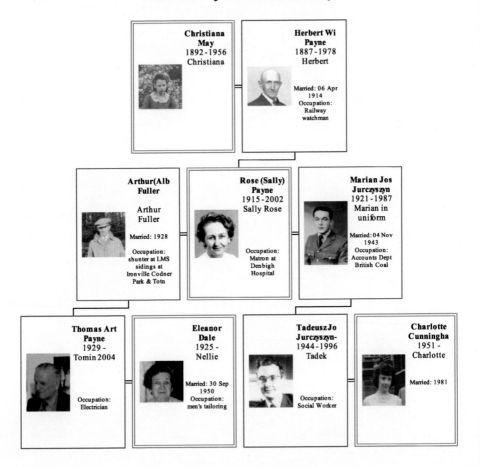

Christiana May
1892 - 1956
Christiana

Herbert Wi Payne
1887 - 1978
Herbert

Married: 06 Apr 1914
Occupation: Railway watchman

Arthur(Alb Fuller
Arthur Fuller
Married: 1928
Occupation: shunter at LMS sidings at Ironville Codner Park & Totn

Rose (Sally) Payne
1915 - 2002
Sally Rose
Occupation: Matron at Denbigh Hospital

Marian Jos Jurczyszyn
1921 - 1987
Marian in uniform
Married: 04 Nov 1943
Occupation: Accounts Dept British Coal

Thomas Art Payne
1929 -
Tomin 2004
Occupation: Electrician

Eleanor Dale
1925 -
Nellie
Married: 30 Sep 1950
Occupation: men's tailoring

Tadeusz Jo Jurczyszyn-
1944 - 1996
Tadek
Occupation: Social Worker

Charlotte Cunningha
1951 -
Charlotte
Married: 1981

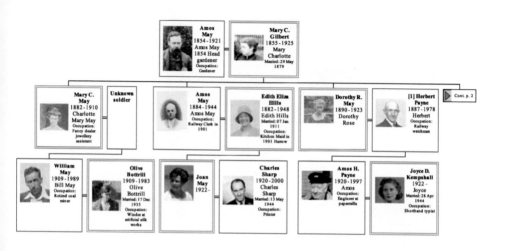

Amos May 1854-1921 Amos May 1854 Head gardener Occupation: Gardener

Mary C. Gilbert 1855-1925 Mary Charlotte Married: 29 May 1879

Mary C. May 1882-1910 Charlotte Mary May Occupation: Fancy dealer jewellery assistant

Unknown soldier

Amos May 1884-1944 Amos May Occupation: Railway Clerk in 1901

Edith Eliza Hills 1882-1948 Edith Hills Married: 07 Jan 1911 Occupation: Kitchen Maid in 1901 Hamow

Dorothy R. May 1890-1923 Dorothy Rose

[1] Herbert Payne 1887-1978 Herbert Occupation: Railway watchman

Cont. p. 2

William May 1909-1989 Bill May Occupation: Retired coal miner

Olive Bottrill 1909-1983 Olive Bottrill Married: 17 Dec 1935 Occupation: Winder at artificial silk works

Joan May 1922-

Charles Sharp 1920-2000 Charles Sharp Married: 13 May 1944 Occupation: Printer

Amos H. Payne 1920-1997 Amos Occupation: Engineer at papermills

Joyce D. Kempshall 1922- Joyce Married: 28 Apr 1944 Occupation: Shorthand typist

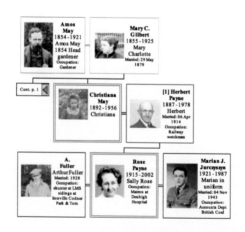

Amos May 1854-1921 Amos May 1854 Head gardener Occupation: Gardener

Mary C. Gilbert 1855-1925 Mary Charlotte Married: 29 May 1879

Cont. p. 1

Christiana May 1892-1956 Christiana

[1] Herbert Payne 1887-1978 Herbert Married: 06 Apr 1914 Occupation: Railway watchman

A. Fuller Arthur Fuller Married: 1928 Occupation: shunter at LMS sidings at Ironville Codnor Park & Totn

Rose Payne 1915-2002 Sally Rose Occupation: Matron at Denbigh Hospital

Marian J. Jurczyszyn 1921-1987 Marian in uniform Married: 04 Nov 1943 Occupation: Accounts Dept British Coal

164

A picture of Plas Mawr in Conway, North Wales, the alleged Welsh 'ancestral home' of the 'twice married' Amos Wynne. Sally spoke of a wealthy slate quarry- owning family connected to the prestigious Wynne family. The 1881 census shows Amos May aged 27, a gardener, now living with his new wife Mary in Windsor, working with the head gardener George Burt.

The undermentioned Houses are situate within the Boundaries of the

[Page 31]

No. of Schedule	ROAD, STREET, &c. and No. or NAME of HOUSE	HOUSES Inhabited	HOUSES Un-inhabited (U.), or Building (B.)	NAME and Surname of each Person	RELATION to Head of Family	CON-DITION as to Marriage	AGE last Birthday Male	AGE last Birthday Female	Rank, Profession, or OCCUPATION	WHERE BORN	(1) Deaf-and-Dumb (2) Blind (3) Imbecile or Idiot (4) Lunatic
25	Do 2 Lodge	1		Colin Turnbull	Head	Mar	47		Gardener	Scotland Lanarks	
				Elizabeth Turnbull	Wife	Mar		37		Berks Sunningdale	
				John L. Turnbull	Son		10		Scholar	Surrey Egham	
				Elizabeth A. Turnbull	Daur			5		Do do	
26	Broom Hall	1		Catherine Black	Head	Unm		28	Housemaid	Scotland	
				Jane Summers	Serv	Unm		16	Do	Middlesex Kensington	
				Frank Woodland	Serv	Unm	19		Cowman	Dorset Winbourn	
27	Do Farm	1		George Burt	Head	Mar	37		Head Gardener	Do Merden Blandford	
				Eliza E. Burt	Wife	Mar		35		Cornwall Falmouth	
				George H. Burt	Son		7		Scholar	Berks Sunningdale	
				Edith I. Burt	Daur			7 Mos		Do do	
28	Do Lodge	1		Amos May	Head	Mar	27		Gardener	Twyford Green Hill	
				Mary E. May	Wife	Mar		26		Berks Windsor Sunningham	
29	Thatch Cottage	1		Mary Olaway	Head	W		80		Surrey Windlesham	
				Thomas Olaway	Son	Mar	39		Gardener Labourer	Do Broom Hall	
				Sarah Olaway	Wife	Mar		41	Needle Woman	Do Stoke	
				Sidney G. Olaway	Son		5		Scholar	Do Broom Hall	
				Arthur F. Olaway	Son		2			Berks Sunningdale	
30	Chequers Inn	1		George Colton	Head	Mar	50		Innkeeper	Suffolk Revonmaids	
				Caroline Colton	Wife	Mar		56		Hants Sleep	
				Ellen Colton	Daur	Unm		21		Herts St Michaels	
				Caroline Colton	Daur	Unm		19		Middlesex St George	
				George Colton	Son		18		Scholar	Do do	
				Esther Alpery	Aunt	Unm		71	Annuitant	Hants Sleep	
				Edwin Smith	Boarder		15		Scholar	Middlesex St George	
	Total of Houses	6				Total of Males and Females	12	13			

Note.—Draw the pen through such of the words of the headings as are inappropriate.

Eng—Sheet H.

Chapter 10 Dear Sir, I wish to bring to your attention!

Throughout her adult life Sally loved to correspond with family and friends, ex-colleagues and fellow members of various organisations. Her flamboyant blue inked flowery scripted letters usually ran over a series of pages as she described, complained, catalogued and confided. She had the power in her writing to make you believe that you were the most important person in her life at that time. She coaxed you to share her feelings and understand dilemmas.

Her phrases often included the sentiments of you both being together against an unfeeling and uncaring world; 'You and I both know' and 'I know you would agree'. The words tied and bound you to her confidences. She allowed you to share her world and you subconsciously thanked her for that. She railed against the constraints on her time that did not allow her to see more of you and allow you to explore, discover and delight in the experiences that you could both treasure. 'Oh how I wish that you and I could see.', 'if only I had a spare room so that you could stay here and we could ….' But there was always something that just stopped this from happening. You were left, wanting more and eager for her next letter to plop onto your doormat. Her visits had that same urgency of restricted time. She would always have to depart from you earlier than she would have wished.

The letters generally ended with a 'God Bless' and again somehow you did feel blessed to have received a letter from her, knowing that she was always so busy with the important matters in life and yet had found the time to include you in her restricted schedule.

However, when it came to business and commerce, officialdom and bureaucracy her letters took on an altogether different tone. They still had passion and emotion but there was the thinly veiled anger and invariably a list of points that punctuated a litany of complaints.

Sometimes she took issue with things that seemed to be of a trifling nature. She objected to her address being Llanrhaeadr or Denbighshire being omitted when the counties had been reorganised into Clwyd, and wrote in a high handed manner to the post office telling them just what she thought about the matter. She would often return unwanted mail into the post box with 'address error' scrawled in large red ink across the offending envelope.

When we visited we would be shown examples of this offence. Wearily she would wave her hand over the letter-strewn table, "just look at these, will they never learn".

"Stage door this way, real actors need not apply" was Dad's whispered response as she swept into her kitchen to make a 'real' cup of special Darjeeling tea, and we giggled at the melodrama of her suffering.

Her bulging address book was stuffed with cuttings from journals, newspapers and pamphlets that required her response. Files containing ongoing correspondence to the BBC, the council tax office, mail order catalogues, charities, garden centres, the Open University, seed merchants, societies, fellow steam enthusiasts, the Franklin Mint, Friends of the Earth, Greenpeace, Clogau Gold, animal sanctuaries, wild life organisations, The Daily Post, The National Trust, Readers Digest, horticultural societies, florists, the social services, RSPB, RSPCA, clock repairers; and so the endless list went on. No one organisation was too small or too large for her not to be actively involved. She read her local papers avidly, scrutinising them for snip bits of information and then would alight upon an article that drew her scorn or derision. Straight away the pen would fly across the page as another missile missive was directed and launched.

Her various positions of responsibility both locally and nationally gave her more scope to intervene and scrutinise. Once she had embarked on her OU course she became an active and vociferous member of the OU General Assembly and the Welsh representative on the OU Senate, and also enjoyed a stint as a member of their Geographical and Philosophical Societies. At home in Denbigh during the early sixties she became the County Nursing Officer for the Red Cross, then in the seventies she joined the Denbigh Borough Council as a councillor. The United Nations took her interest and she became the chair of the local branch. Throughout the seventies and late eighties she often joined in with events organised by the Clwyd Archaeological Digs. Her passion for steam railways ensured that she became a life member of the Llangollen Railway in 1988 and a life member of the Welsh Highland Railway that ran from Porthmadog to Bethgelert.

She never relinquished her enthusiasm for nursing and was for some time an examiner with the General Nursing Council for the area of Yorkshire.

Over the years she got to know some of those whom she was persecuting quite well, and they almost established a masochistic delight in writing to each other. In fact 'disgusted from Tonbridge Wells' should have been replaced with 'livid from Llanrhaeadr'. The thick files grew fatter and yellowed with age and yet if a certain subject arose she could quickly take up the correct file and point to some earlier correspondence that proved that she too had considered that matter at some length.

Whenever Allan and I went to visit her she could be found sitting at the table in her front parlour surrounded with envelopes and writing paper. A cat would be perched by her shoulder occasionally catching the tantalising pen as it swiftly flew across the page. It was as if she was compelled to dash off a missive whilst her passion was still at its height and that she had to seize the moment. She would impatiently indicate that we should be seated until she had finished the correspondence. I would find myself gingerly sitting on a cat fur lined blanket that she had flung over the chair whilst Al's offer to make a 'cuppa' was graciously accepted. From the kitchen he would appear at the door behind her holding a mug and pretending to gag at the state of its cleanliness. I would have to maintain a serene look whilst desperately trying not to laugh. His acting skills would then improve as he made movements to indicate a fresh bout of sickness, as he retched over the kitchen floor and my powers to keep a straight face would be tested to their limits.

Finally he would emerge triumphant from the kitchen with a tray of tea and sugar, having had to scald the utensils, stained teapot and dusty mugs before his entrance. We more often than not brought our own biscuits as a supposed treat for her but in reality so that we could legitimately decline the baked scones that had been lovingly baked but then treated to a gentle stroking by the cats as they walked the surfaces of her tables and kitchen surfaces.

Once the tea arrived we would be treated to a detailed tirade about the letter that she had just received and to which she felt compelled to reply.

She kept all her correspondence; no letter was ever thrown away. Even scraps of paper that incriminated her were filed away in drawers. It was as if they had a life of their own. Her letters from Marion amounted to hundreds of carefully tied envelopes each provided with a number, 567 or 832, and then "replied 13/5/ 65" or "replied 12/10/69" written across the top left-hand corner. And her letters to her friends and family had that same indestructible quality. They too would find themselves reluctant to dispose of her letters, as if the paper held a part of her.

There can't have been a delivery day that the postman didn't beat a path to her door, sometimes bringing special packages containing special seeds and plants and always letters from friends far and wide. Unfortunately the indiscriminate junk mail caught her interest and increasingly she became trapped into sending off for items that caught her attention. Various charities were added to her list and she became an avid collector of china and bric-a-brac, jewellery and unwanted garden tools as the flamboyant claims of exceptional quality and essential usage undid her purse strings.

She was then invited to comment on their suitability and would happily spend time detailing her approval of the purchase.

Her letters to relatives and friends sometimes included a sketch of her particular project and to her cousin Joan she would add spidery family tree charts with dates and names and then would find that she had run out of space so the remaining lines would follow a trail around the rim of the page, almost becoming indecipherable as the size of print diminished.

She had a large stack of notelets, lined blue Basil Bond writing paper and headed note paper that were kept close by on the parlour table so that at any time she could rattle off a letter. When we called unannounced she would often be surrounded in a cloud of cigarette smoke as she completed her writing tasks. Although she was adamant that she had given up smoking she never attempted to explain why the ashtray continued to be full of fresh cigarette stubs and how the yellow nicotine stain on her long elegant fingers continued to remain bright.

It was her concentrated attention to her letters and conversation with Al that afforded me time to slip off to the bathroom and liberally pour bleach around the basin and toilet under the pretence of needing to use the bathroom.

Soon after Al and I had been together he had mentioned about tiling our bathroom and her raised eyebrow had indicated an interest. It wasn't long before she brought up the subject of wanting her bathroom tiled as she had already bought some that had taken her fancy. In the early eighties there had been a boom of imported Italian large tiles that made the small plain tiles of the seventies look quaint and very old fashioned. She had purchased some that could be put together to create a collâge of flowers and grasses as a feature. Al had made a lovely job of the room and had also put in a large mirror, which she had at first rigorously resisted until he persuaded her that it allowed the light to deflect into the room.

Unfortunately despite the walls looking in relatively good condition, the bathroom, as in the rest of the house, was showing some need of some serious cleaning.

Sally was caught up in her twelve hour night shifts at a nursing home in Rhyl, overseeing various gardeners and handymen whom she employed to look after her garden and of course her essential correspondence, which did not leave any time for cleaning even if she had been remotely interested in the domesticity of running a home.

As she scribbled away on her diatribes so the invasion of mice began their work. Once Tadek died she abandoned any interest in the state of property inside. She wanted to talk and debate during our visits; she wove her stories together as we drank the strong tea and munched on our biscuits.

On one particularly cold winter's day the snow that had been forecast began to fall. We went over to see how she was. The outlook promised a heavy blanket of snow for North Wales. We found her huddled in a thick Welsh wool cardigan, hunched over her letters, the many pages strewn across the table. Her ash tray was full; the air thick with smoke. She appeared irritated by our presumption to call unannounced. After she had been carefully coaxed into recognising our concern about her wellbeing we were able to confirm that she had adequate provisions of bread and milk. As the large snowflakes began to thicken at the base of each window and the sky turned a sinister yellow grey, she became aware of her predicament about being house bound for some time. Soon the road would become impassable and I was uneasy about our return journey home. Reluctantly she requested that Al went to the local pub to buy some cigarettes without actually admitting that she was going to smoke them. He returned with the purchase announcing that the road was already so thick with snow that if we didn't leave right away then it would be impossible to drive. We left her in a house blanketed with thick white snow. The slippery slate-covered driveway had become treacherous as we slithered on the ice and snow towards our car.

Her Vale of Denbigh, which never saw bad weather, had decided for once to abandon its claim to be Shangri La and embedded its inhabitants in a cloak of white that took weeks to uncover.

House of Commons

Ms Sally Jay,
Bryn Llwyn A Godwys,
Glyn,
Denbigh,
Denbighshire,
LL16 4NW.

HOUSE O
LONDO

ist Paper

19ᵗʰ January 2001

Mrs. Sally Jay
Bryn L;wum-A-Godwys
Glyn
Denbigh
Denbighshire
LL16 4NW

Dear Mrs. Jay,

Thank you for your letter dated 20 November, to the Prime
Nice. I have been asked to reply and must apologise for the

The Government believes that it is in our national interest t
European Union. Membership provides us with an opport
Europe constructively, without threat to our national identity

The benefits of Britain's membership are clear. Since we
trade with the EU has grown twice as fast as with the rest
crucial factor in attracting inward investment into the UK.
equivalent of a domestic market of 370 million customers.
will expand to almost 500 million people. Denying ourselve
number of British jobs at risk.

The benefits are not just economic. EU membership enhan
It increases our clout in international negotiations, where El
are far more powerful than the UK alone. It helps mak
operation with our partners against cross-border crime, drug
And it helps make out towns and countryside greener, thn
environment and fight pollution.

The Treaty of Nice is a good result for the UK. We wor
through increasing our number of votes in the Council fror
streamlined the Commission. We preserved our veto wher
security, defence, our own resources, border controls Treaty
majority voting where this is in the UK's interests: in a
industrial policy, where UK business will benefit. We have
groups of Member States will be better able to co-operate
opened the door for enlargement of the EU to include the r
The result will be a stronger Britain in a wider Europe.

1

ST. JAMES'S PALACE
LONDON SW1A 1BS

From The Office of HRH The Prince of Wales

17th January, 2001

Dear Miss Jay,

The Prince of Wales has asked me to thank you for your letter of 16th
December in connection with the extracts from "The Garden at Highgrove" which
were published in the Daily Mail.

His Royal Highness is grateful to you for taking the trouble to write and he
much appreciated your comments.

Yours sincerely,

Mrs. Claudia Holloway

Miss Sally Jay

Forei
Commor
Offi
European Union De
King Charl
London SW

CHRIS RUANE M.P./A.S.
Labour M.P. for the Vale of Clwyd / A.S. Llafur i Ddyffryn Clwyd
House Of Commons, London, SW1A 0AA
Tel/Ffon: 01745 354626. Fax/Ffacs: 01745 334627 E-mail: ruanec@parliament.uk

Ms Sally Jay,
Bryn Llwyn A Godwys,
Glyn,
Denbigh,
Denbighshire,
LL16 4NW.

8 December 2000

Dear Ms Jay,

As you have written to me in the past on the subject of fox hunting, I thought I should write to
you with an update on the situation. No doubt you will have seen that in the Queen's Speech this
week, the Government promised to bring forward a Bill relating to hunting foxes with dogs. This
will be, as the Home Secretary said earlier this year, a free vote on several different options: an
outright ban on all forms of hunting with dogs, more limited statutory regulation or self
regulation. MPs will be able to decide how to vote according to their conscience.

I shall be voting for a ban, and I hope that the Bill will soon be brought forward so that we can see
the end of this cruel practice.

Yours sincerely,

HOUSE OF COMMONS
LONDON SW1A 0AA

Ms Sally Jay,
'Bryn Llwyn a Godwys,'
Glyn,
LLANRHAEADR,
Denbigh,
CLWYD
LL16 4NW.

14 March 1990

Dear Ms Jay,

Your letter has been passed on to me as Llanrhaeadr is in my constituency.

I agree with many of the points that you raise in your letter. There is obviously a loss of sovereignty with our membership of the European Community, and as a Member of Parliament I find it increasingly obvious that every piece of legislation we pass has to take into account European views. On the other hand, the existence of minority groups such as the Welsh within Europe actually is encouraged by the laws of the European Community and it is only to be hoped that we can retain our existing British independence as far as possible.

I am personally not pro the European Common Market but it is very hard to see how we can possibly survive outside at this moment.

Yours sincerely,

Martyn Jones
M.P. for Clwyd South West

Various correspondence: on fox hunting, a letter to Prince Charles at St James's Palace, to her MP on the Treaty of Nice and on joining the European Common market

Chapter 11 Money, money, money

Whilst feigning an indifference to money, she and it had a close ambivalent relationship. Sally could not resist buying the best, and yet she regarded anyone who showed a passing interest in retail therapy as quite an inferior being. Perversely she delighted in visiting her local delicatessen shops in Denbigh town and often came to us bearing gifts of pots of fruit or jam. In fact Sally could never visit without bringing a quantity of specially and carefully selected gifts with her which always resulted in several trips back and forth from the car to empty it of its packages. She was generous and extravagant one moment and then be worrying about how she would manage her affairs the next. She avidly read through mail order catalogues, searching for the perfect purchase and yet denied that shopping held any joy for her. "It is something that just has to be got through," she would say dismissively.

Somehow goods on display in craft shops, on stalls at country fairs and in workshops did not count as shopping *per se*. Hours were spent talking to a woodcarver about the method of seasoning timber and selecting the best wood, recognising a piece of turned wood by its grain and colour and then walking away with her costly purchases. Welsh woollen mills held a fascination for her and descending into Llangollen she would buy expensive bed throws, coats, scarves, two-piece suits in one day.

She was well known by the local potters. All the family received gifts from the David Frith pottery. In her kitchen were handmade potato keepers, huge bowls and lidded serving and casserole dishes; a testament to her avarice.Her garage and outhouses bore evidence to her forages into garden centres and hardware stores. The garden tools were of the very best quality and selected with care.

And yet there was never enough money to meet her needs so she spent hours pouring over her accounts looking for ways to save a penny here and there.

My mother found out about this 'spend and save' philosophy very early on. Sally had provided Tadek with an abundance of clothes as a baby. She then found to her horror that he grew so fast that his clothes were redundant. Knowing that Joyce, her sister-in-law was pregnant in the September of 1944 she saw her opportunity. She wrote to Joyce offering the little matinee coats, bonnets, vests et cetera to her. Joyce, although surprised, took up her offer and wrote that she would indeed be very interested. Clothes coupons and rationing were still a great headache to young mothers with growing children. To Joyce's surprise she received a detailed price list from Sally itemising each garment, together with the price alongside and a closing remark that perhaps Joyce would also like to part with some extra clothes coupons to compensate for the 'fair price' of the clothes that she would be receiving.

...... *Well dears, news is scarce, here is a list of the Bits and Pieces:-*

2 Day gowns cost 2 coupons each 3/1 1 would like ½ coup. 1/- each 1 coup. 2/-

3 Night" 3 coupons   7/4 3/4   " " " 3/4 coup 2/- each 2¼ coup 6/-

2 Short dresses 2 coupons   2/11 3/4   " " " 3/8 coup 1/- each 3/4 coup 2/-

Bonnet

Socks } 3 coupons   5/6   " " " 1 coup 3/-   1 coup 3/-

Coat

Bonnet
Socks } 2 ½ coupons 4/- " " " 1 coup 1/- 1 coup 1/-
Coat

Total 6 coupons and 14/-

The little matinee coats etc with the slips of paper on I shall only lend because they are gifts from friends of mine. You can send me the coupons altogether it will be 11 now. I would prefer if you would lend me the book- because the shop folks are very hot on not taking loose ones- I need some things for Master Tadek so I would not keep it long................"

Joyce took umbrage at the 'cheek of it all!' She wrote to say that indeed she could not part with her coupons, especially sending the valuable and much coveted coupon book, and was very surprised to think that Sally had wanted money for the second-hand clothes. Sally retaliated with a long tirade that indeed she couldn't think of parting with the clothes without payment. How would she be able to put more clothes on little Tadek's back if she did not receive a small payment in return! And as she was quite insulted at Joyce's tone, she had decided to offer them elsewhere.

My dear Joyce,

Thank you for the letter I am so sorry if you think I have asked too much for Tadek's things- I quite understand if you would rather have all new things for your coming little one. But as you seemed so keen to have Tadek's little things I agreed to pass them on.

178

However I am very sorry if you think I am being mercenary in asking you to pay the amount I asked. Were I in different circumstances I would be only too willing to give you any of the things you wanted-but times are hard & Marion and I are far worse off than Moss & you therefore I must get a little money for them.

So my dear I am enclosing the 5 coupons you sent me also the P/O for 13/6 (the amount you sent first time) and will you please return everything, as a friend of mine wants them for her baby. I hope you are not offended but you know dear it was your <u>idea</u> <u>not</u> mine.

Thank you so much for Moss's address I really must write to him – but my leisure time is nil and the letter writing has to come out of my sleeping time these days therefore I am, afraid, getting forgetful.

Still I had to go back to work, and although the money is not much (especially when I have paid my fare) it all helps. I should love to come to Maidstone to see you and Joan but the train fare plus time off work absolutely frightens me.

So dear I guess our next meeting will have to be after the war-

. . . .

The two women continued to view each other with suspicion throughout the decades.

Joyce also never forgave Sally for taking Amos's gift from the colliery when he was away serving in the Royal Navy. As Amos had worked at the James Oakes colliery prior to entering the service he had been informed that the unions had made small collections for their work colleagues who had seen active service. A small pot of money was there waiting

179

for Amos to collect. Amos was very touched by the generous gesture and must have spoken to his mother Chrissie about it. Some time later, when Amos went up to Nottingham, Chrissie told him that Sally had gone on his behalf to the colliery and had collected the money. She told him that he needed to go and thank them for it in person. When Amos asked where the money was and how much it had been Chrissie said that she wasn't quite sure. It turned out that Sally had 'borrowed' the money and would be paying it back as soon as she could. Amos then had to set off for the colliery and thank the miners for money, which he never did receive back from Sally. "I felt a right fool not knowing what they had given me" he later told Joyce.

Joyce was more incensed about losing money they could ill afford to lose than Dad's embarrassment, but despite her attempts to cajole him into talking to his sister and demanding it back, he refused to act. Sally had always dominated him and continued to do so during his adult life.

In 1944 Amos was receiving a gross salary of £162 a year with a net amount of just under £142; so his weekly pay was not even £3 according to his Inland Revenue records.

By 1945 his annual pay had increased by just £5 to £167, and by 1955 his wage slips show that he was earning £600 gross a year from the J P Green Paper Mill. With well under £10 a week coming in after tax Joyce had to exist on this very meagre amount. Having two children to support and knowing that 10/- a week from Amos's wage packet was being sent to Chrissie in Nottingham made things very difficult, especially knowing that Sally was being provided with free child care with Chrissie taking on that role for Tadek.

Within a few years, in 1953, she watched as Sally and Marion purchased a large house in Nottingham whilst her family paid rent on their semi detached council house with no hope of buying their own property. The bitterness marked their relationship although she remained tight lipped on the subject until many years later.

"Money went up there whilst my children went without".

In 1976 Amos was earning £3,219 whist working for the Turkey Mill Paper Mill and Sally was receiving almost double that amount of £5,800. Somehow she never reconciled her earning power to her spending power. As her brother often remarked, "too much week left at the end of the money!" His other favourite being "this week I'm working for the cat", having worked out that feeding our cat for a whole year cost about one week's wages.

When Sally had wanted to buy her first property in North Wales she wanted to use 24 Charlecote Drive as security to guarantee a loan from the bank but Tadek refused to entertain the idea. It was a decision that Sally found very hard to accept. Despite all her entreaties and best arguments he put his foot down and would not budge.

Throughout her childhood there had been problems with money. Herbert, her father, had always had the control of the purse strings and been incredibly mean with Chrissie. He resented handing over any money for housekeeping. Everything that Chrissie spent was scrutinised and commented upon by Herbert. He questioned the need for any expenditure until Chrissie grew to fear his interrogations. She resorted to subterfuge in order to maintain some tranquillity in the household but then learnt to fear his wrath once her purchases for small domestic items had been discovered. Sally watched the conflict as her subservient mother attempted to feed her family and provide for her children. She witnessed the relentless oppression that made Chrissie shrink into herself, taking comfort in the family pets who provided her with the warmth woefully lacking in her husband.

Perhaps Sally's relationship with money stemmed from that childhood experience. Her diary entries from the 1940's and early fifties were often punctuated with a longing to buy clothes, for herself and Tadek and large costly items for the house. But she too had to fight a similar battle about money with her own husband. Whereas her mother had had to justify

181

small meagre purchases of food and provisions Sally attempted to justify, often outrageous, expenditure to an increasingly impatient Marion. She, again like her own mother, attempted to deceive her husband about the real cost of items or diverted monies from one bill in order to purchase something that she had not brought to his attention. When eventually found out she would explode in righteous indignation, shouting that as she worked her fingers to the bone to support and clothe Tadek it was right that she should spend her money as she saw fit, often glossing over the fact that the expensive item was completely superfluous to their requirements and did nothing to enhance Tadek's attire.

Herbert wrote a strange letter to Sally, whom he continued to call Rose, in the March of 1972. First he thanked her for the lovely sweater that she had knitted him and remarked upon the fact that she had 'passed another milestone' (her birthday) and then he proceeded to tell her about the financial arrangements that he had made about his house.

"NEWS

I have made over the house and contents immediately to Martin and Mary Duffy so really the house is no longer mine, for looking after me so well, and that of course will stop any grabbing by others later on, when I have stopped breathing you must be on the job when this happens as Tadek will benefit along with the rest of the Grandchildren, to share equal whatever money is in the P Office, which, I might add is quite a nice little sum. It will mean of course they should all get the same.

Heather, Julia, Wendy. Dawn, Ruth, Tadek.

Well this is not much of a solicitor's letter but its plain enough to understand. In the will I have left Martin's 3 girls a sum of 50 £ each Kathleen, Karen and Rita.

Well that's it this time. From

Somehow he saw plotting against him; fearful that his life savings would be snatched away and yet he parted with his most valuable asset without establishing some legal undertaking that they should care and provide for him. Eventually he railed against the Duffy family when he found that he had no means of ensuring that they would continue to care for him. He wrote to Sally complaining about their callous treatment; that the house was dirty and that he was lonely and neglected.

By the late 1990's Sally relied increasingly on the mail order catalogues and began to buy outrageously expensive ornaments, china plates, jewellery and coins, and on receiving them began to pile them up in her back bedroom. Once the Millennium bonanza started to kick in she bought Millennium gifts without regarding the costs at all; her failing health led her to give up accounting and attempting to balance the books. Her bank statements showed a deficit in her account but she took no account of them; she had run out of time and money for, finally, both had ceased to matter to her.

Chapter 12 Religion and politics

Sally also had an ambivalent relationship with church and religion. She admired the beauty of the buildings and loved to visit cathedrals and chapels. She abhorred those whose hypocrisy allowed themselves to be married in church and then declared that they had no interest in God. She ensured that her patients in Denbigh Hospital regularly attended the Sunday services and yet left, to her own devices, worship did not form part of her everyday life. She loved the natural world and felt the magnificence of the creation but this did not endear her to listening to sermons delivered in the main by crusty old dry men; her relationship with a God was forged by Mother Nature.

A kiss of the sun for pardon
A song of the birds for mirth
One is nearer God's heart in a garden
Than anywhere else on Earth

By a strange coincidence Patience Strong's real maiden name was May; Winifred Emma May. We buried Sally's ashes in her garden under a tree with a stone inscribed with this sentimental but apt Patience Strong poem denoting the spot.
She married Marion, who was brought up as a Roman Catholic, in a civil service at the registry office. Through out her life she spoke against the Roman Catholic faith and the Pope's dictates and yet she was quick to list as one of her famous moments her meeting with the Polish Pope John Paul in Krakow, Poland whilst they were holidaying there in the early 1960's. He allegedly, according to her story, chatted to her quite animatedly for some time.

"Of course he was just Cardinal Karol Wojtyla of Krakow then!"

She said that he had been fighting the communist regime and was, "incredibly brave and modest. Such a little man but with a huge personality; we hit it off straight away."

In later years, once he had been ordained as the Pope John Paul the 2nd she collected mugs and plates rimmed in gold depicting his image. She was so proud that he had been the first non- Italian Pope and that she had met him. Again, who was to say if her story was true?

When Tadek met his future wife and Sally found out that she too was a Catholic she made her extreme displeasure well known. The wedding was set for 1981 but she found that due to pressure of work she would not be able to attend. It was left to Dad, Mum, Allan and I, his father Marion and Uncle Zygmunt to support Tadek's side of the family; Sally was conspicuous by her absence.

In Wales she delighted in poking around in the little churches and said that the little chapel situated just next to her cottage in Llanrhaeadr conducted their services in Welsh. "And I told the vicar not to worry since I would be able to follow the Welsh even if I didn't always join in". She did own some 'Teach Yourself Welsh' tapes, and later attended some Welsh classes in Ruthin, but I never heard her speak a word in conversation, just the odd greeting of "Bore Da, and Sut dych chi?" or the odd "Diolch." I think she had a smattering of vocabulary for food and counting but she always declined to engage in any Welsh with me even although mine was also set at the basic primary school level. She did have a good ear though, just as her brother did for Arabic when he was stationed in Egypt.

She favoured the idea of Christianity and celebrated the festivals, especially Easter and Christmas, when she sent cards to her family and friends, and yet spiritually she did not speak of having a faith. As the church was directed and managed by men her feminist side was affronted. She preferred people to speak directly to her and not through a series of catechisms or a script. When she and Amos were together they spent hours discussing the creation of the world and the stories of the early scriptures. Dad was convinced that the world was just one such populated planet and that there were an infinitesimal amount of galaxies with their own worlds such as ours. Sally favoured the uniqueness of just the one world. His ideas seemed too seeped in science fiction for her liking. They agreed that the man Christ existed but whereas she believed him to be the son of God Dad would not accept the concept of an all powerful all seeing God the creator. She had some suspicion of Judaism, feeling indignant that they saw themselves as the 'chosen people'. She was piqued at being excluded. Dad was more interested in the science explaining the wonders of the parting of the Red Sea and Noah's Ark on Mount Ararat.

For her, 'being English' and being a Christian was one and the same, although she allowed for the Church of Wales to be part of that establishment. She viewed nuns and priests with suspicion, feeling that although being essentially good people that they should be actively involved in the real world. Strangely she did approve of them establishing monasteries, although was not keen on nunneries, and for tilling the land and harvesting honey for mead and for creating illuminated manuscripts. The Holy Island of Lindisfarne had her seal of approval as did the Salvation Army and their work against the evils of drink. Dad also spoke up for the 'Sally Army' as he said that they went into places where 'angels would fear to tread'.

When it came to politics however they became divided. Sally was a staunch Conservative and Dad was equally staunch in his devotion to the Labour party. She felt that that the Conservatives, having natural leadership quality, had what it took to made the empire strong. They were solid and dependable. Unions were divisive, meddling and small minded, run by self seeking publicists who were only interested in the overthrow of management and would ultimately destroy the wealth of the country. Chamberlain had been a weak fool, Churchill was magnificent, as was Thatcher, but as for Wilson he was just a nasty little man. Dad spoke for the miners' champion Arthur Scargill and said that Thatcher had ruined the mining industry. He believed in the work of the unions to better the conditions for the working man.

But they both agreed that Enoch Powell was absolutely right when it came to his 'rivers of blood' speech as the country was too full of immigrants already. Sally quoted at length from the articles that she had read in her 'This England' magazine and they were both more than happy to accept that England was the best country in the world. Sally had a grudging respect for Aneurin Bevan with his vision for a welfare state, and it helped that he was of good Welsh stock. Dad agreed but believed that the vision had been initially hampered by Churchill's interference.

Sally championed the ruling classes and the establishment of large country estates and spoke up for them employing so many working- class people. She spoke of their philanthropy in setting up hospitals and schools, museums and art galleries. There were many examples; one had only to look at the Rowntree family, the Cadbury family, Lord Lever and his wonderful village and art gallery in Port Sunlight, and, of course, the town of Saltaire built by Sir Titus Salt for his workers, to illustrate the vision of these people.

Dad had to agree but countered her arguments that for every one philanthropist there were hundreds of others who had no thought for the ordinary man and had only interest in profiting from the labour of underpaid workers.

"Look at how long it took for them to establish safety measures in the mines, Sally! And the mills; don't forget they had to be forced to stop child labour. And what about all these Lady Bountifuls going around with their baskets of food; if they had paid their farm hands properly there wouldn't have been any need for charity".

"No, if it hadn't been for the co-operatives and the unions we would still be there cap in hand to the Lord and Master_ 'if you please Sir." Dad doffed his imaginary hat at her.

"Well so many of those so called 'good' working men used to drink most of their wages. The families wouldn't have seen much of it; spending all their time in the pubs," she blazed.

As for women's suffrage, they came to a happy resolution. If she had been born a little earlier she would have been campaigning along with Emily Pankhurst's suffragettes and Dad would have supported her. They both believed in universal suffrage agreeing that it was a scandal that women had to wait until 1928 in Britain and that equal pay for equal labour was still haphazard despite the headlines in the 1954 Daily Express that heralded 'Civil servants to get equal pay'.

Education and equality for women in all walks of life they both agreed upon. "If you educate a woman you educate a family," was his favourite mantra.

Sally and her brother discussed everything from MG cars to Arthur Scargill, striking miners, unions and women's emancipation.

Sally argued with her brother about the Pope and if there was a God. She did not attend Tadek's marriage to Charlotte because she was a Catholic and yet she collected memorabilia about Pope John and spoke of meeting him in Poland. She took the magazine This England, but endeavoured to convince her friends that she was Welsh.

Chapter 13 Llanrhaeadr 27th May 2002

It was a bright, warm morning. The bumble bees lazily buzzed around the tall purple comfrey as we stood on the side driveway, uncertain as to what to do.

"We've measured up the chapel doorway and there's no way that we can bring the coffin through because the entrance splits into two side doors. It's just too long". The undertakers seemed apologetic for troubling us with the news.

I had a sudden urge to laugh as an awful vision of upending her coffin and taking it in vertically suddenly sprang into my mind.

"Well what about this drive?" We considered the area. The large wooden-gated drive was shaded by the tall oak tree to the right. Her cottage stood before us and to the left was the grassed unkempt but natural area dotted with buttercups and daisies. Heavy drooping bluebells and red campions fringed the drive to either side, surrounding the oak in its mantle of bright new leafed green. It was a tranquil spot; shady and surrounded by the garden that she loved. To the left we could just see the Clwydian range, misty in the morning dew.

Marcus, her black, white-socked cat walked towards us, his tail held high, inquisitive and friendly. He rubbed his warm body against my legs, purring, pleased to see us.

"What do you think Marcus_ a good spot for your mistress to wait?"

The undertakers watched as he lay on the ground rolling and stretching, waiting for another caress.

"Yes she'll be safe here," we had decided. She'll still be able to hear the service and the music."

As people assembled in the road later that day the air was filled with a mixture of accents and conversations. Her friends and colleagues from Denbigh were there, representatives from the council, old friends from her nursing and Gwilym from her Open University days, a local drinking friend of Tadek, her family from Nottingham; Tom (her son), his wife Nellie and their three daughters, Wendy, Dawn and Ruth, whom I had never met, the son of her dear friend and wedding witness Ivy Humphries. Then there were the neighbours from Llanrhaeadr, from the small hamlet of The Glyn and from the town of Denbigh, and representatives from the Red Cross. Finally there was our family, all of us mingling with strangers and friends, all brought together for the first time. I was surprised by such a large gathering of people, so many I had not been able to directly contact although notice of her death had been put in the local Daily Post. We had attempted to go through her most recent address book, sending them a copy of the letter which she composed in readiness, insisting that it should be sent after her death.

Dear.........
Because the "Writing is on the Wall" I have time to prepare
this letter, which will be sent to you when I go to the
"Promised Land" by my niece, Julia.
Over the years I have taken great pleasure in our friendship,
and feel it is only right to give you the news of my demise. I
know only too well how unsatisfactory it is to write to
someone and have the letter returned marked "Gone away
or not at this address" by the Post Office.
Thank you for the many years, which I have enjoyed your
friendship.
Goodbye, God bless you...

193

Even after death she had continued her correspondence, reaching out to so many who valued and cared for her.

The service began in the little chapel. The congregation listened as the précised history of her life and achievements were read out; the sound of singing must have been carried down the vale into Denbigh itself.

People spilled back out into the narrow lane after the service, filling the road, their chatter breaking the spell of late spring's peace. We had planned to take her to the Pentre Bychan Crematorium; cars and transport needed to be arranged. People were allotted roles as drivers and passengers. Al became a chauffeur to some whilst Heather and I were designated to travel with Tom and his family as I could navigate the journey to Wrexham for him.

The conversation was strained at first. We barely knew each other. Somehow we had always accepted the fragmentation of the family. Sally had never spoken about Tom and his family to us. We were still strangers. Tom and Nellie had spent their honeymoon in Maidstone, staying with Mum and Dad, but during our trips to Nottingham we never once met up together when staying with Sally and Marion. We had never questioned why this was so. It would have been a perfect opportunity to get together. Why had we had this distance put between us? Was it conspiracy or merely laziness? Did we have anything in common save our association with Sally? Pleasantries were exchanged within the confines of the cramped space in the car and our own timidity. The journey took us through the pretty wooded countryside and moorland separating Denbigh from Wrexham.

Finally we arrived at the crematorium, awkwardly waiting together before the other cars came into view. Further meaningless pleasantries were exchanged as we fought to find some common ground. Strangers attempted to decide whether the other groups standing around were there for the same funeral or stragglers from the previous one. Women viewed other women's outfits and figures considering the fashion, colour, fit, size, shape and suitability of the garments and accessories. All was taken in at a glance. Various dark-suited men came together introducing themselves with a handshake or a nod before falling silent again and rocking back and forth on their heels, fixing a smile and gazing with some concentration into the distance. Stilted conversations came and went as faltering attempts to prolong them petered out and people regrouped according to some mutual attraction or recognition. Others kept apart as they waited for the hearse to appear.

An audible thankful sigh signalled the arrival of the gleaming black car as it slowly wound its way round the carefully tended flower beds.

The brief service seemed over before it had begun and once again strangers mingled with the new arrivals for the next funeral.

Hurriedly, explanations about the funeral wake to take place at Brookhouse Mill in Denbigh were given as cars were once more filled with a mix of Sally's mourners.

Once we had squeezed back into Tom's car we began to relax; the thought of welcome refreshments and the knowledge that the worst of the day was over seemed to loosen our tongues. Tom's girls were our age. They all looked completely different to us and to each other. Tom's voice, though, had the same light tone as our father's with just a different accent. If I closed my eyes I could almost feel him there. He had the same awkward, shy manner; the same small stature, or was my memory just playing tricks? It was their daughter Dawn who had an uncanny likeness to Sally. She held herself straight and erect. Slim but fair haired she could have been Sally in her prime.

We started to talk. At first we spoke of our trips to Nottingham and then of staying with Sally in Denbigh in the matron's apartments. Our recollections were exact replicas. They had been in awe of her. They had thought her so aloof and

195

cultured and had been so impressed with her position and lifestyle that had been such a contrast to their own family situation. They too had never heard Sally speak of us.

"It's the same with us!" We shook our heads in disbelief. The exchanges of confidences thawed our conversation. We began to talk of our own upbringing as young girls. How strict Dad had been when we had been children!

"Yes, yes, the same with us!" Anecdotes, uncannily similar to our own reminisce of childhood, set us off in gales of unrestrained laughter. If ever there had been any doubt that we were tied together by common family traits there was no doubt left now. We were as peas in a pod.

"You were never allowed to miss school and say that you were ill!"

"No,oh no! If you were ill you had to stay in bed and do jigsaws on a wooden tray."

"We did that too!"

"I remember that one night I felt so sick but wasn't allowed to get out off bed. Dad said that I was making a song and dance about nothing and then, the next moment, I was sick all over the bed!"

"Ugghh. Never!"

"And we never had holidays, just off days away with a packed picnic and thermos of Heinz tomato soup!"

"Yeah, same as us."

"Oh and do you remember? Tadek was so spoilt wasn't he? He broke our bike when he came to stay with us because he was so fat!" We shook with laughter.

"Oh yes," began Heather, "When we used to live with my grandparents at 49 Plains Avenue, he and Sally came to stay when I was playing with my pram in the back garden. I'm not sure where Sally went on that afternoon but Tadek wanted to push the pram and tried to get hold of it. There was an old pond in the middle of the lawn, and when he pulled it away from me he ended up walking backwards and landing in the pond!"

We could hardly contain ourselves.

"Oh our Mum got into trouble with Gran. She was shouting 'why weren't you watching him Joyce!' to her and he was soaked to the skin!"

"I think he had to wear some trousers of Dad's until his were dried."

"Oh yes, we always wearing 'hand me downs'. Mum used to get them from that wealthy family where she used to do part-time cleaning in Willington Street."

"Do you remember getting those lovely hampers from Sally at Christmas?"

We chattered all the way back to Denbigh, but still the intimacy was just too fresh for me to ask questions of them. Did they know that they were Sally's grandchildren and not her nieces? I wasn't sure; I couldn't ask, and I couldn't spoil the fragile bond that we had established.

Sally's death had momentarily brought us together as a family. I hoped that in time we would pick up the threads and know more of each other.

At Brookhouse Mill the atmosphere had lightened. Sitting at circular tables people reminisced as they nibbled sandwiches on small plates. I spoke to Ivy Humphries' son, surprised that he had made the special long distance journey.

Yes, Sally had been very special to their family too. He couldn't have let the occasion go past without honouring her memory.

I mingled with the other mourners. The stale beer breath of one caught at my throat.

"She was so good to me you know." He attempted to keep me by him. "She believed in me and gave me a second chance you know. If it hadn't been for her........"

His eyes slid away from my face and then back again as he attempted to refocus. "It hadn't been for her..."

He waited for my response and burped.

My mask of civility strained to stay in place. I was furious that he was there at all. How dare he think that his sycophantic gestures could engage my sympathy?

"Erm excuse me; I need to just see to the coffee and ...." I smiled and turned away, feeling his eyes on my back.

Charlatans and scoundrels, I felt myself chanting the words going over and over. Looking back into the room I saw that he had moved on to someone else.

Yvonne and Phil were there. She had watched my brief encounter.

"Surprised that he has showed his face, still drinking I see".

"Oh yes, and reeking of it too."

"He's in with a bad lot down in town, not sure where he's staying at the moment tho'."

"I thought that he had set up in his chiropody business."

"Mmm, not sure what business he's in but you can be sure it will be with little old ladies to be sure, bound to be squeezing some money from them." She sniffed and shook her head.

"Good job that you changed the locks or who knows what he would have carted off! A nasty piece of work, him and his drinking pals, he'll never change, mark my words, and to think that she thought so much of him!"

We shook our heads.

"Well, a good conman if nothing else!"

"Perhaps she thought that she could save him from himself. She was always trying to rescue waifs and strays."

"Now don't forget, we'll be back tomorrow and then perhaps we can arrange a time for you to bring the trailer down for the clock?"

I continued circulating. Gwilym caught my eye.

"Thanks for coming Gwilym, she would have been so pleased to know that so many people were here."

"Well we knew each other for years you know. A grand lady, difficult to find you know. A rare breed. Such an individual. We had some spats tho', did you know?"

I shook my head.

198

"Ah yes, very head-strong and determined when she wanted to be. But then that's real character for you."

I smiled and agreed. "She certainly knew her own mind."

"Oh yes. Wasn't many who could put one past her. She had her finger on the button. And so many different interests you know. She never stopped wanting to find out about things, A real enthusiast. Don't know where she got the energy from." His eyes twinkled at the memory.

"I know she puts us all to shame"

I've had to slow down but she just seemed to keep on going. We lost touch a bit over these last couple of years you know but she's always had a special place in our hearts."

"She wanted you to have that carved dining room sideboard."

"Did she, did she indeed? Well then."

"There are a lot of pictures you know, you might like to come up to the house at some time and see if there are any that you would like".

"Yes, well thank you for that. We will see what we can do then."

After the wake we returned to the house quite tired by the tension and emotion of the day. The cats eyed our arrival.

"Your mistress has gone," we told them. It is all over.

CERTIFIED COPY OF AN ENTRY
Pursuant to the Births and

COPI DILYS O GOFNOD
Deaths Registration Act 1953

DEATH - MARWOLAETH	Entry No. Cofnod Rhif 106

Registration district Dosbarth cofrestru DENBIGHSHIRE SOUTH

Administrative area

COUNTY OF DENBIGHSHIRE

Sub-district Is-ddosbarth DENBIGHSHIRE SOUTH

Rhanbarth gweinyddol

SIR DDINBYCH

1. **Date and place of death**
Dyddiad a lle y bu farw

Eighteenth May 2002 Denbigh Infirmary Denbigh

2. **Name and surname** Enw a chyfenw

Sally Jay otherwise Rose Sally Christiana Mary JURCZYSZYN - JAY

3. **Sex** Rhyw Female

4. **Maiden surname of woman who has married** Cyfenw morwynol y wraig sydd wedi priodi PAYNE

5. **Date and place of birth**
Dyddiad a lle y ganwyd

15th March 1915 Nottingham Nottinghamshire

6. **Occupation and usual address**
Gwaith a chyfeiriad arferol

Matron and Nursing Officer (Retired) Widow of Marian JURCZYSZYN Bryn Hwnfa a Godwp Y Glyn Denbigh Denbighshire Accounts Clerk (Retired)

7.(a) **Name and surname of informant** Enw a chyfenw'r hysbysydd

Julia Dorothy BOTTERELL

(b) **Qualification** Cymhwyster Niece

(c) **Usual address**
Cyfeiriad arferol

11 Hazelwood Crescent Hawarden Flintshire

8. **Cause of death** Achos marwolaeth

I (a) Carcinomatosis
(b) Carcinoma of colon

...ONES M B

Sally's ashes were scattered underneath this tree in the garden.

JAY – SALLY, May 17, 2002, peacefully, at the Denbigh Infirmary, aged 87 years, of "Bryn Llwyn a Godwys," Glyn, Denbigh (former Matron N.W. Hospital, Denbigh). Beloved mother of the late Tadek, and fond aunt of Julia and Heather. Funeral on Monday May 27. Service at Glyn Presbyterian Chapel, at 1.45 p.m., followed by committal at Pentre Bychan Crematorium, Wrexham, at 3.30 p.m. No flowers, please, but donations in lieu, gratefully accepted towards Denbigh Infirmary, Macmillan Unit, per R W Roberts & Son, Llys Aled, Denbigh (812935).

Chapter 14 Three weddings and two funerals

Goudhurst 1971

How strange that we found ourselves living in the same village. To think that exactly seventy years ago my great grandfather, his wife and two girls had walked up the same hill from their tied cottage and watched the ducks swim in the village pond. And I had not discovered this until a new millennium had begun. I knew that the May family had lived in Cranbrook but not that they had settled for a short while just south of the village that was to be our home for the next three years.

Sally arrived at my first wedding, with Tadek and Marion in tow. The pictures, taken in Mote Park, show her girlishly leaning against Charles, her cousin Joan's husband, her arms draped over his shoulders. She was wearing a Welsh woollen tweed suit, her wavy hair cut short. Terry was tall and thin in his new suit and I was dressed in the flower power hippy fashion of the times with a medieval styled dress. The bodice of brown velvet was trimmed with gold, as were the long sleeves, the white skirt flowed to the floor. The sides of my long hair were plaited and tied at the back of my head as I attempted to resemble Sir Walter Scotts' 'Lady of the Lake'. A style that was at complete odds to my mini skirted female friends and the family relatives who had sensibly let the flower power movement pass them by.
 Somehow Sally found out that we were going to drive down to Goudhurst as we had no money for a honeymoon. She insisted that Tadek and she would accompany us to our rented school house attached to the C of E Goudhurst Primary School. At my interview at the school I had been asked about

where we proposed to live and so we had been lucky to secure this house; with the headmaster deciding to vacate the property earlier that spring.   Terry, my first husband, had successfully been interviewed for a teaching post at Angley School in Cranbrook.

 After the tea in the dilapidated village hall in Willington Street, Maidstone we changed and drove off down the winding roads towards Goudhurst, finally passing the crowded duck pond and turning in at the school gate.

The car contained the David Frith Denbigh pottery and the wooden Welsh love spoon that she had purchased for us along with other wedding gifts from our friends and family. I had thought it strange at the time that Marion had given us a separate gift of Prestige kitchen tools but hadn't realised how separate they both were.

Our rented brick house was masked by an ugly temporary mobile classroom and a beautiful cherry tree. A large moss-covered brick wall surrounded the garden making it quite private and secret. As I was uncomfortably and awkwardly carried over the threshold, not feeling in the least bit romantic, Sally and Tadek gleefully took snaps of the event, sending us copies of the pictures later. Marion had been totally excluded from the venture; it was as if he had not been there.

"We were the only ones to witness that, weren't we!" She had taken great delight in the 'scope' recording the event. When I look at the pictures I just remember a peculiar embarrassment. Somehow it all looked so stage managed. Later we had planned to celebrate our nuptials with a meal at the Star and Eagle Hotel at the top of the hill only to find that they couldn't accommodate us that evening, so we had to settle for a tinned soggy Fray Bentos meat pie as we had nothing else stocked in the kitchen cupboards. I can't think why I look back at those photographs with such dislike. Was it because I was so unnerved by her 'sisterly act' that I had never encountered before?

Streatham 1972

Heather looked beautiful in her lace wedding gown but I could see that Sally was not impressed. The room was full of wedding guests. Our side of the family had travelled up together in a coach. My father looked particularly ill at ease in his new jacket. Stuart's parents kept apart from the crowd. Sally made no attempt to engage in general conversation although she drew Terry to one side for a private chat.

Finally she found her way to Mum's side.

"It's rather a grand affair seeing that they have been living together for some time already - haven't they?"

Mum took in a sharp breath. "Well, if they are going to buy somewhere they need to save every penny. And good luck to them."

"Oh I see, so different from our day," and she turned to talk to someone else.

"That Sally! Who does she think she is?" Mum was pink and furious.

The hotel had laid on a magnificent spread on white damask table cloths. The beautiful cake was set to one side. On the main table a decorated poached salmon curled on a large platter surrounded by a generous buffet of cold meats, salads, sandwiches, delicately produced pastries and savouries. An array of desserts lined the side table together with cups and saucers.

I watched despondently, unable to sample the magnificent fare as I had been rushed off to the dentist that morning and had a tooth extracted after spending an agonising night suffering from an abscess.

The waitresses passed between the guests offering drinks balanced on silver trays. At the smaller grouped tables, fragrant flowered centre pieces had been placed. Each small detail had been considered.

Happy conversation lingered in the air but Sally left earlier than expected.

Holywell 1982

Al and I had lived together for over three years in Mynydd Isa and decided that the time had come to formalise the relationship. The very small guest list had been drawn up to help us celebrate the simple ceremony at the Holywell registry office. Al looked handsome in his light blue suit and I had chosen a grey knee-length dress and a light cream jacket.

Sally arrived in a short fur coat. We looked at it twice; Sally in a fur!

She explained. "Oh no it's a faux fur, I couldn't wear a dead animal, but I needed something a little warmer with you choosing to get married in the autumn." It was an aimed reprimand and we smiled.

Sally and Al had met a few times and had hit it off. She approved of him. He was tall and direct with a military RAF background to which she could relate. After the short marriage ceremony we drove back to our house to share an afternoon buffet. We had said that we didn't want expensive wedding gifts, just a gathering of friends, in order to keep things simple. Sally had other ideas. As we handed round the plates of sandwiches Sally could hardly contain herself. Her boxed present sat conspicuously on the lounge floor. We were encouraged to open it in front of the assembled guests. A large grey and fawn pottery plate emerged from the newspaper wrappings. Terra cotta brown slip work decorated the plate. In the middle was a crudely drawn church, the outer rim proclaimed 'Julie + Alan' at the top and '22nd October 1982' at the bottom whilst the inner rim declared 'were married at Holywell'. We didn't have the heart to say that both our names were misspelt; somehow it seemed to be churlish to point out the glaring error. My mother spotted the plate and was about to comment as we quickly ushered her away.

We had arranged to have the evening reception at the Plas Hafod hotel in Gwernymynydd just outside Mold, with just a small family and a few close friends. Sally watched as the waitresses came around with the steak fillets and glared at the table set with wine glasses.

"Oh - she's going to make a fuss!" I warned Al, but he had assessed the situation. Going to her table he put his arm around her.

"Now something special for you Sally. A veritable vegetarian delight. They have been warned; said if you weren't happy there would be trouble."

She allowed herself to be pacified; pleased that she had been given priority treatment and the evening passed peacefully without incident. She had decided to enjoy herself.

Nottingham May 1996

We travelled from Denbigh to Nottingham together. Sally sitting in the front with Allan and me at the back with a friend of Tadek's whom he used to meet up with when staying at Sally's. I disliked the man intensely. He reminded me of one of Willie Collins' Victorian villains. His face was ruddy and pock marked. He tried too hard to endear himself; his voice was oily slick and his breath betrayed the enjoyment of many recent drinks. Sally found him sincere. She had recently enjoyed more of his company. As she explained; he was endeavouring to kick his drink habit with her support, and had begun a chiropody course so would soon be qualified to set up his own business. He was effusive in his praise for her. Without her 'help and support' he could not have embarked on such a venture. At that time we had no idea how practical her support had been. He spoke of Tadek and how they had had some marvellous times together. Her son had been a chip off the old block and he would miss him more than he could say. But what strength and fortitude Sally was showing. Such an amazing woman! His voice droned on throughout the journey.

Finally we reached the cemetery. Standing away from the crowd I recognised Tadek's ex-wife, Charlotte, and her son David. The service was short but the crowd of people filled the chapel and spilled out into the entrance. Sally looked about her; so many people that she did not know all coming together to celebrate the life of her precious only son. Friends from Nottingham Social Services Department looked quite distraught. They wanted to speak to Sally and tell her what an impact Tadek had made on their lives. Not just professionally, but personally, for they each had a story of his generosity, his unfailing support, the fun and laughter they had shared, his wonderful music, his larger than life personality. He had been a marvellous companion and they would miss him so much. One girl grasped Sally's hand as if holding on to her for support as she told her tale of her part in his life.

And it undoubtedly helped Sally to get through the day. She did gain in strength as the conversation buzzed around her. People wanting to be able to shake her hand, knowing that it was she who had produced this wonderful man.

At the graveside Tadek's youthful son David timidly attempted to offer her a handful of soil to scatter on the casket but she turned away from him. My heart went out for the gesture that was so obviously snubbed. He returned and stood by his mother, her pale face showing no emotion. Charlotte was surrounded by a sea of people who had not acknowledged them; indeed they probably did not know who they both were. He so resembled his quiet mother with her dark eyes and slight form. He had no features of his father, dressed as he was in his smart waistcoat and dark jacket. He was her son. Sally could not bring herself to speak to them.

Congregating at the pub afterwards was difficult but we managed to find the tables outside and with tea and coffee she continued to bask in the adulation of her son. We were pleased that for a short while some of the pain of losing him had been replaced with the comfort of these genuine accolades, but I was saddened that an opportunity for reconciliation had slipped away. I spoke for a few minutes to them both. My words hung in the air. Stilted pleasantries between total strangers were exchanged, empty phrases left our lips merely to emphasise the gulf between the two sides of the family. I knew that we would never meet again.

Maidstone 1997

We eventually managed to find some accommodation for Sally in the town that suited her requirements. The first bed and breakfast had steep stairs and I could visualise her pitched headlong down them so we duly gave our thanks to the owners and moved on.

Dad had said that he didn't want to be buried; "can't have dead bodies littering up the place, just a black bin bag will do."
He disapproved of good land being used as cemeteries.

Despite his lack of organised faith the service was held for him at St Martin's church by the 'new top shops' as we still called them. It was Mum's church so she had comfort in being in familiar surroundings. The congregation consisted of friends from the Maidstone Model Engineering Society as well as family, friends and neighbours. They had lived a modest life together in Oxford Road for forty-seven years, celebrating both their Ruby and Golden Wedding Anniversaries with family and friends. Sally sat by her cousin Joan and Joan's oldest son Kevin, her nephew.

She was looking quite frail. The journey down the night before had sapped her strength. It was going to be another difficult day. During the service the vicar remembered our earlier conversation, neatly bringing together his life's achievements for us to celebrate.

Afterwards, at Vinter's Park crematorium, we again mingled with those who wanted to share their thanks for the little things that Dad had done for them. Sally was not feted, she had only Joan to speak to and Joan was accompanied by her healthy son who served as a reminder to Sally what she had so recently lost. We had been caught up with friends and family whom we hadn't seen for a while.

She was very quiet on the journey home. It had all been too much for her.

OBITUARY Tad Jay

Members that knew him will be saddened to learn of the death of Tad Jay (T.J. Jurczyszyn-Jay in the membership list), larger than life character, talented pianist, organist and treasurer of Butterley Garden Railway Association. Tad suffered a fatal heart attack on the 7th May at the age of 51 while on holiday at the 7¹/₄" gauge railway at Hemsby in Norfolk.

His father was a Hurricane pilot in the Polish Air Force (younger members may not be aware that 5 per cent of R.A.F. pilots in the Battle of Britain were Polish and accounted for 7.5% of enemy losses); but it was from his Welsh mother, Sally, that he acquired his love of railways and steam. Mrs Jay is still a shareholder in the Llangollen Railway and a member of the Welsh Highland Railway.

"Converting" to 16mm in 1984, he could be found most weekends at the Midland Railway Centre with his son David in recent years, either camera in hand or steaming on the garden railway. He was also a member of Chesterfield Society of Model Engineers, where he indulged his taste in larger gauges. His passion for old cameras was widely known. Tad spent the last 24 years as a Social Worker in Nottingham. He will long be remembered by his friends and greatly missed.

Max Bryce

Tadek's obituary stating that he had a Welsh mother!
Amos, her brother, who died in 1997, *and right*, Tadek's gravestone at the cemetery in Nottingham.

Julia and Terry's wedding in Maidstone 1971; Heather and Stuart's wedding in Sutton,1972; and Sally wearing her faux fur at Allan and Julia's wedding, 1982

Chapter 15 In this will I bequeath……..

During her lifetime Sally rewrote her will on numerous occasions. Sometimes a copy would be written out only to be discarded and left incomplete in a drawer. She had at one time circulated copies of the most recent will to those whom she had chosen to benefit from her estate.

At first she made a small provision for her *two* brothers, Amos and Tom. They were to receive £100 each with the remaining estate to Tadek her *only* son. When she found out about Marion's affair with Barbara she drafted a new will. Tadek was still the main beneficiary but she inserted a clause that Marion was only to receive £500, that being the money that had been held by them in a past joint account with a building society. She wanted nothing to do with the 'contaminated' money.

When Tadek died in 1996 her plans to leave her entire estate in his hands fell apart. She considered leaving the estate as split shares between friends and family. Then another bombshell fell. The following year in 1997 she lost her brother 'Moss'. Once again she had to plan for her estate and pets. She set about writing another will, sending copies of it to the named beneficiaries. Her sister-in-law, Joyce, received the following communication with her copy:

Dear Joy,

Just a 'quickie' to go with the enclosed copy of my will. Next time you come to Alan and Julie' spend a few hours with me to see if there is anything you would like. I am trying to give away as much as I can whilst I am alive. It will make my life easier-so much less to clean etc. There were quite a lot of things to be decided upon when T J retired to keep or not.

Now that is all done with. I hate Friday's because when he came he would stand on the front doorstep smelling the air and looking at the view saying" Mum it is so peaceful, I can't wait for the time to retire"."

I can't still realise this will now never happen- I try but its no use, I see things and think-next time TJ comes......then remember it is not going to happen.

No more news.

Don't forget next time you come to Hawarden,

Love Sally

The new will dated the 21st August 1997 gave all her personal chattels in clause 4 to;

i)   her *'brother'* and sister in law Mr and Mrs T Payne,
ii)   her sister in law Mrs J Payne,
iii)   her said niece Mrs A Botterell,
iv)   the husband of the said niece Mr A Botterell,
v)   her niece and her husband Mr and Mrs S Johnston,
vi)   her friends Mr and Mrs G Roberts
vii)   her friend Mr Roy Noon.

 She stated that the residue of her property, including her house, would go to any of the above persons who would look after her animals during their lifetime or to an animal charity willing to do the same.

If she had no animals at the time of her death she wanted £500 to ten listed charities and then the remainder paid to the seven named beneficiaries named in clause 4.

There was no mention made of her grandson David and his mother Charlotte. Once Tadek had died she never made any attempt to contact David or Charlotte.

By the end of the 1990's there were a couple of acquaintances who started to visit more regularly as her health declined. She used to discuss her affairs with them and share her concerns about her feral cats. He was a woodcarver whom she had met at one or other of the country fairs that she had frequented. Like Tadek he sported a full set of whiskers and was loud and jovial. His wife was quiet with small inquisitive dark eyes. Increasingly they spoke about their love of her house and how they could imagine setting up their woodcarving business on the premises.

A newly qualified chiropodist also became a more frequent visitor as the entries in her old cheque books revealed. He also managed to coax her into him driving her car for her as a way of thanking her for her kindness. She finally found that she was unable to cope with gear changes after she broke her wrist. He would come up the drive in her car and take her to the shops or into town but kept the car with him to save her the bother of it standing on the drive unused.

She began to worry about the treasures that she had taken a lifetime to collect. Increasingly she would ask me if I liked a particular picture or ornament and if I agreed that it was good she would urge me to take it home.

"No Sally, not now, one day, but not now. It is for you to enjoy;" I would protest uneasily, thinking how other things seem to have disappeared from her house since our last visit. She pressed me to take her collection of herb pots. "I don't cook much these days," she insisted.

When Sally died Al and I were ushered into the solicitor's office in Denbigh.

"Sally Jay made a new will last week," he announced. We were astonished at the news.

"I went up to her house to draw it up and it was witnessed this week". We couldn't believe that once again she that decided to change her will after circulating a copy to friends and various members of the family. Who did she leave everything to? We looked at each other, eyebrows raised in query.

"You will see from this document that Mrs Jay has named you both as sole beneficiaries to her estate."

"She has stipulated that the Richard Griffiths Denbigh clock should be given to Mrs Yvonne Johnson in recognition for her kindness to her and there are a few small cash gifts to some animal charities, but otherwise it is for you both to enjoy."

I felt my throat constrict with emotion.

"No doubt that you were aware that she had this in mind?"

We shook our heads, unable to think what to say. We had been chosen by Sally to receive everything but how could we then face the other relatives who had thought that they were to inherit a share of her estate?

"We need to make some arrangements," Al spoke slowly.

"I think we need to arrange another meeting with you as soon as possible."

As we drove away we came to the same conclusion. Here was our chance to right some wrongs. That the chiropodist and the woodcarver and his wife had not been mentioned was a puzzle, but we were thankful that she hadn't finally been deceived by them.

It was agreed. The family members who had been put into the previous will would receive a share of the proceeds when the house was sold. We would arrange that her grandson David, who had never featured in any of her wills, would also receive some money. In this way we would be ensuring that family discord would not continue after her death.

It was on our way back to Denbigh to keep our appointment with the solicitor the following week, just as we turned off the main A 415 towards Denbigh that a blue streak flashed in front of the car, swooping down towards us and then flying high above us until it disappeared from sight.

215

"Did you see it?" I was mesmerised and a large lump unexpectedly came into my throat.
"It was a beautiful Jay!"

"It is a most strange request that you are making"; the solicitor pressed his fingertips together when we outlined our plans during our next visit.
"Usually I have family members demanding to know why their share is not larger." He smiled ruefully.
"Still, if you are sure about this I can certainly proceed with the paperwork and you will be able to issue the cheques accordingly from Mrs Jay's estate."
"No we don't want that." We both agreed.
"The cheques will come from this office and a letter from you confirming that this is a payment from her estate. It is not from us to them, but from Sally directly to them.
In this way we are complying with her wishes but just diverting some of the funds which are ours to give."
"Again I have to reiterate that this is most irregular and I need to consult my colleagues but I'm sure that we can accommodate both your selves and at the same time comply with Mrs Jay's wishes." He allowed himself a faint smile.
The interview was at an end.

We then had to consider her cats. One cat, Marcus, was extremely tame and housetrained but the others rarely came too close to strangers.
During that summer whilst we were cleaning and sorting out the house we made arrangements for them to be fed by the neighbours on the days that we could not go to the house. We changed the locks and made the house secure and pondered on what to do.

Finally, during one day of cleaning we mentioned the affectionate cat Marcus to our friends Margaret and Reg. They had a suggestion. Their daughter Debbie might like to take him. So Marcus found a very loving family. Despite some scares at the vets when it was pronounced that he was on death's door, having contracted a form of feline Aids, he continued to live a contented, pampered, and healthy life with his adopted family.

Then there were two others that the neighbours said that they would look after as they were becoming fairly tame, but the remaining very old and ill-looking feral cats needed more care. Finally they were caught and taken to the North Wales Animal Rescue together with a sum of money to ensure their wellbeing.

The wood carver and his wife came to the house after Sally's death and said that they had been promised some furniture and the large Tiffany- style lamp shades which we agreed that they could take.

Yvonne had the large Denbigh clock that Sally had wanted her to have, along with a few trinkets that she admired.

We than wanted to ensure that apart from the money that each family member had received from the estate, that they would also have a more personal kind of memento.

Sally's' son Tom and his family had the silver, some jewellery, the gold and silver coin collections, some ornaments, the grandmother clock, various commemorative plates, some Hornby trains, and other pieces that they chose after the funeral. Gwilym Roberts had the big oak dining room side board, and finally other bits and pieces were distributed according to taste and desire; hopefully complying with her wishes expressed whilst she was alive.

Her jewellery was distributed between her grandchildren, Tom's daughters, Ruth, Dawn and Wendy and his wife Nellie, then to my sister Heather, and her daughter Rachel; to Mum and Sally's irrepressible cousin Joan; and finally a small emerald ring to Janet the daughter of Bill May. I had never met Janet until we finally wrote and arranged for her to come and stay with us. She had been completely unaware of our existence and that she still had remaining contacts with the

May family. She did not realise that Bill had had a cousin Joan, née May, daughter of his Uncle Amos; and that she was still alive. I was saddened to find that her father Bill (William) had died before I was able to show him pictures of his ancestors. I had been so surprised to find that she and Tadek had shared much of their childhood; that her mother Olive had been involved in helping to look after Tadek despite a terse entry in Sally's diary that stated that she didn't want Tadek to be looked after by 'that Olive'.

And then there was her grandson David and his mother Charlotte They had already received the estate from 24 Charlecote Drive following the death of Tadek, but David had nothing directly from his grandmother. We decided that he might like to receive either her car or for us to sell the car and pass over the proceeds to him. Having consulted Charlotte the latter course of action was taken.

Each family member had in some way received something from Sally, and we were sure that Mal and Morwenna, the new owners of Sally's home, would make a magnificent job of tastefully renovating the house and gardens.

And so the estate was cleared and distributed.

Chapter 16 Denbigh lacquer

It was the first time that we had entered the house after her death. Whilst she was in the Denbigh Infirmary we had gone in as the caretakers, feeding the cats, checking the locks on the doors before departing for the night. Now we were the owners but it did not feel like our house. It seemed so quiet. The sun attempted to enter the house but even it seemed reticent to shine too fully. It still seemed an intrusion to move from room to room without a direct invitation. Marcus followed us around, pleased to have our company. His lithe body circled our legs; his black coat glowed in the morning sunshine.

"You'll take us round Marcus?" His green eyes blinked in recognition of his important role.

We opened the door to the lounge. The acrid smell of decay and mouse urine swirled around us. I looked at the little litter-strewn games table where she used to write up her diary each day. Instinctively I went to the table and opened the battered book. I was bitterly disappointed. Page after page denoted the weather each day, birthdays and anniversaries were underlined but no trace of her prose took up any page. It was merely an impersonal journal of weather patterns and appropriate times to plant seeds.

The sun was casting faint beams of sunlight into the room from the stain-glass window in the back door. Ragged curtains, rust stained from the radiators, limply hung from their rails. Books piled on the pianola and piano showed nibbled edges, dust and marked covers. We stood and surveyed the room once so well furnished and warmed by a log fire. Trays and books were scattered over the floor. The wooden ceiling beams were punctuated with hundreds of hanging mugs. Cushions on the sofa exposed their stuffing. The smell was suffocating. I put my hand over my nose attempting to block it out. Everything was covered by a layer of thick dust. Lining the wall above the impressive fireplace, perched on wooden shelves, were finely crafted oasthouses, cottages, and miniature buildings which had once been internally lit by their tiny concealed lamps at Christmas. By the sofa, areas of the floor looked wet and shiny. To the left by the window stood the large and impressive oak cupboard with a collection of garish pottery cats assembled on the top. A large black cat had lost one green glass eye and winked at us balefully. The top drawers had been wedged open and as we attempted to pull one open it disgorged its flaky contents of papers and photographs; ghostly sepia faces spiralled to the floor. And as we looked down we saw that the skirting boards were thickly glazed with waxy elm-coloured urine.

"Looks like a lacquer veneer." A faint sad smile played around Al's lips.

"Perhaps it's Denbigh lacquer," I replied, and we slowly shook our heads in disbelief.

Al pulled at the drawer again and it jolted free of the papers to expose mouse nests and one stiff skeletal mouse.

"Oh God!" I was repulsed. "Leave it Al, ugh, don't touch it please!" I shuddered again; the hairs on my arms raised themselves in horror.

The green rug in front of the fireplace was patchily threadbare in places. Windows were encrusted in grime; trailing plants that had abandoned hopes of thriving sat on the sill, their dried wrinkled leaves drooped down from the window ledges and remains of previous flowerings lay on the floor.

Dispirited we turned and closed the door. Going back into the more familiar sitting room we went up the stairs. Her bedroom, empty of its occupant, the bed still unmade, mourned her departure. We opened the door to the bathroom. Various dusty jars of ointments, bars of soap and thin towels showed signs of use. The warm airing cupboard door swung open. The cat had made his bed amongst the tea towels and bed linen. His black hairs coated the nicely rounded depression on the second shelf. Sally's emerald dressing gown, that I had never seen her wear, hung from the back of the door. Cloths for cleaning were carefully laid over the bath; stiff with age. The well-tiled wall with its pastel beige and delicate grass and wild flowered panels still showed signs of previous care.

We walked further along the landing. To the left was the shower room, rancid with old soap, the slip mat dark with dried mould. Backing away from the claustrophobia of the musty space we passed Tadek's bedroom. A fine woven Welsh tapestry had been lovingly smoothed over the large double oak bed. On closer inspection mouse droppings and dried cat faeces covered the floor and bed. Books assembled along the length of the leopard print *chaise-longue* appeared to be also covered in a black treacle substance. Inside the black ebony wardrobe a large collection of Welsh wool coats, two-piece suits and dresses, men's suits, an undergraduate gown and mortar, a faux fur coat and various shoes, handbags and scarves hung forlornly from the rails. Mouse droppings coated the dusty floor. In the black iron grate a basket of fir cones had once been carefully arranged; they too now spilled out from the fender and onto the dull floorboards, adding to the air of neglect.

We backed out of the room and turned to our left and peered into the room that seemed to have been set aside for David, her grandson's visits. The small room contained a narrow bed covered with a grey tinged mattress. A little shelf contained Rupert Bear annuals and a hard copy of The Water Babies. Huge looped cobwebs swung catching in the movement of air, the little window that had once looked out towards the back of the house and the orchards was clouded with a film of cobwebs and weathered grime, giving the room a cold dismal aspect. Carpeting the bare floor were tiny black pellets and in one corner was a beautifully carved stool, the seat one sheet of exquisite whirled and circled oak, stained black with urine which held a hanging ragged comic in its gluey substance.

On the landing area had been a library of books and magazines stored on free-standing bookshelves that lined one wall. They too had seen the attentions of the mice. Each cover had been gnawed and the crumbled deposits scattered underneath.

Further down the corridor a bedroom faced us with its door half opened. As we came closer we realised that it had been chaotically stacked with boxes, tables and stools, cabinets, a red 1977 Caernarfon Investiture chair, blankets, throws, hat boxes, plates, mugs, Christmas tinsel and baubles; electrical cables tangled themselves around each other having spilled out from their cases of toasters, kettles and electric blankets. An assorted pile of purchased goods not yet unwrapped had been placed around the room and then had collapsed into the room as the growing weight began to destabilise the intended arrangement.

Inside four identical Royal Crown Derby blue boxes the tissue paper surrounded gold embellished loving cups. The crumpled invoice proclaimed that each Millennium mug had cost over £100; the first two in the consignment, including VAT, were £250 and the others 'to follow' would total £500 in all.

Peeping out of another large box was the proud honey coloured head of a lion, and as I attempted to pull the box clear, I found a perfect group of lion, lioness and their cub nestling in tissue; a Sherratt and Simpson commemorative collector's piece designed to celebrate the Millennium. Amongst the debris and decay another long box exposed a large magnificent male pheasant, its long tail feathers seemingly gossamer soft, totally intact and perfect, designed once again, according to the box, to celebrate the Millennium.

"My God look at it all!" Al's disbelief at what he was witnessing evident. "Who was she buying all this for?"

223

"Goodness knows." I shrugged helplessly. "She must have spent a fortune on this lot, and so recently too."

"But why?" We were both baffled. "If she had someone in mind, then why didn't she give it to them before now?"

"Look in that box with the pheasant, Al. Is there a certificate or anything?"

He delved into the tissue paper" Nope don't think so. Oh hang on, there is something here. He drew out an invoice. "Says it's a Limited Edition from Border Arts for celebrating the Millennium. My God!" A sigh of pent up frustration punctuated his sentence," she spent over £500 quid on this piece alone!"

"Oh look there's another one! He pointed to another larger box. "Another pheasant!"

"I can't believe it!"

He turned over a dark blue box. "I think there is a bowl in this one."

"Careful. It might break."

Al steadied himself as he bent over to reach the box and brought it closer to him.

"Urgh!" he shuddered as mouse droppings cascaded over his trousers.

"Gawd, they're everywhere!"

Opening the blue box he drew out the Aynsley Certificate of Authenticity and started to scan read. "Hand painted ....male and female pheasant....typical country setting....erhmmm...embellished with 22 carat gold. Blimey. The edition is strictly limited to 75 pieces, each bowl being individually numbered."

"Turn over the bowl. What does it say?"

"Number 20," he announced.

"No invoice with this one then?"

"Nope can't see one."

"Oh come on. Let's go down and make a cup of tea. I can't stand too much excitement in one day."

We retraced our steps along to the landing and as I went to go down the stairs I glanced to the right.

"Oh, I didn't realise that there were more cupboards here and a little writing desk. What's inside this one?"

I pulled open the heavy top drawer. Inside were carefully folded trousers and jumpers. Some still with the remains of cellophane which had been chewed and nibbled. All the clothes gave off a stench of mice.

"Ohhh no.....all these are brand new and they are just covered ......just look at them!"

We stared in dismay at another discovery of abandoned purchases.

"Some of these, they've never been worn."

"Oh what a shame," my heart sank at the thought.

"There she was, wearing the same old scruffy things and all these things were here all the time, oh what an awful waste."

I felt both irritated and saddened in equal measure,

"to think that she could have been so comfortable, but left all of it to the mice to ruin."

"C'm on," Al pulled at my arm, "Come on leave it now. We'll do more tomorrow. We need to clear up the sitting room so that people can come in case it rains."

We looked at each other wide eyed. "How can we make it presentable, the smell is everywhere?"

"We'll just have to keep the other doors closed and hope that the sun shines for the funeral." He bit the back of my neck.

"Can't let the mice out then!"

Downstairs Marcus had waited in for us; he languidly stretched himself and stared up.

"Perhaps we can get Marcus to do his stuff" Al suggested. Marcus turned to Al enquiringly. "What do you think Marcus, a good day to hunt?"

Marcus blinked.

"We'll take that as a 'Yes' then," and stoked his head.

Chapter 17 Confidences and discoveries

Sally wanted to write a letter to her friends. "I need to let them know what is happening," she was adamant. Her voice was faint and husky over the phone and she attempted to clear her throat.

I waited until she was quiet. "Why not let us bring you back over here and we can have a little bit of lunch and you can explain what you want to do," I suggested, waiting for the usual refusal and then the inevitable cajoling until she allowed herself to accept an invitation. She surprised me with her reply. "Yes, come tomorrow for me about ten o'clock. It will give me a chance to see to the cats, and sort out a few things."

"Fine Sally, we'll be there." I put down the phone. She had seemed very different. I couldn't put my finger on it, there seemed to be a new determination, like a last stand before charging into battle. Did she want something else? It was as if a bit of the fiery Sally had returned, positive and sure of herself.

In the kitchen I looked in the cupboards. Once upon a time Sally had a healthy appetite and would devour the food put in front of her. Al would always say "I don't know where she puts it all. She must have hollow legs." But for the last couple of years she seemed to have lost the habit of eating. She always enjoyed my cheese and mushroom quiche and liked plenty of the vegetables so I decided on that, with jacket potatoes, which was another of her favourites. In the past she had allowed herself to commend my pastry and so I thought I'd make an apple pie then she could take some back home with her.

We drove up the lane to her house and knocked on the front door, then on the sitting room window and then walked round to the back door, letting ourselves in with our usual shout: "It's only us, Sally we're here", before going through the kitchen and into the warm sitting room.

She had collected some things together to put in some carrier bags. "I've got a few things for you to take back with you."

"No I want you to have them;" she wafted away my attempt to speak.

"Okay, okay." I attempted to pacify her.

"It's pretty nippy outside Sally."

I tried to be jovial but it hurt me to see how painfully thin and grey she looked. Large dark circles ringed her eyes. Her long legs had their thinness accentuated by the close-fitting green trousers. Her elegant nicotine-stained fingers showed that she had succumbed once again to a habit that she denied having.

Al drove through Ruthin on the way back to our house. "Thought you would like to see the views Sally."

Usually Sally would be attentive and inquisitive if we drove her anywhere. She would point out places of interest and provide us with a running commentary, but this time she settled herself in the seat and seemed resigned to complete the journey in silence. Al attempted to provide some dialogue but even he found it hard going and lapsed into longer and longer silences.

On the dining room table Sally brought out sheets of paper covered in her usual flowing script.

"I don't like sending letters and cards to someone and not knowing if they are dead or alive!" she announced.

I want to have something sent to people when I am dead to say that I have gone. But I don't want it to be morbid; something short and sweet."

She showed us some of her jottings;

"something along these lines."

"We could always add a picture of you if you wanted it to be a little less stark Sally" I suggested tentatively.

"Mmm." She considered the idea.

"We have a lovely one of you that we took in the conservatory last Christmas, that's a good one," Al assured her.

227

"Tell you what, I'll go up on the computer, write down a couple of lines along the way you have put it, find the picture and bring it down for you to look at."

"He can do that and then afterwards we can have a spot of lunch. Okay?" I suggested

She mutely nodded her agreement. I sat with her at the table. She seemed so lonely and frail.

"Funny how things turn out Sally, huh?"

I looked across the room at the photograph of Dad on the sideboard. She followed my gaze.

"I miss him too," I said sadly.

"I could always talk to him about everything. He didn't allow the shadows of the past to worry him you know."

Sally pursed her lips together, "Mmm."

"He gave me all his letters and things from his mother. Did you know?" I queried gently.

"He wanted me to have all his mementoes. One day I will put them together to celebrate his life," I smiled.

"I hope that I will be able to do it justice."

She watched me through half closed eyes. I started again.

"He told me about his own illegitimacy and about Tom." I probed. Her eyes widened almost imperceptibly and I waited for her to speak.

"About Tom?" she asked huskily, clearing her throat.

"Oh yes," I dare not break the spell. "Years ago he told me, and of the sadness for you."

The room waited for a response. "You were just a young girl then." I breathed quietly, "just a girl."

She drew herself up breathing in heavily. "Yes."

"These days children are acknowledged to be blameless you know." I looked at her profile; she did not face me. I tried again. "Men have always taken advantage of the silence of their victims."

Her face turned towards me and her eyes hardened.

"He said that he would kill my rabbits" she hissed.

A cry of a child in the body of a dying woman. My eyes welled with tears for her grief and for her destroyed childhood.

"You weren't to blame Sally. He was the adult. You were just a child."

"It was a rape," she blazed.

"Yes it was. He abused you. It was a criminal act."

She allowed me to touch her hand. I could feel the dry paper thinness of her skin under the palm of my hand.

"And all these years you have had to carry that weight around with you. Nobody should have to do that."

She seemed to soften and, in breathing out, lost some of the tightness in her body.

"You should have been protected from that guilt."

Slowly she nodded again.

"And all that time you have thought that somehow you had provoked it?"

Hoarsely she grunted her agreement.

"You were just a child. Children have crushes, they idolise heroes. They don't deserve to be abused for childish fantasies. It was never your fault."

We looked at each other and for the first time I felt that she had been able to forgive herself. It was as if a physical weight had been lifted from her.

Al came downstairs with the letter.

"I'll make lunch," I smiled at Sally, but I'm not certain that she smiled back.

....

We went in to tidy her front sitting room, the parlour.

"If we shove some of the stuff upstairs for now there will be room to sit in here." Al tried to reassure me.

We had brought some bin bags and some cleaning cloths. "If we clear the table and sort the chairs out, they could come in the front door, then in here, and back out the same way."

"There's no way we can do anything to the kitchen, it will take days to do that." Marcus darted to the door as we spoke and

229

sat by the small swing bin, his ears pointing forward, alert and quivering.

"I think he has found a mouse."

We opened the lid of the bin and the mouse attempted to jump out, losing its grip on the smooth sides.

"How did it get in there?"

"Take the bin outside Al; don't let it be killed in here."

Marcus followed Al as he carried the bin out; the mouse kept jumping up and down as they went.

I took some of the covers that had been thrown over the chairs and took them upstairs to dump out of the way whilst we were preparing for the funeral. On the landing I glanced again at the little writing desk. Curiosity took over. I pulled open the front of the desk. This time the expected rush of mouse droppings did not follow. Envelopes and papers were tightly crammed into the little compartments. It was neat and tidy but looked as if it had been undisturbed for years. I carefully pulled out a long brown envelope from the nearest compartment. Inside there was a thin folded green certificate. A wedding certificate.

'Certificated copy of an entry of marriage' 'When married.... 4th November 1943...marriage solemnised........Registry office, Bingham in the County of Nottingham. Marion Joseph Jurczyszyn 22 years bachelor, Rose Christiana Mary Payne 28 years spinster.' I was bewildered, where was the name Sally? There had been just two witnesses, Ivy Humphries and Rudolph Scatkowski.

I pulled out another slip of thin beige paper folded carefully twice into a square.

Bath House, Mansfield. October 9th 1943 'I certify that Sgt Payne is an expectant mother about 3 months,' signed PM G......... MD. I stared at the paper, slowly realising that Sally had been four months pregnant when she had married Marion. Something that I needed to remember stirred in my brain; something to do with Tadek. What was it? It just wouldn't come. Someone had said something about Sally and Tadek;

was it about her being pregnant or was it about the mystery surrounding the date of her marriage? I just couldn't bring the conversation back; it had been years ago, perhaps I had imagined it. Try as I might nothing came back. Did Marion know that she was pregnant? Had she confided in anyone? At four months surely she would have begun to show. Had they brought the marriage forward? Had it been a terrible mistake and that is why she and Marion had been such an unsuitable match? So many unanswered questions circled round my head.

Putting the papers back in the desk I went downstairs. There was plenty of time to unravel all of this, now it was time to prepare for her funeral.

....

We had started to sort out the house. There was the immediate concern of eliminating any remaining mice. Marcus had made a sterling start. He was a champion mouser; quivering with expectation and excitement he dispatched them cleanly as if he had been born to it. Well I suppose that he had! We explained our predicament of the soft furnishings that contained the mice to Phil and Yvonne, her hairdresser. Phil had the answer. He had a large wire caged trailer that he would bring to the house and help Al to take out the chairs and sofa in the lounge. He had protective clothing and large rat-proof rubber gloves.

It was a glorious day. The sky was powder blue and a warm caressing breeze lightly danced with the leaves. Marcus stood on the warmed tarmac watching carefully as Phil and Al came struggling through the front door, faces pink with the effort of holding onto the sofa. Their gloves were wet. Grey stuffing burst from the bottom. Suddenly Marcus darted forward; leaping and then twisting around as a tiny brown body shot between Phil and the sofa.

231

"A mouse!" I pointed, and in that moment Marcus had turned and had run into the back yard.

"The sofa is full of them," Al puffed with the effort. "It is so damn slippery; can't get a proper grip!"

"Why are your gloves wet?"

"Well what do you think it is?" Al shook his head. "The thing is wet through with them, no wonder it was stinking in there."

I left them to it and resumed my cleaning duties.

Later that day I went upstairs to look inside the desk again. Taking out the certificate and the scrap of paper I attempted to concentrate. It was to do with the name Tadek. I was sure that it was Dad who had said that he had never been told about the date of Sally's wedding. Perhaps he had been at sea when they had been married and she knew he couldn't attend. Possible, but then they had always been so close it didn't really make sense. And no church wedding which suggested haste, or was it that as Marion being Polish and a Catholic they couldn't agree about a Church of England service and had left things so late. Perhaps he had to apply for special permission. Somehow I wasn't getting anywhere.

Go back to Tadek and his name. Why was that special? Who had chosen that name? Was it a family name on Marion's side? His father perhaps? I looked at the certificate. Marion's father was…Hilary.

Perhaps a friend of Marion? A friend! That was it! Suddenly I had remembered. There had been another Polish airman; a pilot, and his name was Tadak. Everything came flooding back; why had I not remembered before? She had been sweet on this Tadek and there had been talk about an engagement. So why had she married Marion? Did Tadek die on one of his missions? This had been discussed when Heather had wanted to do the family tree all those years ago. Nearly forty years had gone by and I was trying to recall things said at that time. Yes, Sally had talked about her pilot Tadek to Dad. I was positive that this had been said. So perhaps Tadek, the pilot, had died or he had ditched Sally for someone else.

Too much supposition. I needed more evidence. In the desk I pulled out letters from the hospital to Sally; something about salaries and pensions, letters in blue envelopes from Marion to her with postmarks of the 1960's, another brown envelope. Inside was a thin pink certificate; a birth certificate. Whose? Excitedly I unfolded the paper. Could it be Tadek's? No it was Sally's; a certified copy of Rose Christiana Mary born in.........I couldn't believe it! She had been born in Willesley Green, Cranbrook, Kent and not in Nottingham. Only a few days ago I had completed her death certificate with the registrar and had now got two main facts wrong. Not only was her name incorrect, so was her place of birth. I had given her name as Rose Sally Christiana Mary when Sally was never a given name. Her father was listed as Rifleman 7363 2nd battalion Kings Royal Rifles and Railway watchman. Why were they living in Kent and not in Nottingham? That was strange. Were Herbert Payne and her mother Christiana living with the May family during her confinement?

Everything that I thought I knew was in a terrible complicated muddle.

In the next compartment was a small dark blue Aero diary and I opened it to find the date 1943. As I turned the pages it became apparent that she was waiting impatiently for a Tadek to speak to her and couldn't wait to see him again. A Flt/Sgt Bowen had said that she was the kind of 'girl that men dream about but seldom see' and that she was bored to tears with him until a little 'Polski officer' rescued her. Every day she commented about her health, her duties at the hospital, staying at RAF Hucknall, going to dances and the cinema, seeing her family, and about various men who were getting too serious for her liking and many times she wrote about how Marion was always 'talking his head off' going on about the future and wanting to be with her. She included sentimental poems by the popular Patience Strong which had been printed in the newspapers;

Yours Ever
Every moment brings you nearer
Every hour that passes by
Draws you closer to my heart
And speeds the day when you and I
Will walk together once again
With minds at peace and hearts content
Looking out into the future;
Hopeful, happy, confident
Bitter is this separation
But my thoughts are all with you
Faithful to the pledges given
To my promise always true
In a swiftly changing world
Love changes not with joy or pain
Whether parted or together
Yours forever I remain

She put in pressed flowers, four-leaved clovers and cuttings from magazines. On the 4th March she made an almost illegible comment about; 'it will be Sally if girl and Tadek if boy'. The pages were filled with comments until the 15th September when suddenly all the entries stopped.

Tucked inside the back cover was a signed photograph of Tadek Ciszcwski. A lean young uniformed man stared wistfully out at the camera. His lips were full and his hair combed back from a crow's beak. Was this the Tadek of her dreams? On the 24th September she wrote, 'I wish I knew for sure and really what to do'. If she had found out that she was pregnant on 15th September why was she so desperate? Was this child Marion's or Tadek's?

Then as I took out another scrap of paper it contained the date and details of the child's birth but then I looked again at the entries and found that she had written:

'Thurs 11th Great fun and games all day, pains worse, took two tabs. Violent pains started 1pm. Vomiting and continued pain. No start 5.30 until at last 8.30 T born about 10pm. What a sight 7/8 dead 1/8 alive.

Fri 12th Mum came brought lots of bits feeling lousy (cried why).'

Marion could not be with her as he was attending her cousin Joan's wedding on the 13th with the family oblivious to the fact that she had just given birth the previous day.

She continued to write up the account of each visitor and the type of flowers that they brought in for her, and then on the Wednesday 17th *'The umpteenth letter from poor old M.'*

By the following week she reported that T was *'looking more like a human being'* and on the 19th wrote starkly, *'news on the wireless rather startling; 76 Allied RAF prisoners of war shot in Germany. Poles have had smashing victory in Italy.'* By the Sunday she received her visitors with good humour. *'Mum, Dad, Rudolf, Tom and Laura arrived; my God what a crowd _ Rudolf gave Tadek 10/-.' And by the 25th of May she noted: 'Paid up and ready to go. Taxis came at 2pm home about 2.30.'*

In Germany on the 24th March 1944 there had been a breakout of 76 RAF and Allied POW's from the Stalag Luft III POW camp in Germany. At first it was argued that 50 had been shot whist attempting to escape but it was finally found that they had been murdered by the Gestapo after they had been rounded up. Three managed to escape completely and the rest were returned to the camp. It took a few weeks for the event to be uncovered and it was finally announced by the BBC in May. This was named the Great Escape. D Day had yet to take place in June. Finally, in the July, Anthony Eden the Foreign Minister announced in parliament that the perpetrators would be brought to justice. After the war a special team of RAF investigators did find some of the perpetrators and they were brought to justice.

What an odd mix; of sentimental poetry, a secret birth, against the backdrop of the horrors of war; bombings and massacres. No wonder normal behaviour was out of kilter and yet the cultural taboos that surrounded a child born out of wedlock were still very real. Perhaps her own mother and father had not been made aware of Sally's wedding date, thinking that she had been married earlier in the Autumn of 1943, and believing that Tadek had been premature instead of being late. And what had been Sally's state of mind knowing that Tadek had been the second child to have been conceived out of wedlock. Yet another secret to be kept. She had used Marion to cover her tracks knowing that he continually irritated her and jarred against her sensibilities but there had to be a father for the child and she needed to be married. But the audacity of choosing the name Tadek was quite staggering. Did she insist that it was to honour the death of a mutual friend? How had Marion been so blind about her passion for Tadek; how had she concealed that from him? Surely her friend Ivy and his friend Rudolf knew something, or perhaps they conspired in their silence with her against him.

In the desk there was a thin drawer. It resisted my first tugs and then shot free. Inside there were some thick papers. I opened one. Inside there was a beautiful seductive portrait of Sally, aged about twenty, tall and slim. Wearing a long fitted gown, her face slightly averted, she gazed over her left shoulder, smiling into the distance. It was such a shock. I had never seen her looking so glorious. I could see why men had swooned at her feet. She was an exotic mix; cool, clever, sometimes passionate and seemingly unobtainable. Marion must have been blindly in love, unable to believe that she had finally accepted him; he, like so many other young men before him, must have found himself head over heels and totally captivated by her. Perhaps he did know the truth but chose to believe that they had a chance together. She had the ability to persuade, despite all the times that she had been scornful and disparaging and he still returned gratefully to her side to do her bidding. Her personality was so strong and vigorous; she was impossible to resist once she had decided upon a course of action. He would have been swept up in the intensity of the excitement. The chance to hold her in his arms and make love to her would have thrilled him. She had the power to make him a man and yet reduce him to a boy, so he took his chance.

I took out more large portraits of her. First she was dressed in late Victorian costume holding a parasol, then as a flapper, next in a fur-lined astrakhan coat, and then in a ball gown styled in the 1930's. Somehow these portraits showed a more innocent charm. She still looked beautiful in each one; turning over the first picture it was inscribed 20th November 1932. She would have been just seventeen. There was the name 'Peacocks' above the date. I realised that I had been told that she had worked for a store in Nottingham with that name. I think it had been a dress or a milliners shop.

So Sally had commissioned a series of prints of herself dressed in the fashions of different eras. Here was another side of her that I didn't know had existed. That she had been interested in fashion was at odds to the haughty distain that she had shown of overt femininity. Yet there she was again, holding seductive poses, her large liquid eyes gazing up from a coyly lowered head. It was as if she had a compulsion to reinvent herself in every picture. Which was the true Sally or was she the sum of all these personalities?

Underneath a bundle of more letters there were more photographs in cardboard sleeves. Another sultry portrait of Sally stared at me but this time it was just her head and shoulders. Her hair was carefully waved and two large 'buns' were plaited at either side of her head. Turning it over to look at the date I found a torn piece of printed newsprint that had been stuck to the back.

"Daily Mail"
National Beauty Contest
Name...................Nurse Sally Payne
Address ....RSI Woodbeck
.........................Near Retford
.........................Notts
Competition...........Face

State section for which photograph is entered:
(Face, Hair or Smile)
I would like to be trained as:-

Sally had not ticked the box 'I would like a film test' but for the choice of Mannequin, Beauty Expert, Manicurist or Hairdresser she had ticked the box for the Beauty Expert.

I found myself smiling back at her. You dark horse Sally; wanting to be trained as a beauty expert! I am sure that she must have entered this for devilment, just to see how far she could get. If I had said to her that I wanted to go into hairdressing or be a mannequin she would have snorted with derision at the idea. Yet there she was, as large as life, entering a beauty competition. What next? It was a veritable Aladdin's Cave of surprises.

Yet I really should have anticipated this muddle and confusion of identity; only months before her death she had informed the neighbours that she had been born at the foot of Snowdon. When they told us it had been difficult to keep a straight face, we had shrieked with laughter for much of the way home, winding our way along the Denbigh to Mold road. "Perhaps she would like to be buried with Gelert the faithful hound," Al had suggested. That set us off again.

"'Here lies Llewellyn's descendant Sally Rose Christiana Jurczyszyn-Jay née May Wynne,' et cetera. 'She never spent a Christmas outside Wales until she was seventy-two!" Al intoned as I giggled helplessly.

"Oh look, Bronwen; a dear little baby girl here at the foot of Snowdon. The stork must have dropped it on his way back from Narnia!"

"And what is this that she is wearing round her neck? A silver love spoon, entwined with the two masks of tragedy and comedy forsooth. Methinks she must be of noble birth!"

"We will place her with a humble family in far off Nottingham so that she can come to no harm."

Our stupidity lasted for most of the journey that evening.

....

The Denbigh 'clean out' took months. During most of the time the other feral cats of Sally's kept their distance. We were able to feed them but they were still wary of our presence. Marcus continued to rampage around the house on his killing spree but despite our best attempts to open all the windows and air the rooms the acrid smell still lingered. We once again enlisted the help of Yvonne and Phil and together with our friends Reg and Margaret from Mold, we filled just over five hundred bin bags with an assortment of ruined clothes, videos, books, kitchen paraphernalia, bed linen, broken ornaments, carpets and rugs, and bags of nibbled pictures, photographs, letters and files. Those things that we thought we could salvage we washed and boxed. Her son Tom came and stocked up his car with odds and ends, treasures, and the modern grandfather clock, and on leaving resembled the car featured on the BBC 'Antiques Road Show' with the long-case clock sticking up out of the car.

Finally, most things had been boxed or dumped, leaving the attic and the outhouses to be investigated. Al couldn't face the attic on his own and said that he needed another strong pair of arms to lower some of the heavy items down from the attic and into the bedrooms. Our son-in-law Chris volunteered his services and later that summer whilst I harvested her rampant runner beans, broad beans and raspberries in the front garden, Chris and Al heaved the pictures, crates and boxes through the small attic aperture and completed to fill the two larger bedrooms that we had only just emptied.

We stared at the clutter that had spread itself across the two rooms, hardly able to believe that so much had been stored up there. We were once again faced with the prospect of sorting it all, going through it carefully for any important treasures and memorabilia and then cleaning those things that were going to be sold or kept. Our hearts sank at the prospect. We had spent so many months doing just that for the main house and still we hadn't tackled the outhouses.

In one battered old suitcase we opened it to find fine laced and satin underwear in lilac, pink and blue. Delicate slips and petticoats lay nestling in the remains of tissue paper. That Sally had owned such things was difficult to believe; that she had worn them was quite beyond our understanding. Sally had always despised such overt femininity.

We had had to return items that she had ordered just prior to her death. Expensive rings were sent back as there was just no money left in her bank account to cover the cost of them. Various societies and charities had also had to have their requests turned down as there was no money left to pay for good causes and raffle tickets that had been delivered with alarming regularity. Every donkey, pony and wild life sanctuary in Great Britain had beaten a path to her door requesting help with their work; it was quite staggering how many there were and how many we had never heard of before. We cancelled ongoing subscriptions to 'This England', some gardening magazines, the WWF, the Radio Times and the many steam railway societies that she had joined; being a shareholder in name only to some. She would have never realised a return on the shares but societies like the Llangollen railway provided free train tickets to her as a shareholder and life member, which pleased her sense of propriety.

As we worked in the house her feral cats became emboldened and would come to the house whilst we were there, although they still would not allow themselves to be stroked, and any sudden movement would send them leaping back into the garden, hiding under bushes where they would watch us with wary eyes.

Downstairs the rooms contained various boxes and crates crammed with china, paintings, ornaments, kitchen ware, lamp shades, and other artefacts that we had decided would be taken to auction. And the pieces of salvageable furniture stood around in each room waiting for the van to take them away. The family members had been asked what pieces they would like. Coins, silver and jewellery, decorated limited edition plates and embroidered linen had been distributed as keepsakes to family members but still there was a vast amount of junk that needed to go. Old battered suitcases that were never going to go on another holiday stood empty. It was a forlorn collection that finally was loaded onto the furniture van. Two strong local lads drove up the drive one early morning. Mum and I were in the garden still picking the remaining garden produce. Marcus was lying amongst the large onions that had yet to be lifted and watched as we walked over to the men to acknowledge their arrival. It was another glorious day. The trees were in full leaf, providing a nice amount of shadow as we bent down to reach the peas.

We explained that there was a great deal of things to be loaded but it wasn't until they saw for themselves that they realised that we had not been exaggerating.

"All this lot for just one woman!" They shook their heads in disbelief.

"And this doesn't include the outhouses, we haven't started those yet," we explained.

By midday they were showing signs of heat exhaustion. Heaving the pianos onto the lorry had sapped their strength. We kept up a steady supply of lemonade and refreshments but they were plainly overwhelmed by the task that loomed in front of them. We felt quite guilty to witness their weariness; almost feeling the need to apologise for the task in hand. Finally the last piece was loaded up and then they attempted to drive back down the drive but found that the turning was more difficult than it had been on driving in, for some inexplicable reason. It was as if the van itself had gained in size now carrying its full load, which was nonsense, of course. Two very weary men finally negotiated the van onto the road and turned for home that evening. They probably spent the rest of that week recounting to their friends and family about the day spent emptying a house in Denbigh.

A few weeks later we began the outhouses. In the first area it housed mostly garden furniture, parasols, chairs, hand tools, a ten foot tree lopper, an extendable fruit picker, rolls of chicken wire, bamboo canes, rolls of log paving, earth sieves, a heavy red rotovator complete with battery and other expensive equipment. The other side was piled to the ceiling with boxes and trunks. We could just make out the shape of an old cream Aga and a rusty old oven behind them, and a dilapidated desk and a cupboard containing papers and files from Denbigh Hospital were propped against one wall.

I had never realised that there was another back door to a separate part of the outhouse and as we pulled that open we found old rusting leaded windows in beautiful octagonal designs. Piled against the wall were ceramic tiles and wood block flooring, brown glazed rounded edging stones, milk churns and a collection of very old wide-necked milk bottles. Crates of them were stacked precariously on one side, threatening to overturn as we attempted to back out of the little cobwebbed shed.

We could only wonder what plans she had in mind for such a collection of things. Al had attempted to lift the rotovator.

"Bloody 'ell, it weighs a ton!" he gasped.

"Leave it or you'll have a hernia!"

We went back to the right-hand side part of the outbuilding and started to prise apart some of the boxes that had crushed the boxes wedged beneath them. As we lifted out the top one, we found heavy crockery wrapped in newspaper. The crockery revealed their shapes. A rich purple face stared from one beetroot-shaped pot. The next celery designed jug, on turning around, also displayed a face.

"My God they're horrible!" said Al disapprovingly.

In the box must have been half a dozen pots and containers each fashioned as a gaudy vegetable; a turnip, cauliflower or potato.

"Well somebody must love them," I spoke without conviction.

We heaved the box to one side and gingerly opened the next box. It contained more of the same.

"There's a veritable garden of them," we giggled.

The next box had been considerably squashed but once again the items had been carefully wrapped, this time in tissue
paper. Al unwrapped the first piece gingerly; inside nestled a piece of pastel green Carlton ware decorated with foxgloves.
The next piece was a large dish of the same design but a large piece had been chipped off.

"Oh what a shame,"

I recognised the china from the BBC Antiques Road Show. Another smaller parcel contained a tiny spoon with the bowl snapped off. "All these pieces must have been here for ages and then this other stuff dumped on top.

Oh what a shame!"

Three boxes contained various Carlton ware in varying degrees of preservation. Underneath them a box housed fine glassware; dainty blue Edwardian style wine, champagne and liqueur glasses. Those with slender stems had suffered badly. Why had Sally collected wine glasses when she was so opposed to drink? And they were blue.

We mimicked her, "I can't abide anything blue and certainly wouldn't give it house room. Your sister likes blue doesn't she?"

We continued to unearth treasures. What were we going to do with this lot? Finally the last box was set aside and a battered trunk emerged as the last layer.

"Enough for one day," Al announced, "Let's get some fish and chips on the way home." We left the wooden trunk for the following day.

245

Sally & Amos; the note confirming her pregnancy in Oct '43; Arthur Fuller with Tom their son; Sally in costume (abt. 1930

Chapter 18 Inheritance and history

Nature or nurture? The eternal question that has puzzled many psychologists.What had shaped Sally and the rest of the May and Payne family? The Mays had been involved in flora and fauna for two generations and yet my father said that they held no interest for him. I could never walk in a park or wood without having to touch a leaf or gaze at a tiny wild flower; a chance of seeing a squirrel close up still had the power to enchant me.

So what is it in us that makes one person desperate to entertain, sing and tell jokes and another happy to work diligently in a quiet space without the company of others? Do we inherit the passions and interests of our forbears or is it all a matter of conditioning and living in close proximity with other family members and absorbing the stories of the past? And how did Sally's character develop? Was it due to the inherited genes of the Mays and Payne's or was she shaped by the pressures and tensions of her upbringing. Did the politics and fashion of the 1930's weave their influences on her intellect and emotions or did the intensity of war challenge her natural inclinations and aspirations? She had natural intellectual intelligence; she could absorb detailed information and disseminate the facts. She could utilise that knowledge and relate it to other facts. She had a phenomenal memory and was able to quote back things that she had read weeks or years before and yet her emotional intelligence was fragile. She liked to have power and used it wisely on a professional level but in relationships she tyrannised those who worshipped her. As a young woman she was very attractive, being tall and slim with regular features, dark wavy hair and large round grey blue eyes. As a mature woman she was proud of her trim figure.

"When I was young I had an eighteen inch waist," "she would boast, and yet she could not abide chatter and gossip and despised 'female' conversation. She was attracted to powerful, intelligent men but hated to be dominated by them. Her sense of humour was not apparent. I can't ever remember her doubling up with laughter or giggling at a joke. Her sense of fun was a fairly dull affair. Whilst Tadek, her son, would wheeze and laugh until tears ran down his face Sally would remain quite distant, and yet when she 'held court' everyone in the room would listen to her performance.

Around children she looked uncomfortable and they seemed wary of her. She watched from a distance. I never saw her encourage David, her grandson, to play with her or to enter into his games. And when he was engaged in play in her company she seemed to be assessing him for his skill, prowess or understanding. The concept of her being able to gather a child in her arms and smother him with kisses was quite ridiculous.

Had she been happy and carefree as a child or had she always been grave, reserved and older than her years? Her brother Amos had been more than happy to lead his two girls in childish pursuits. He made us bows and arrows so that we could go hunting with him. He led us on sledging expeditions in the snow and engaged in our games. He lost himself in the games of chess and playing cards, making us theatres and forts and encouraging our artistic skills. As children, Amos and Sally probably knew something of their father's unhappy childhood with his violent father. Charles Payne, a miner, and his plump Scottish wife Mary produced a large brood of ten children. As a youth Herbert and his brothers had not only had to fight his own father but had also been embroiled in brutal skirmishes during his army days in India. Herbert was a stern disciplinarian and all in the household suffered from his uncontrolled outbursts. His temper was not improved by the lack of money and he watched every penny that was spent, resenting every outlay of funds. Chrissie had spent her childhood in more cosy surroundings. She had witnessed at close quarters the life style of the owners of the large estates for whom her father had worked. She had more contact with nature and appreciated being in the countryside. She must have hated the 'back to back' house in Nottingham where she was brought to by Herbert. Her southern accent would have been resented by her neighbours. Certainly my father Amos remembered with some wry bemusement how his teachers had whacked his knuckles when he spoke with a Kentish accent after a short holiday spent with the May family.

"It's not barth lad, it's a bath!" And the strokes of the ruler accentuated each word. Although one Amazon female teacher preferred to chastise his southern ways with thumps into his spine, which allowed him to receive a two-way punishment as each stroke to his back sent his stomach into the unforgiving desk in front of him and so he ricocheted backward and forwards until she was satisfied that he could adopt the acceptable mode of Derbyshire dialect.

Sally always spoke with a very pronounced Derbyshire accent so perhaps she was able to blend in more easily after her sojourns in Kent. Perhaps she displayed more strength of character and people saw and respected her independent spirit.

Later, when she went to live in Wales she became more bohemian, happy with her own company. We could never call unannounced and on the rare occasions when we did pop in because we had been passing by she let her displeasure at being interrupted show. Her love was in tending a garden. She planned and researched the varieties that would be sown and her fine long fingers would always show signs of recent gardening; the dirt lodging in the cuticles. Avidly she watched the Chelsea Flower Show, visited nurseries and garden centres, always on the lookout for the exotic and rare. Was this due to her natural inclination or a desire to emulate her grandfather? I think it was in her blood. She was drawn to the natural world like a moth to a candle. I believe that it must have been in them both.

Then there was the tendency of being overwhelmingly generous on one occasion and then begrudging a penny spent here and there. When we took her to Bodnant Gardens she imperiously informed the startled attendant that she had life membership and had been a member for countless years. When the attendant questioned her and asked her to produce the card or pay the fee she had to admit to not carrying it with her. We could see that a full blown battle was about to commence as she drew herself up to full height. Al quickly whisked her away whilst I struggled to calm down the offended National Trust volunteer, paying the money that was due for the entry fee and apologising profusely for the misunderstanding. Sally was indeed a life member, but the fact that every volunteer manning the entrance to each property would not be aware of that, escaped her. She still believed that each AA man on the road should offer a salute as she drove by as she had fastened her original AA badge to each successive car that she owned. That the combined speeds of two cars passing would be in excess of eighty miles an hour and the fact that most AA men drove around in vans not encased in leather leggings and wearing goggles whilst riding on a motor bike, seemed to have also escaped her.

She delighted in carrying a trug filled with her fresh vegetables and fruit from the garden and presenting them to us on her visits. On the occasions when purchasing from a farm shop she almost invited the assistant to carry her goods to the car, and sometimes the suggestion was actually carried out. Sally was born to be served and somehow she found many willing servants amongst us.

In the family members, Dawn, her granddaughter, most physically resembles her, being tall and slim. My sister Heather still has the same penchant to gather and collect objects around her and is happy in her own company. Sally's son Tom and my father had the same voice tone and shared some musical prowess, more developed and trained in Tom and very apparent in Tadek who had the flamboyant skill of a confident jazz performer. They all loved steam trains although it was my father who showed a real talent for making them, producing beautiful modelled and faithfully replicated 'black five' engines in his small and cramped workshop.

Sally's grandfather May wrote with flair and emotion, demonstrating the grand style, and Sally wrote in a similar fashion. Amos, her brother, favoured a more poetic style but his letters were often awkward and hesitant; he was conscious of his poor spelling, his punctuation haphazard. Sally's letters flowed with ease; she did not seem to strive, her letters exhibited a stream of consciousness as if she cared little for the effect her words would have on the recipient.

Families have shared mannerisms, modes of speech, shared shorthand of memories and jokes that are a mystery to the outside world. It would be unreasonable to think that Sally had not inherited certain traits and views, and that in growing up together, similar interests would not develop. Experiences of poverty certainly affected my father. He feared debt and dare not take risks with employment despite being over qualified for so much of the work that he did. The memories of seeing the out of work miners, squatting on their haunches as they talked to each other at the end of his street haunted him. Sally was more circumspect and confident in applying for different positions. But whereas for my father his family was his world, Sally could not be constrained by domesticity. She liked the idea of family and tradition but railed against it when she perceived that it would imprison her.

Tom grew up in the shadow of Sally and Amos. He must have been quite lonely when they excluded him from their company. For him his family and his wife Nellie became his source of stability. How much he must have resented Tadek when he realised that his childhood had been an entire masquerade is difficult to assess. Even as an adult he had been denied his rightful place as her eldest child. No wonder his visits to Denbigh had been infrequent. Sally looked down on Nellie although she had been more than happy for Nellie to take on the housework for her father Herbert. She was equally dismissive of Olive, who was the wife of her cousin Bill May. Again she had been happy to let Olive do the housework for Herbert and let Tadek play with Olive's children, and yet when it came to the time when she needed a more permanent arrangement for Tadek she wrote that she did not think that Olive would be 'suitable' to provide the proper care for him.

....

The secrets of the trunk had to be investigated. Would it contain yet more china, crockery and glassware? We opened it up. The musty smell that escaped proved that it had been kept closed for years. Would it prove to be Pandora's Box or just plain disappointing? We looked inside. Large framed photographs, peeling and torn, were stuck together bound by age. The faded sepia print showed a young uniformed Herbert standing behind his seated wife, Chrissie, holding her child Sally by her knee. The little child stared solemnly at the camera. Another large framed print depicted Herbert with the Kings Rifles Regiment. Then there was a little worn leather purse. I turned over another photograph, unframed and badly torn. A young woman posed by her bicycle. She wore a long heavy dress and a feathered hat. At her waist was caught a purse fastened by a little chain. It was her purse. As I looked closely at her I recognised her features. Sally's Aunt Lottie, the woman who had born an illegitimate child, William May, and then died the following year. Charlotte Mary May. How had such things survived through the upheaval of moving? How had Sally taken possession of these things? Her mother Chrissie must have brought them back with her to Nottingham after her own mother had died. Under some more photographs of the May family standing outside a grand house were little envelopes. Carefully I opened the first one. It was written in pencil and the writing had faded with time. It was by Mary Charlotte, Sally's grandmother. She wrote about her concerns about Chrissie's health and her little ones needing to see a doctor. Another letter informed Chrissie and Herbert that they were being turned out of their cottage and that the police had been called. What was this! I had imagined a wealthy grandfather well set up after his work as head gardener in stately homes. How had the family sunk so low? What had caused their ruination? I was shocked and saddened by the revelations. The May family had been held in such high esteem, for Sally had spoken of how important they were. Now here they were being portrayed as little more than beggars having all their belongings piled onto a cart.

I realised that we were running out of time to sift through all the memorabilia. The urgent priority was to clear the house and get ready for a sale. We decided to leave the items inside the trunk and take it back to our garage. There was so much left to do. The box would have to wait.

From top left: Sally and her mother Chrissie; Sally, Amos and Tom; Marion (best man) at Amos and Joyce's wedding,1944, with Joan.

Top: Tom and Nellie's wedding, 1950, with Tadek as their pageboy.
Far left: Olive and Bill (William) May (son of Charlotte May) who, as a child lived with Amos and Mary May in Kent, then as a youth, went to live with Chrissie and Herbert.
Above right: the Payne family in Nottingham about 1950: Herbert, Sally, Tom, Chrissie, and Tadek in the foreground.

The painting is reputed to be that of John, who served in the Navy and his brother Amos May, born in 1833. The back of the picture is marked 'Valletta, Malta'. Joan's father, (Sally's uncle) gave her the painting.

Below: Charles Payne and his Scottish wife Mary with Herbert. Herbert Payne played both the violin and this mandolin.

Some early pictures of Sissinghurst Castle and Cranbrook High Street. Amos May worked at Bedgebury Pinetum, just outside Goudhurst, Kent, featured on the left. He may also have worked at Sissinghurst castle before Vita Sackville-West purchased the property.

Chapter 19 Pandora's box

I had spent six years going through letters, photographs and paperwork, attempting to make sense of the profusion of information. I consulted family members of their recollections and started an intensive compilation of the family tree via the internet. For the first few years there was set-back after set-back as dates and information refused to be reconciled. The Payne and May ancestors were determined to remain in the shadows. I read through all the correspondence between my father and mother during the war years and went through envelopes and albums of photographs piled into large stacking boxes, attempting to identify the individuals who stared back at me.

The family tree work progressed. Pictures and certificates were scanned and the censuses from 1841 to 1901 were searched. We visited the Family Records Department in London and the National Archives in Kew. I spent fruitless hours in the Maidstone Town Hall. It became finally evident that most of the stories were based on myths. Names were incorrectly spelt or transposed and locations just plainly wrong. Summers were spent poring over the evidence, and winter evenings saw me sitting for hours at the computer only to be discontinued as everyday life beckoned.

Finally it appeared that I had found as much as there was to find. The ancestors for both sides of the family had been traced and inputted into the family tree file.

I began to write Sally's story, weaving in some stories that had been told by other members of the family. I used the correspondence and certificates to bind the picture of Sally together. All the memorabilia was housed in boxes by the study within easy reach. We had a new study built to make scanning and writing easier. I reread the letters and tiny delicate fragile scraps of paper again and again. I sat trying to recall conversations of the past as they wilfully slipped in and out of my mind. Sometimes startlingly clear other times so hazy and elusive.

I forgot about the box.

I had thought that it had been more or less excavated and had contained just the dusty and stained old albums of Victorian scraps and postcards, the formal photograph of Sally with her father and mother, Herbert with his regiment, the purse of Mary Charlotte, and the letters to Chrissie that I had removed, and that was about it. I was convinced that there had been nothing else that could be useful. The box stayed unopened in the garage, covered with plastic sheeting, forgotten.

....

It was only to retrieve the picture of Herbert, Chrissie and Sally that I decided to re-open the box. I thought it would be an opportunity to clean them up and put things in order. As I opened it up I had the strangest feeling that it was different. It was as if I had never seen things before. Had it been that all those years ago when we were dealing with the loss of Sally and trying to empty the house that I had formed an erroneous impression of the contents? Surely it was just the battered old picture frames and a few tattered postcard albums that were inside. I reached inside and took out a dusty grey cardboard box. I just know I had not seen that before. The box had a picture of an Egyptian sphinx and the words 'Charta Egypta'. As I looked closer there was a blue pencilled letter 'T' at the top and then a 'W' written at the bottom. I opened it up. A small stained wedding cake box sat on the top of some papers inscribed, *Tadek's curls 1946*. Inside nestled two brown coils of hair tied with blue ribbon.

I placed them back inside the box and put them to one side. Next was a badge with a metal embroidered phoenix rising from the ashes; a Polish airman's insignia? Underneath a folded piece of paper money; Eine Mark. It looked German. As I unfolded the next scrap of paper my heart contracted.

"RAF Station,
Abingdon 23/1/41,
Dear Sir,
I have just received your letter and it is with deep regret that I have to tell you that pilot Walczak Tadeusz was killed in an air accident a week before Christmas."

My head reeled. Tadeusz? 1941, killed in 1940. Which Tadeusz was this? Certainly not the one that she had been meeting in 1943. Were there two different men? I went back to the diary of 1943 and looked again at the photographs of Taduesz. One was inscribed on the back, 'Best love from your loving son Tadek Ciszewski' and as I looked at the other smaller picture I realised that they were totally different men. On the back it had 'Sally' and then a Polish greeting, signed Tadek.
I unfolded another piece of paper that lay in the box; this time written in Sally's distinctive hand.

Crashed Stratford on Avon

December 14th 1940

Buried Cleott College cemetery near Birmingham

By Father Horton of the college

Grave No 642

I went to the computer and typed in Tadeusz Walczak. The information came straight back.

'On 14th December 1940 Dragon AW173 (G-AEMI) of 7 Anti Aircraft Co Operation Unit crashed in forced landing at

262

Pillerton Hersey Pilot P/O Tadeusz Walczak and Sgt T Tubis, both Polish, both killed.'

Next in the trunk were two Royal Air Force passes from RAF Hucknall provided for Corporal S Payne, one dated 31st January 1941 and the other for March of the same year; the first valid for the month of February and the next for the month of April. She had been given two months compassionate leave.

I placed these to one side. There were one, two, three........nine envelopes addressed to Miss S Payne, either to 29 Albert Avenue in Jacksdale Nottingham or the WAAF detachment Hucknall, dating from the 27th August until the 8th December 1940. I started on the first letter,

Tadeusz wrote from the Officers' Mess at Hucknall, and described how he was longing to arrange a meeting to see her.

In the next letter he apologised for not being able to see her and of sending a colleague in his place but that despite explaining what Sally looked like, his friend did not find her. His letter exploded with frustration of not being able to get leave to see her as he planned their next rendezvous

'My only forever Sally,' it began on headed note paper, from 'T Walczak, Royal Air Force Station, Castle Bromwich, Warwickshire, 24th October 1940'. In small careful script he poured out his heart for his darling Sally, apologising for his poor English and lack of a dictionary to help him express his thoughts and longing for her.

'I cannot sleep for I see you in my dreams...........I am not belonging to myself now I feel that I have lost something, full of hot blood, yes I am sure, I am thinking of our future, yours for ever Tad.'

263

On the 30th October his next letter was composed in very good English. He wrote from the New Inn, Pembridge, near Leominster, Hertfordshire.

'Sally my darling,
…………..Sally! How I would be happy when I could see you in here, when I could look at your loved eyes, when I could keep you near my heart. Although sometimes life is sometimes very nice, sometimes it is cruel. I would like to ask you darling, ending this letter for sending my best remembrances to your parents, your brother ….remember darling, that somewhere in wooded hilly country, and far, very far away from you, somebody is thinking always of you and expecting your letter.'

By the beginning of November he was thankful that 'Lady Weather' sometimes allowed him some time off from flying and that he was thinking about his emigration from Poland. He was amused by her attempts to write in Polish and explained that the grammar was very complicated but that he too was having problems with translation as he had lost his dictionary.

During the middle of November he was stationed at Abingdon and wrote how busy he was but at least his luggage had been found and he had been reunited with his dictionary. He sent her all his love.

As he was so busy Sally was beginning to believe that he was forgetting her. He wrote to reassure her that he thought about her all the time.

'Every morning and every evening I am thinking about you. I putted your photograf on the writing table in my room and every time I am looking at it I remember you.'

He added that he was soon to be transferred to a place in Lincoln.

There was a note of distrust and discord in their next correspondence on 4th December when Sally suggested that he was cooling off and he wondered if there was someone else in her life. The difficulty of trying to see each other was proving to be a great strain on them both. They wanted to spend some time together at Christmas. Four days later, on the 8th, the silly misunderstanding was cleared up. He looked forward to meeting her brother, who was going abroad, before he had to go back to Hucknall and was hoping to arrange more than just 24 hours leave.

Just six days later, a week before Christmas, he was killed.

So the 'TW' on the sphinx box had been the initials for Tadeusz Walczak containing her treasured love letters from him.

Inside the wooden trunk box there was a rusty tin containing two dusty letters from Sally addressed to her mother. The first one, written on 1st August 1940, contained an amusing account of how Sally had tried to smuggle Tadeusz into the sick quarters at Hucknall for an illicit liaison but there had been an emergency call just as he had knocked on the door to say that someone was suffering from dysentery. That meant that the duty doctor had to be called and her poor Tadeusz (Taddy) was left outside kicking his heels for two hours, unable to gain entry. She completed her letter with the hope that he would attempt to see her again.

really it is all so funny I think I shall write a book about it after the war is over. . I do hope Taddy will be able to come tonight because the poor little man is awfully shy.

And then added a post script hoping that Moss, her brother, would complete a painting of the Hawker Hurricane,

Tell Moss if he does not do my Hawker Hurricane painting for the mantle piece soon, I shall die of a broken heart because I am simply dying to get it hung up.

Her next letter contained more serious news saying that she was going to respond to Tadeusz's offer of marriage and had discussed the business of her past history with him.

Old Moss kept his word and wrote me a letter as soon as he arrived and gave his address so I kept my word and sent him the photo. I am so glad he likes Tadpole [Tadeusz] because I have promised to give him a definite answer next week.

By the way he likes Moss very much. The other night he got very worked up and forgot himself, when I refused he was very, very, sorry and started to cry saying that he had never intended to insult me with such a suggestion and I really believe that he meant it.

What is more I have told him all my past history, and he was furious to think any man could possibly be so low as to make a fool of a young girl. I told him that was the reason I had not given him an answer before and he said 'I was not to even think about it any more as I was only a child'. But we must make sure that he never meets Arthur because I am afraid he would murder him.

One thing I an sure of if I refuse him my secret will be quite safe, He was absolutely overwhelmed to think I would make such a confession, but mother I had to because he could not understand why I was so cold with him even though I loved him (which by the way I know I do)......................Don't tell dad anything about this yet because I want to make sure before I tell him. Taddy wanted to give me some money towards keeping Tommy when he knew because he was sure I couldn't manage on mine but I told him it was alright you had always kept him for me and always would. He said,

266

'I am longing to see the little fellow, is he like you or his father' you know he really is a dear but I shall not bring him home until I have thoroughly made my mind up......................

PS I told him I thought it was only right he should know, because I did not think I had any right to marry anyone and he was furious, said he had never heard such nonsense, my life had been rough enough, he thought it was time I had someone to take care of me even if it was only to prove all men were not alike.

Beneath the tin box were two identically framed portraits; one of Tadeusz Walczak and one of her son Tadeusz. The serious, strong, hawk nosed face of Tadeusz, turned slightly to his left, stared into the distance. His lips were full and his hair was swept back from his high forehead. Was this the same face as was in the smaller print that I had discovered earlier? I placed the two pictures together. As I looked closer the differences appeared to mock my earlier casual conclusion. It was obviously not either of the men; it appeared to be a totally different face. Surely three different men; it didn't make sense. So I tried to reconcile the puzzle. She had been engaged to this Tadeusz and then had tragically lost him in 1940. By 1943 she must have met another Tadeusz whilst being pursued by Marion. Then in the September she had realised that she was pregnant and married Marion in the November. A couple of years later she had put her son's curls into a box with Tadeusz Walczak's letters and proceeded to put a large portrait of them both in identical RAF frames. She just had never given him up. He must have haunted her throughout her marriage to Marion; the husband whom she felt was unable to arouse her; to be sexually exciting, according to another piece of damning evidence in Pandora's Box.

Her love for Tadeusz Walczak had been untested; their passion was still fresh and exciting, the intoxicating frisson exaggerated by the dangers of war. She had kept alive a hopeless fantasy, trying to recreate him through her son Tadek. Death had snatched him untimely from her. He would never grow old; his youthful face would stare back at her reminding her of her loss. She would think of him as her impetuous, shy but heroic pilot who would have cared for her and protected her as only a hero could, in direct contrast to the reality of living with her husband who wearied her with his demands on her affection and their frequent clashes over money.

The second Tadeusz may have been a passing fancy; someone who tantalised her by his frequent absence. Again it was the thrill of the chase, the hope of being pursued and then to capture his heart just as she had been able to do with so many other young men; but a dangerous game to play with Marion so close at heel. Her reputation could have been ruined in an instant. The discovery of her pregnancy sharply reminded her of the vulnerability of women of those years. Unmarried motherhood was a despised position for girls to find themselves in and many hurried arrangements were made to escape discovery. It was all well and good playing fast and loose but to be shamed as being loose was not something that a working class girl could risk. Abortions were still illegal and dangerous. Those with substantial funds still had serious difficulties in finding a doctor who would be willing to carry out the procedure. The gin and hot baths methods were not reliable and a desperate 'do it yourself job' with knitting needles would have only been contemplated by those for whom life itself had lost all meaning.

And then there was the matter of age. She was no longer a mere slip of a girl who could plead inexperience or innocence. At the age of twenty-seven it would have been difficult to have reconciled her with the notion of seduction when the young men with whom she was associating were mere youths in their late teens and early twenties. She ran a serious risk of ridicule and scorn. Her parents had already brought up one son for her and it would have been impossible for her to have brought illegitimacy to their door. Besides, she was a well trained nurse who had studied anatomy and biology so to have not understood the importance of contraception would have been extraordinary. She was trapped and she knew it. Marion had been brought up in the faith of Roman Catholicism. For him sex outside of marriage was a sin. His attachment to his church was as strong and unshakable as his faith, his love of his family and for his tormented country Poland. Sally did not choose an option, she had it forced upon her, and had to accept the consequences of a loveless marriage. Tadek, born in 1944, remained an only child. They fought over him but left his upbringing to Chrissie and Herbert until Chrissie's health declined to such an extent that they had to farm him out to other family members. Chrissie was dead by 1956; her thin body ravaged by cancer. Marion and Sally had contributed a weekly sum of 10/- towards his upkeep to Herbert and Chrissie, reflecting the exact sum that his brother-in-law Moss sent up from Kent; Moss who was the sole wage earner supporting a wife and two children.

Then I found an envelope with a magazine article alongside a scribbled message which had never been sent,

Darling,

Please find time to read this article, study it, the advice is sound. Had we lived together perhaps we could have worked out our differences; but your stupid refusal to come out of the air force-to leave me to do all the planning- and then to turn round and tell me I had all my own way spoiled any chance we had in the past to get really close. When you did feel closeness to a woman it was not me. Now after our talk this weekend maybe that there is a chance because as I have told you I do

269

feel insecure and unwanted and I always have. I have lived on
Hope for years I can't any longer,
love Sally
PS You always say you are not very sexy this may well be true but
is it so, or is it that I am not and never have been attractive to you?
Be honest because you found energy for Barbara!!

The magazine article was entitled 'Sexual incompatibility_ the discord that leads to disillusionment'.
Pandora, your box contained some dreadful secrets.

As I delved in deeper in the trunk I found three dirty blackened illuminated certificates belonging to Christiana Edith May announcing her full attendance at school in 1905, 1906 and 1907. One dirty dishevelled photograph album threatened to dissolve as I attempted to bring it out for examination. The pictures were so faded and cloaked in grime it was almost impossible to distinguish any features. A large scrap book with its contents of postcards was in a similar condition as was another smaller black book, threatening to part company with its back cover. I carefully turned it over. 'Holy Bible' it announced heroically in patchy gold leafed script. I turned the flimsy front cover. 'Elizabeth Ann May, presented by her father on 20.2.75.'The writing in perfect copperplate ended with a flourish. I knew this name. She was the sister of Sally's grandfather, the distinguished gardener. Chrissie had obviously assumed ownership of the bible and had copied her name underneath. For some reason Elizabeth's sister Isabel had also had her name inserted with the date 1884.
So there was no large family bible and in fact there would not have been one showing any Welsh heritage as Amos, Ann, Cecilia, Elizabeth Ann and their brother Joseph were the children of Amos May, born in 1833, and his wife Ann, born in

1828. Amos May was born in Boxley, Kent, near Maidstone, and his wife came from East Peckham. Sally had known that this small, insignificant bible was in the trunk. She knew its contents well. The fiction of a huge bible inscribed with the Welsh ancestry was pure concoction. My research into the May family had been vindicated by this find. I had no other source documentation prior to this bible that these siblings and Amos May,1854, were of the same family, only that they were listed together in the various censuses and that Amos May, 1833, was a nursery man and plant propagator.

Sally had brought the trunk back from Nottingham with her and knew its contents well. She knew that Herbert and Chrissie's family pictures and their odds and ends were kept in it and added her own things. Time had not been kind to the contents, first homed in the dirty unkempt surroundings of Herbert, her father's, house and then being consigned to the damp outhouse in Llanrhaeadr.

And then there were her diaries written in the early fifties. Constantly the refrain of hopelessness and weariness of her life was bleakly recorded. 'I am so tired' or 'I feel that I am trapped' appeared over and over again. Her life had appeared to be so glamorous. She had money, status and position, and seemed so successful in achieving her goals yet even then with a young child and only ten years into marriage her life was unravelling from the web that she had woven. Perhaps she did not have the nature for marriage; for certainly domesticity did not suit her. Her aspirations for promotion drove her to take more exams and yet the ordinary day-to-day routine of work depressed her. She noted her patients' developments and improvements and yet seemed not to take pleasure from her occupation. She wanted more but nothing seemed to satisfy her. At times she appeared to note with some surprise that her own child had been a 'good kid' today, as if he was outside her life. And then there was her relationship with Edna. In her diary she appeared to look forward to their taking tea together and sharing home life and yet to Marion she complained about her

271

heavy handedness and her manner with Tadek. It was as if she practised some deception with her own feelings, wanting the help and support of a colleague and the very welcome extra revenue that having a lodger provided, but unable to control a destructive force within her. At first she welcomed the camaraderie and friendship but then cooled towards her as if afraid of getting too close. Once again her seesaw of emotions unbalanced the relationship. Marion could have been jealous of them sharing his home and making decisions that didn't include him or he may have merely been used as a pawn in Sally's tangled machinations. She perhaps wanted to have her own space in her home; the novelty of sharing time together having worn off, and subconsciously allowed Marion to give Edna her marching orders. Then, as he had taken the lead and done that which she had been reluctant to do, she resented his interference and flew to the defence of her friend.

Whatever were her motives and intentions it was certain that Marion could never second guess her. He would always find himself on the wrong foot and then be perplexed and angered by her change in stance. He was damned if he acted decisively and damned if he didn't. They both wanted to build a home that reflected their aspirations but somehow always ended up pulling in different directions.

Sally told him that she was tired of having to manage everything on her own but once again resented his interference when he was there.

And then there was love. Did she ever love him? I don't think so. Perhaps there had been some affection at first; some pleasure in seeing the adoration in his face and knowing that she had some power over him. But was there that strong magnetism that draws lovers together to the exclusion of all else? No, sadly probably not on her part. Perhaps the trauma of her first abusive sexual encounter had been too damaging. As a young woman she certainly had a romantic streak as autographed photographs of the film stars of the day, carefully preserved amongst her papers, bear testimony. She and her friends swapped photographs of each other as keepsakes and she pressed little wild flowers in between the pages of her diary to act as an *aidé memoire* of significant encounters and events.

Perhaps her first Tadeusz had provided that fission of passion that she found so elusive with Marion. She had needed someone who could lift her spirits; could be decisive without dominating her, whom she could respect and trust. Marion continually attempted to cajole and command but she found his attempts to be masterful irritating and futile. And who could compete with a dead hero?

When she left Nottingham she knew that there was nothing there to hold her. Perhaps she had finally decided that the deception of playing happy families took too much energy and that the freedom to be herself and start all over again would perhaps give her back some purpose and dignity.

Two months went by before I returned to the trunk. Family matters and a brief spell abroad interrupted my quest. I was impatient to scan some of the photographs that I had found for the family tree file on computer. I opened the box and once again the feeling of not seeing the contents before swept over me. It was as if they had been shifted around. The order was not as I had left it. My mind must have been playing tricks again. I took out the Egyptian box and there underneath were two small navy blue pocket diaries. Had I seen them before? Casually I flipped through the pages before studying the dates. Nothing that I read seemed familiar. The first, thicker, diary was written in 1947.

The brief lines on each page seemed to emulate the entries that I had read in her later diaries. The smaller diary was dated 1946. But I was impatient to find the photographs to scan and almost put the diaries to one side when a full page of writing written on the 9th February caught my eye.

I feel utterly fed up with life sometimes, I wonder why God so cruelly allows people like me to live on and on- I don't think I am ever to have happiness_ the only bright spot was, or ever will be, May to Dec 1940. Marian has at last told me the truth about his past- I felt very sick at the thought afraid our life together is doomed, I no longer feel safe in any way. Oh God why was I so foolish _if only he was older I would feel a little safer.

Set against a background of the long harsh cold winter of '47 she struggled to fetch hundred-weight sacks of coal and coke, reach work and return home despite unannounced bus and train strikes.

The end of the war in Europe in the May 1945 had been a source of instant celebration but the ensuing peace and a change to a socialist Attlee government had had little effect on the hardships faced by the ordinary families. Rationing continued just as harshly as before and the welfare state had yet to be introduced. Bread, potatoes, fresh fruit, cheese, milk, eggs, fats, meat and sugar were all in short supply. People bitterly resented the vast amount of necessary aid that was going into rebuilding a devastated Europe. The despised and distrusted prefabs were being built to rectify the housing shortage and there was wholesale animosity towards the lingering immigrants, resentment of the old order crumbling, fear about rising communism, strong anti-Semitism despite the pictured horrors of the concentration camps being shown at the cinemas, whispered fascism and concern about the nationalisation of the mines and railways. Stories emerged about the treatment of the people caught between the Soviets and the Germans. There were alleged atrocities and stories of massacres. Some spoke about a Cold War. People had expected a cessation of want and were unprepared for the hardships of peace. Some of the more fortunate children who had been evacuated to wealthy families brought stories of the war having had no effect in the more remote areas of the countryside and that indeed they had not experienced any rationing. This brought a new wave of bitterness to struggling families. People at work found themselves bickering over the fate of their enemies. For some, nothing short of annihilation of a nation would suffice. They wanted retribution; for somebody or some country to pay heavily for the state in which they now found themselves.

The heavy snowfalls in the February 1947 made the effects of industrial strife harder to bear. Any medical intervention meant paying out a fee to the doctor. Just one visit would result in handing over at least half a crown so the early symptoms of illness were ignored until they became acute.

Sally's health was compromised by coughs, colds and her crippling monthly pains which frequently resulted in her taking to her bed. The long hours at the hospital caused her feet to ache but more worrying was the effect on her mental health that living with her parents was having. Marion was stationed away. Sally and her young son Tadek lived under a cloud of rows and tension. She relied on Chrissie to look after the young toddler whist she was working shifts at the hospital and was constantly reminded of her obligation to them. The household strained against being able to contain a lively, inquisitive but spoilt three-year-old, a demanding, querulous husband, an antagonistic daughter and Tom, a young teenager. Chrissie became worn down under the strain and her health too was beginning to break down. She grew visibly thinner as the winter continued to keep them cooped up together inside the house.

It was no wonder that Sally longed for the return of her carefree flirtatious years and the summer of 1940 spent in the company of her beloved Tadeusz.

I went back to the 1946 diary and started to read more carefully. On the 14th January a dotted star appeared next to the date together with the entry 'saw Czy's in E'Wood'. I was intrigued; who was this? 'E wood' would be Eastwood but Czy? The usual routine of snow, frost, work, washing hair and feeling tired followed before the next remark made on the 28th spoke of their best man Rudolf having made plans to get married. I read on. Then on 2nd February Czyz's name appeared again, going with her to Map (Mapperley?). By the 6th of February she wrote that Czyz was at the house.

'Czyz here. More rows in house. Heavens I am sick of it.

And by the 8th she wondered if Czyz would be 'going overseas' and then arranged to meet him on the 16th but just missed him. She met him on the following Monday, the 18[th,] but noted that she was disappointed. On the 23rd she noted that Czyz was in a good mood. On the 25th she wrote that he was late home and then on the following day that he did not turn up at the Palais. On the 2nd March she went into Nottingham and put down £5 on the £45 silver tea set that she had previously seen, bought a serviette ring and put another £1 down on a tray and then said how pleased she was that Czyz came to the Hall.

By the 6th March she and Czyz went to the pictures to see 'Arsenic and Old Lace'. She went to the RAF Hucknall camp the following week to meet Czyz and on her birthday on the 15th March he gave her a frock.

The pattern of working, over-spending on shopping in Nottingham and rowing with Marion every time he returned home continued, as did her assignations with Czyz. He celebrated his birthday on the 24th March but she had to miss it because, as she remarked ruefully, she was working. Not a week went by when she was not commenting about Czyz.

In May she arranged to go down to Maidstone to visit her brother Moss and his family. Arrangements were made to stay at the 'Star Hotel 'in the town and she duly went along to Plains Avenue for tea and met her cousin Joan Sharp later that day. She had planned to visit Cranbrook and to meet up with an Ellen and Syd. Then just at the bottom of the entry penned on the 17th May she wrote that she had promised Czyz to "become a RC and that TJ would also become one". I could hardly believe my eyes. The next day she and Czyz went for a walk in Angley Woods and she remarked that she thought that he enjoyed it. Czyz was with her in Kent! Where was Marion during this leave of hers? How did the family not know that she was with him? Did she meet him down there and stay with him in Cranbrook?

How was it that she hardly ever wrote about her dearest son TJ and yet every other page mentioned Czyz's name? Was she having an affair, a brief flirtation or something more serious under the noses of her family, friends and husband? Suddenly, on the 1st June, a warning crept in; she and Czyz had a row and she said that she found the insurance money short, but unusually optimistic she wrote that things 'must go right one day'. As ever money and men, or bed and work, seemed the two tied constants in her life.

Then on the 19th June she wrote that Czyz had written home and had had a reply to say that there was good news as they (his family) liked the look of her.

Once again she managed to confuse me in her next two entries for the 28th and 29th June. On 28th she wrote,

Czyz came with me he gets worse all he can talk about is 'our future

and then on the 29th:

Czyz home all day nice to see him, made me late going to bed though, still who cares tired but not too unhappy.

Ominously by the late July Sally wrote that she and Czyz were rowing more often and wished that they could agree. She embarked on a Polish course in August; perhaps hoping that their communication would improve but by September Czyz was described as being in a 'blinding mood'. Things took an upward turn in October when she and Czyz went shopping into Nottingham and brought back the coveted silver tea service.

Running alongside this relationship with Czyz was her marriage to the unsuspecting Marion, whom she showered with presents, hoping that he would be happy with her choices of gifts. It was as if she had put her life into different compartments. She happily went shopping with Marion to buy a fur coat for herself despite all the money worries that she constantly claimed left her chained to a life of drudgery and unremitting work.

On the 18th December she and Marion had the 'row to end all rows'. Christmas came and went without comment and Czyz was conspicuous by his absence until the first entry in 1947 when they went to Nottingham and had a cup of tea at Billy's. Then on 4th January, she, TJ and Czyz went into Ripley and bought a hot water bottle for his mother in Poland before he accompanied her back to work at Mapperley Hospital.

On 3rd February she noted that it was still snowing and by the next day she was alarmed to find that TJ's temperature had risen to 103. It was confirmed by the next day, by the doctor who was called in to attend to him, that he had contacted pneumonia. Unusually Sally realised that she had to take time off work; she paid the doctor £1 for his visit and waited in for some coke to be delivered as the weather worsened. Being at home with TJ and Marion drove her to distraction. She was fuming about the fuel situation and felt that her work at the hospital was the only worthwhile thing in her life.

Once she returned to work she had a row with the staff nurse as the snow continued to fall. By March she had decided to purchase a watch and clock, Czyz returned to her diary, and still it continued to snow. She said that they had rowed before he went out to fetch the watch and clock. The weather again disrupted the transport system and Czyz had to walk home through the snow.On the 8th March she wrote:

'Came prepared to stay the week (at the hospital) if the weather does not improve. Ye gods what a year! "Snow for ever" should be the slogan.

By the end of March they were able to get out and about and she went shopping to buy sandals for herself and TJ and a fountain pen for Marion's brother Zygmunt.

In April she was allowing Marion to massage her feet and bring her breakfast in bed, reporting that Czyz was at home, that she was preparing chocolate Easter eggs for TJ and wishing that she did not have to go back to work. An Aunt who had rowed with her husband was also staying with them so there must have been a household of different personalities under one roof which made life difficult for everyone. She visited the Citizens' Advice Bureau and the Technical College about Marion but by the beginning of May the rows with him began again after she spent over ten pounds on a tricycle for Tadek. She noted that the differences in their temperament caused the divide and continued to see Czyz.

She had leave arranged for the middle of May saying that she had gone to RAF Hucknall to meet Czyz and then they had 'both gone' to the Technical College and that 'all was fixed'. The next day the journey to Portsmouth and then on to the Isle of Wight took place. Cryptically a bright dotted star appeared on the top of the page for 22nd May and continued to appear until the 25th when she and TJ returned home. She did not say if Marion came with them on the trip but seemed particularly pleased with herself. When one of her friends, who had been seeing a Polish Officer at Hucknall, was ill on 27th May, Sally noted that actually the friend had had a miscarriage, writing:

and I had to be very careful to cover it up

Marion was still uncertain about his 'move' and on 4th June she wrote,

'Ye Gods I wish our future would settle itself

and then cryptically on the following day

I wish I could finish- but I dare not risk it.

Finally she arrived home from shopping on 7th June to find that Czyz had been posted.

What a life

was her only comment on receiving the news, but the following day she noted that she had such a pain in her chest. By July she appeared to have made an assignation to see a Pana Szefa; on 12th July she wrote,

to Nottingham to meet F/Sgt Wieczorek -missed the bus (it was full) caught the train, we were late I was afraid Pana Szefa might be gone

By the beginning of August she wrote that things were still very unpleasant at home, and on the 9th the weather was lovely but the atmosphere was,

too thick for comfort

On the 11th she wrote ominously

saw Marion about the Rumours

And on 14th August she wrote,

wish Czyz was here to keep me warm.

The entries from then until they stopped in October seem to show that she and Marion managed to rub along a little better and she actually said at one point that perhaps things could be easier between them. She merely wrote of films that she had seen; how things were progressing at work, and about her colleagues who had been to see the Polish pianist, Henryk Mierowski, at the Albert Hall. Apart from having a leather coat altered and buying various clothes and gifts her entries ceased to remark on anything substantial.

And so, what to make of the diaries and her life? And then I finally realised! It was so obvious. Why had I missed it! Czyz was Tadeusz Ciszewski, the third man of the pictures in the diary. So there had been Tadeusz Walczak who died in the air crash in December 1940; then she had some romantic trysts

280

with another Tadeusz in 1943 just before she married Marion; and then in 1946 she met Tadeusz Ciszewski. Perhaps he became their lodger and the daily intimacy had produced romance for them both during those two bleak winters of 1946 and 1947.

It appeared that she liked the idea of romance but could not cope with commitment. As a young woman of just thirty-two, she felt trapped by her lifestyle and the constraints of living at home with her parents. She hated not having money and not being able to spend as she pleased. She yearned for her independence; liked the idea of a career without the daily grind; thought herself as being strong and self possessed and yet in reality she complained incessantly about not being well, constantly being tired and seemed to suffer very poor health with a multitude of concerns about bad teeth, aching feet, headaches, colds, pains in her chest and generally 'feeling lousy'. She managed to fit in trips to the cinema and shopping trips to the local towns which gave her a great deal of satisfaction, as did her liaisons with various young Polish airmen whom she met through friends at RAF Hucknall who were still attached to the service.

I put down the diaries and reached down into the box. This time I found a piece of folded black plastic. Thinking that it was a small wallet I opened it and there staring back at me were two photographs framed by the wallet. Tadeusz Walczak on the left and Sally on the right. Her dark coiled hair was swept up away from her young smooth face; her eyes held the camera and a faint smile lifted the corners of her finely painted full lips. They were both in uniform. His photograph appeared to be slightly at an angle and as I went to straighten it my fingers felt a piece of paper underneath the picture.

I pulled it out. It was a cutting from the newspaper.

'A Quiet Corner' By Patience Strong

281

Here on your grave I place the flowers you loved. Each flower a pledge of faith and constancy.....Grief yields to Time -but Love within the heart -lives and abides in sweetest memory. Drear is my world and dark without your smile. This is your grave - and yet......there are no dead. God, for some reason not revealed to me-beckoned you on a little way ahead.

Carefully I tucked the little cutting back under the photograph. There was no doubt at all. This was her Tadeusz whose life was cut short on that fateful December day in 1940.
She had ensured that they would remain side by side after death had taken both of them.

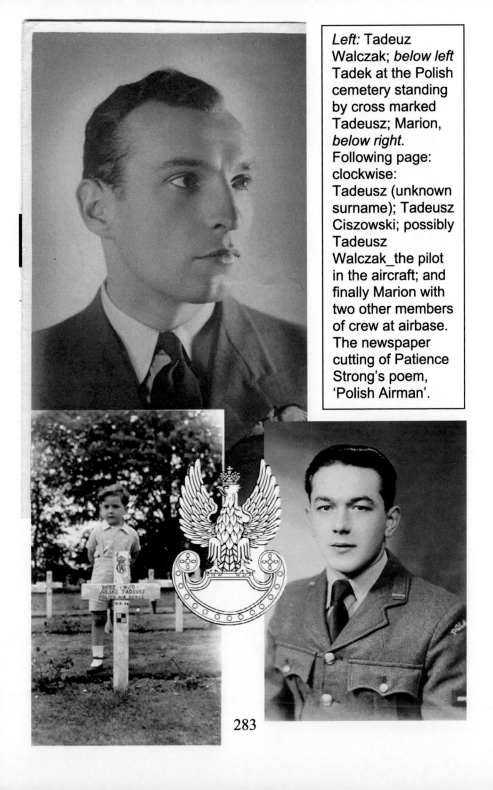

Left: Tadeuz Walczak; *below left* Tadek at the Polish cemetery standing by cross marked Tadeusz; Marion, *below right.* Following page: clockwise: Tadeusz (unknown surname); Tadeusz Ciszowski; possibly Tadeusz Walczak_the pilot in the aircraft; and finally Marion with two other members of crew at airbase. The newspaper cutting of Patience Strong's poem, 'Polish Airman'.

283

nd sits at a large mahogany

B. B. B.

284

Chapter 20 Summer 2008

Just as I thought that there was nothing else to add to my story of Sally a letter arrived from Hubert, the son of Zygmunt and nephew to Marion. He, his brother Marek and their father Zygmunt were travelling from Poland to Nottingham. They wanted to go to the Polish War Memorial site, to see Charlotte and their blood relative David and visit Marion's grave. They also wondered if there was any possibility that we could meet up. We exchanged emails and I invited them to stay with us for a couple of days.

Feverishly I began delving into the box of memorabilia to see if there were any photographs that I could give them. Once again I trawled through the letters, photographs, documents, postcards, newspaper cuttings, old birthday cards from Tadek's 4th and 5th birthday, invitations and other paraphernalia.

I scrutinised the small indistinct pictures of family gatherings, women in headscarves, men in uniforms, groups of people on snowy ski slopes and a couple kneeling in front of a priest. All were strangers, the only clue of their origin being a script of Polish and a date, 1946, 1948, or 1950, written on the back of each photograph.

Perhaps they would be pleased to think that Sally had kept and treasured them. I decided to sort them out.

I found pictures of Marion looking fit and athletic when he was stationed in Malta, postcards that he had sent to her, an aerial photograph of a ship purporting to be carrying Churchill on board, a picture of a group of men who appeared to be digging at a graveside; all pictures and bits and pieces that I had discounted as adding anything to my quest to find the essential Sally.

Then I was faced with a dilemma.

To Zygmunt and his family, Sally had been almost revered and I didn't want to shatter any of their illusions.

My recent findings in her 1946 and 1947 diaries had exposed her ex marital longings for romance during her early years of marriage with Marion and of course there were her earlier liaisons. Perhaps they had no knowledge of her other son Tom. How much had the family been told?

Sally in turn had always spoken with great affection of her Polish in-laws. Her visits to Poland with Marion during the late sixties had been a great success. She had attempted to learn some Polish and had been admired for her efforts and enthusiasm. They had thrilled to receive her into the family, wanting to protect her from the frailties of their wayward son Marion, pleased to show her their home in the forest and take her to places of national importance.

Now, here in 2008, were the three Jurczyszyn men wanting to meet with Tadek's son David and to renew their cherished memories of a dearly beloved Aunt and sister-in-law.

My quest to unravel her past had even called into question the ancestry of their cousin Tadek. It had almost denied them blood ties to both Tadek and his son David.

I needed time to think. How much had been to do with my own desire to create my own web of intrigue because it seemed more mysterious and exciting?

Could that be that Sally indeed knew that she was expecting Marion's child and that her dread was purely to do with the fact that her carefree days of freedom as an attractive, desirable single woman were over? Certainly the Tadek, whose name she had entered in her diary during the weeks of 1943 before the discovery of her pregnancy, seemed more absent than not. There was nothing in her diaries that suggested great intimacy with him other than the occasional dance or cinema date. And there again, even these meetings were few and far between. Had she been so desperate to rekindle the old romance that she had enjoyed with Tadek

Walczak in 1940 that she had managed to fool herself that this was more than just a brief flirtation. That indeed their relationship was merely platonic despite her romantic urge to take it to another level; and that in longing for romance and wanting to be cherished she had allowed herself to consummate her relationship with the ever vigilant and present Marion. She was staring into the abyss of marriage with a man whom she knew she did not love.

Many young women during those war years had allowed the uncertainty of tomorrow to tip them into unwise liaisons, and for some the outcome had been more terrifying than the one that Sally had found herself in. The infamous GI's 'over paid, over sexed and over here' had undone the strict morals of the time. Unmarried girls and married lonely women found to their shame that their 'intended' had intentions elsewhere. Their glamorous hero did not possess a fine ranch back home but in fact had a wife and child in a small city apartment waiting impatiently for news of their husband and 'daddy'.

With the Polish airmen, they were for the most part well educated, quiet, polite, and obsequious; a combination of qualities rarely to be found amongst the ordinary working-class man in Britain. The working-class girls were dazzled by the charm of the Polish men; humoured the easy manner of the 'yanks' and finally seduced by their strange and romantic sounding accents. If they had been subjected to that kind of treatment by more upper class British men they would have been more defensive and wary. 'What does he want and what do I have to do for it' would have been their first thought, followed rapidly with 'and what's in it for me?'

So I waited, with some faint misgivings for Zygmunt, Hubert and Marak to make their way from East Midlands Airport, near Nottingham, anxious to make them welcome and resolved to maintain a status quo. The past, as they knew it, would be left undisturbed.

Thinking that in some way they would be handicapped by strange road signs and with lack of local knowledge it was with some surprise that I saw them draw up outside the house within the appointed time of arrival. Their hired car's GBS system had guided them throughout the journey and had allowed them to visit the Polish War Memorial in Newark and to find their way to our Hawarden address situated in the Ewloe area without a problem. Three men stepped from the car. The tallest, whiskered Hubert introduced me to his distinctly sprightly elderly father and his dapper smaller brother Marek. We kissed, following the Polish tradition, and I could feel myself falling for their quaint courtesy and respectful familiarity. I struggled without success to see the similarity between Zygmunt and Marion as I ushered them into the house.

They had brought us carefully chosen gifts in return for our proffered hospitality and the thoughtfulness of their actions once again melted me.

That evening we sifted thought the dog-eared photographs and memorabilia that I had collected for them.

"Yes, here is Hubert as a baby, and there, yes it is me, Zygmunt". The old man smiled at me. He was tired from the long journey but determined to examine every picture. A baby swathed in bonnet and shawl smiled from its warm pram and a handsome dark haired man gazed back at the camera.

"It is my mother, and there my wife, Ludomira", Zygmunt formally announced, as I struggled to catch the strange sounding names whilst looking at the two serious women staring at the camera. They spoke amongst themselves; their words and sentences dissolving into a wave of sound until Hubert carefully translated.

The Polish family started to form a pattern. They were foresters living in a part of Eastern Poland close to Germany. Zygmunt had come from the Ukraine to live in Poland. He had become a scout. He was pictured in his uniform.

It was then that they started to explain their lives. Immediately after the war the Soviets closed in and maintained marshal law. For those young men who had fought for the Allies in the

289

Polish Air Force alongside the RAF a return to Poland, despite the Yalta Agreement, meant a certain prison sentence of at least ten years, if not exile to Siberia for an indeterminate time, or even execution. They were viewed with extreme distrust by the British working classes and some Communist-controlled Trade Unions who saw that they were prepared to work hard and were well qualified to embark on any given task, therefore putting British workmen out of jobs, and by the Soviet-controlled Poland who regarded them at best as fascists and reactionaries and at worst traitors to their country. Marion could not return to see his family. Zygmunt had to wait for years until Marion could finally come home to see him and his family. Hubert calmly translated the awful facts. Yes it was so. And then he explained the German Soviet pact of 1939 that had resulted in more than fifteen thousand Polish officers being taken to prisoner-of-war camps in Kozielsk, Starobielsk and Ostashkov. The Germans had invaded from the west and the Russians from the east. Poland was caught in the pincer movement. There in the woods at Smolensk the three thousand Polish officers had been massacred. Shot in the back of the head with their hands tied behind their backs. In 1990 Yeltsin finally admitted that it had been a Soviet massacre of the Polish officers in the Katyn Forest; a crime that had been attributed to Germany for all those years. Zygmunt's voice was harsh with emotion. The Russians had taken the Polish intellectuals for mass deportation. I was appalled and shocked both by the stories starkly told and by my own woeful ignorance. I had no idea that it was Polish mathematicians who had helped to break the Enigma code, nor that the Polish allies had not been allowed to take part in the London Victory Parade in June 1945 for fear of upsetting the Soviet leader Stalin.

No wonder Marion had always seemed so paranoid about his country. He was convinced that the Secret Service and the spies were still following and watching him throughout the late forties, fifties and very early sixties. He had waited for so many years before applying for permission to travel to Poland with Sally. And for Zygmunt it had been the same. He too had had to go through the laborious red tape in order to obtain visa and permission to travel to Britain in 1968.

I didn't tell Zygmunt that Sally had kept his letters about Marion's affair. I didn't say that I had seen the documents about her pregnancy and marriage in 1943. The knowledge of her diaries and the framed pictures of her lover Tadek Walczak stayed confined and secret. They deserved more than these unkind disclosures. I could not hurt Zygmunt who had travelled all this way to light a candle in the chapel to honour Sally's memory. He was eager for me to find a way to do this. "Is this possible?"

"She was such a great lady," his eyes appeared to mist over. "She worked so very hard, so very, very busy".

I nodded, "yes it was so, yes it was as you say" 'and nodded again.

"We will take you to see her house that she had in Denbigh. We can take pictures from the road if you like. Perhaps the owners will not mind".

Al rang Mal and Morwenna. It was fine. Generously they had invited us over for morning coffee and would be delighted to meet them.

The next day we travelled to Denbigh, following the road to Ruthin and taking in the magnificent view from the track to Moel Famau. Dotted white sheep stretched across the green fields and mingled with the purple heather. Shafts of sunshine moved across the hills and swept over the town of Ruthin far below us.

"I remember this!" Zygmunt was delighted, "Sally showed me all this. We went to the Eisteddfod". He beamed at the memory.

Driving up the steep road into the small square of Denbigh Hubert too was able to recall his visit to Sally.

"We will see the castle and the hospital soon," I explained as Zygmunt became intoxicated by the wine of his remembered youth.

The car crawled through the narrow Castle Street and reached the brow of the hill. Below us sat the untended, deserted, magnificent buildings of a once busy hospital. We got out of the car and surveyed the scene. In the foreground young bullocks quietly munched on the grass, untroubled by our sudden appearance close to their fence.

Sally's domain where she had ruled with such authority had been abandoned. From the distance its desolation was not so apparent but once we reached the padlocked sign-posted gates, warning us to keep out and not to enter the premises as trespassers, the destruction of neglect was obvious. Zygmunt was indignant and visibly shocked.

"Nobody seems to want to buy it," we explained. "Denbigh has built new council offices on the other side of the town, probably because it would cost too much to refurbish and repair this building," we explained.

We went forward and began to slowly wend our way along the narrow road that led to the house. Al attempted to lighten the mood.

"These hedges still bear the scars of Sally's journeys," he joked. "Her MG often had to be pulled out after she had plunged through following a spot of night duty!" And we all smiled at her feisty resistance to part with the unsuitable car.

At last the house came into view, and Zygmunt and Hubert both confirmed that they remembered it well. For Marek it was a different adventure. He had not been to visit Sally in Wales and so for him it was all new and uncharted territory.

Mal and Morwenna met us at the gate. A young brown Labrador strained at her leash, wagging her tail to provide her own welcome for us. The house looked well. The blue sky set off the warm grey beige stonework. We were ushered into the polished and tidy lounge and sat on the comfy cream sofa. Zygmunt spotted the glazed window in the door. 'East or

292

West; Home is best' written under the brightly coloured billowing sails of a ship. "I remember that, it was my idea!" he was happy to confirm another memory.

Morwenna delighted him by announcing that she had worked at the hospital with Sally and that she had been very firm but fair. The three Jurczyszyns were pleased to acknowledge the compliment. They nodded their approval and carefully drank their coffee. Mal arranged for the chapel to be opened and we trouped into the tiny, pew polished, high ceilinged, room as I tried to explain how it had been impossible to carry her coffin inside and that there had been so many mourners they had to stand at the back during the service.

Zygmunt reverently ran his hand over the gleaming wooden altar. He decided that he could not light his candle safely in such a beautiful place and would be happier to stand it on the step outside to burn. We stood awkwardly in silence as he remembered her.

We continued our travels across Denbigh moor and down to Betwys y Coed in the pouring rain before travelling up the Conway valley to Conway Castle and then on the A55 to Chester.

By the time we arrived back to Hawarden Zygmunt was satisfied but tired. He had relived the past and was ready for bed before starting on the next adventure, to be reunited with his great nephew David. I hoped that he would not be disappointed.

In no time morning arrived. The little red car was packed with suitcases and the Polish party disappeared. Their eagerness to celebrate Sally's memory had seemed a rebuke to my voyeuristic probing.

I spent the morning piling the bedding into the washing machine and thinking hard about their visit. I finally decided. I had to tell her story as I saw it through my eyes, however distorted, and could not now be deflected from the task. I saw her, warts and all, and despite all the misgivings from what Tom and his family would say, and her cousin Joan in Kent.

This was my version of my Aunt Sally. Better to tell some of the tales, however incomplete, than to let her slip unknown in to the shadows of the past. Why had she kept all her letters and papers if it was all to be consigned to a dustbin?
Her life had become my obsession and I could not and would not let it go.

Denbigh Castle; the Jurczyszyn family, Zygmunt, Marek and Hubert during their visit to Flintshire and Denbighshire before they returned to Nottingham; Zygmunt pictured as a young man in the 1940's.He signed his photograph for Sally.

Index

2

24 Charlecote Drive · 65, 94, 182, 219

A

Abersoch · 51, 54
Al · *132, 133, 134, 135, 136, 137, 139,*
   170, 171, 172, 195, 206, 207, 215,
   216, 222, 224, 225, 226, 227, 228,
   230, 231, 232, 233, 239, 240, 243,
   244, 245, 252, 293
Albert Avenue · 76, 264
Amos · 22, 23, 25, 26, 28, 29, 30, 31,
   32, 33, 34, 35, 68, 75, 76, 78, 79, 88,
   102, 103, 104, 114, 143, 144, 146,
   147, 152, 156, 157, 159, 160, 180,
   181, 182, 187, 213, 271
Amos May · 22, 34, 114, 143, 144, 146,
   159, 160, 272
Aneurin Bevan · 188
Angley School · 204
Ann · 145, 271
Anna Pavlova · 16, 155
Anthony Eden · 237
anti Semitism · 275
Arthur Fuller · 76
Arthur Scargill · 188
Attlee · 275
Auxilliary Territorial Service · 82

B

Barbara · 104, 105, 107, 108, 111, 112,
   213, 271
Bedgbury Pinetum · 144

Bedgebury · 22, 35, 129
Bill · 25, 26, 28, 29
Bodnant Gardens · 137, 252
Bryn Llwyn â Godwys · 122, 125, 131

C

Caernarfon Investiture · 224
Cardinal Karol Wojtyla · 186
Carlton ware · 244
Cecilia · 271
Celtic romanticism · 145
Chamberlain · 188
Charles · 88, 158, 203
Charlotte · 23, 25, 26, 31, 32, 108, 109,
   113, 147, 157, 158, 160, 214, 219,
   254, 287
Charlotte Mary · 23, 31, 254
Chris · 240
Chrissie · 22, 25, 32, 33, 75, 76, 77, 78,
   79, 87, 93, 94, 96, 98, 99, 100, 147,
   148, 153, 157, 158, 181, 254, 262,
   270, 271, 272
Christianity · 186
Churchill · 188, 287
Ciszcwski · 235
Clogau Gold · 168
Clothes coupons · 178
Clwyd · 137, 153, 168, 169
Cold War · 275
colliery · 180
Conservative · 153, 187
councillor · 151, 169
Cranbrook · 18, 21, 25, 27, 29, 30, 31,
   32, 36, 63, 143, 203, 204, 234, *278*

D

David · 37, 129, 137, 177, 204, 208, 214, 216, 219, 223, 250, 287, 288, 294
David Frith · 204
Dawn · 194, 196, 218, 252
Daybrook, Arnold · 158
Denbigh · 11, 15, 17, 18, 41, 46, 51, 52, 54, 102, 103, *108*, 113, 121, 122, 128, 129, *137*, 144, 149, 150, 151, 152, 153, *169*, *173*, 177, 185, 194, 195, *196*, *198*, *204*, 207, 215, 216, *218*, 221, 222, 239, 240, 243, *254*, *292*, *293*, *294*
Denbigh Hospital · 51
Denbighshire · 168
Doncaster Royal Infirmary · 80
Dorothy Rose · 25, 26, 28, 147, 148, 157, 158
Duffy · 183, 184

E

Eastwell Manor · 22, 143
Edna · 94, 95, 96, 98, 99, 272
Elizabeth · 271
Emily Pankhurst · 189

F

First World War · 24, 81
Folkstone · 159
Friezeland · 37
Frith pottery · 177

G

gardener · 22, 23, 35, 36, 143, 159, 160, 255, 271
General Nursing Council · 130, 169
George Hotel · 29
George Neve · 35
German Soviet pact · 291
Gladys Smith · 7
Goudhurst · 22, 35, 36, 122, 158, 203
Great Depression · 80
Gwilym · 194, 199, 218

H

Harold Nicholson · 144
Hartley · 24, 143
Heather · 47, 51, 54, 60, 62, 63, 68, 69, 70, 147, 195, 197, 205, 218, 233, 252
Henryk Mierowski · 281
Herbert · 18, 22, 23, 24, 25, 26, 27, 32, 75, 76, 77, 78, 94, 98, 99, 100, 147, 155, 160, 234, 254, 262, 270, 272
Hollingbourne · 159
Hubert · 287, 289, 290, 291, 292, 293
Hucknall · 82, 234, 264, 266

I

International Eisteddfod · 51, 107
Isabel · 271
Ivy Humphreys · 82, 86

J

J P Green Paper Mill · 181
Jacksdale · 29, 76, 98, 264
James Oakes · 180
Janet · 93, 218
Janet May · 93
Jarrow March · 81
Joan · 29, 32, 88, 144, 145, 147, 157, 180, 203, 209, 210, 236
John May · 144
Joseph · 86, 108, 231, 271
Joyce · 61, 68, 88, 104, 178, 179, 180, 181
Julia · 132, 194

Jurczyszyn · 86, 102, 108, 113, 231, 239, 288

K

Kent · 16, 18, 22, 23, 24, 29, 30, 31, 36, 37, 102, 122, 129, 143, 144, 147, 158, 234, 270, 272
Kentish cob nuts · 37
Kevin · 209
Kings Royal Rifles · 22, 234
Krakow · 16

L

Labour · 80, 187
Llangollen Railway · 152, 169
Llanrhaeadr · *115, 121, 149, 152, 154, 168, 169, 186, 193, 194, 272*
Ludomira · 290
Lynford Hall · 22, 23, 28, 143

M

Maidstone · 34, 59, 60, 93, 159, 160, 180, 195, 204, 209, 261, 272, 277
Mal · 219, 292, 293, 294
Mapperley Hospital · 87, 93, 124, 279
Marcus · 193, 217, 221, 226, 230, 231, 232, 240, 242
Marek · 106, 108, 287, 290, 293
Margaret · 217, 240
Marion · 65, 67, 68, 70, 83, 86, 87, 88, 93, 94, 96, 97, 99, 100, 101, 102, 104, 105, 106, 107, 108, 111, 112, 115, 134, 154, 170, 180, 181, 185, 186, 195, 203, 204, 213, 231, 233, 234, 235, 236, 237, 268, 269, 270, 273, 274, 276, 277, 278, 279, 280, 281, 287, 288, 290, 291, 292
Mary Charlotte · 22, 25, 27, 144, 146, 147, 255, 262
Mary Payne · 18, 22, 231

Mary Smith · 158
Matron · 23, 41, 51
May · 16, 18, 22, 23, 24, 32, 69, 76, 78, 80, 83, 86, 88, 93, 115, 121, 143, 144, 145, 146, 147, 148, 185, 193, 203, 207, 234, 236, 237, 239, 254, 261, 271, 272
MG · 129, 134, 293
mice · 13, 116, 172, 224, 226, 232
Midland Railway Company · 22
Millennium · 184, 224, 225
Model Engineering Society · 209
Moel Famau · 292
Morwenna · 219, 292, 293, 294
Mote Park · 64, 203

N

National Archives · 261
National Trust · 52, 115, 168, 252
Nellie · 7, 79, 93, 99, 194, 195, 218, 253
Norfolk Railway · 152
Nottingham · 18, 22, 24, 26, 27, 29, 30, 32, 34, 65, 68, 75, 79, 83, 87, 102, 104, 108, 112, 114, 115, 147, 148, 152, 154, 157, 158, 181, 194, 207, 208, 231, 234, 238, 240, 254, 264, 272
nursery man · 272
nursery propagator · 159
Nuttery · 36, 144

O

Olive · 219, 254
Open University · 152, 153, 154, 168, 194
Oxford Road · 60, 209

P

Payne · 7, 8, 18, 59, 94, 100, 157, 158, 159, 214, 231, 234, 239, 249, 250, 261, 264
Peacocks · 79, 238
Pen–y–Graig · 45
Plains Avenue · 197, 277
Plas Mawr · 143, 144, 146
Poland · 54, 70, 102, 104, 185, 265, 270, 279, 287, 288, 290, 291, 292
Polish Air Force · 291
Polish War Memorial · 287, 290
Pope John Paul · 185, 186
Princess Alexandra Hospital · 136

R

RAF · 82, 87, 137, 206, 234, 236, 263, 264, 268, 277, 280, 282, 291
Rampton Hospital · 81, 82
Rationing · 275
Rectory Cottages · 27, 28, 29, 31
Red Cross · 21, 151, 153, 169, 194
Reg · 217, 240
Retford Hospital · 80
Robert Wynne · 143
Roman Catholic · 185
Rose Christiana Mary Payne · 21
Rose Cottage · 26
Royal College of Nursing. · 125
Royal Kings Rifles · 159
Royal Navy · 85, 180
Rudolph Scatkowski · 86, 231
Ruth · 194, 218

S

Sally · 1, 5, 12, 15, 16, 18, 23, 24, 25, 26, 28, 29, 30, 31, 32, 35, 37, 38, 41, 42, 43, 44, 45, 47, 51, 52, 53, 54, 59, 60, 61, 62, 63, 64, 65, 66, 67, 68, 69, 70, 71, 75, 76, 77, 78, 79, 80, 81, 82, 84, 85, 86, 87, 88, 93, 94, 95, 96, 97, 98, 99, 100, 101, 102, 103, 104, 105, 106, 107, 108, 112, 113, 114, 115, 116, 121, 122, 125, 127, 129, 130, 132, 133, 134, 135, 136, 137, 138, 139, 143, 144, 145, 147, 148, 149, 150, 151, 152, 153, 154, 155, 156, 158, 160, 167, 172, 177, 178, 179, 180, 181, 182, 184, 185, 186, 187, 188, 195, 196, 197, 198, 203, 205, 206, 207, 208, 209, 210, 213, 214, 215, 216, 217, 218, 219, 223, 227, 228, 229, 230, 231, 233, 234, 235, 237, 238, 239, 240, 241, 244, 249, 250, 251, 252, 253, 254, 261, 262, 263, 264, 265, 266, 270, 271, 272, 273, 276, 278, 279, 282, 287, 288, 289, 292, 293, 294, 295
Salvation Army · 187
Second World War · 36, 70
Secret Service · 291
Sissinghurst · 16, 23, 34, 35, 36, 52, 63
Sissinghurst Castle · 35
Snowdon · 51, 52, 239, 240
Social Services · 101, 114, 208
Soldiers, Sailors and Airman's Family Association · 100
Stalag Luft III · 236
Stalin · 291
Stuart · 205
Suffragettes · 21

T

Tadek · 13, 16, 60, 61, 62, 63, 67, 68, 69, 70, 83, 84, 87, 88, 93, 94, 95, 96, 97, 101, 102, 104, 109, 111, 112, 113, 114, 115, 116, 127, 129, 144, 178, 179, 181, 186, 194, 203, 207, 208, 213, 215, 223, 231, 233, 234, 235, 236, 237, 250, 262, 263, 269, 270
Tadek Walczak · 289, 292
Tadeusz Ciszewski · 281
Tadeusz Walczak · 263, 266, 268, 269
Tall Agrippa · 149
Terry · 203, 204, 205

Thatcher · 188
the Bedgbury Pinetum · 22
The Household Means Test · 80
Tom · 7, 78, 79, 93, 99, 147, 148, 156,
   194, 195, 196, 213, 218, 229, 236,
   240, 253, 276, 288, 294
Turkey Mill paper Mill · 182
Ty Mawr · 16

U

unions · 45, 180, 188, 189
United Nations · 153, 169

V

Victoria Sackville West · 16, 34
Victoria Sackville-West · 16, 34
Vita Sackville West · 144
Voluntary Aid Detachment · 21

W

Wagstaff Lane · 98
Wales · 24, 29, 32, 34, 41, 46, 52, 53,
   102, 108, 109, 114, 115, 123, 130,
143, 149, 152, 153, 157, 186, 187,
   239, 251
Welsh · 12, 16, 32, 46, 51, 52, 115, 129,
   130, 143, 145, 146, 149, 151, 153,
   157, 158, 159, 177, 186, 188, 223,
   271
Welsh family bible · 143
Welsh Highland Railway · 169
Wendy · 194, 218
Wollaton · 65, 104, 108, 112
Women's Army Auxilliary Corps · 21
Wynne · 143, 144, 145, 146, 239

Y

Yalta Agreement · 291
Yvonne · 101, 108, 199, 216, 218, 232,
   240

Z

Zygmunt · 105, 106, 108, 186, 280,
   287, 288, 289, 290, 291, 292, 293,
   294